# Finding Loopholes

## in the Bible on Divorce and "Re-marriage" is like ...

## Riding a Bike to Jamaica

**Judith A. Brumbaugh MHE, MBA**

Copyright © 2014
Committee for the Restoration of the Family

Distributed through:
RESTORATION OF THE FAMILY, INC.
PO Box 621342
Oviedo, FL 32762-1342 USA

www.RestorationOfTheFamily.org
blog.RestorationOfTheFamily.org
blog.familiesRusKJ.org

This manuscript represents opinions of the author
based on Scripture from the King James Bible.

All rights reserved. No part of this book may be reproduced or transmitted in any form or by any means, electronic or mechanical, including photocopying, recording, or by an information storage and retrieval system, without written permission from the author, except for the inclusion of quotation in a review but that quotation must include the immediate context surrounding the quotation and not an isolated phrase or sentence.

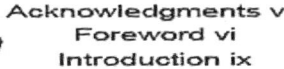

Acknowledgments v
Foreword vi
Introduction ix

1  It's Necessary To Study Loopholes. 1

2  Use Biblical Guidelines To Study
   And Interpret Scriptures. 7

3  There's Nothing New
   Under The Sun! 15

4  Let's Begin At The Beginning:
   A Very Good Place To Start! 25

5  Biblical Guidelines To Scripture Interpretation Become Very Important. 37

6  "ER" Is More Important Than
   The Emergency Room! 49

7  Jesus' Warning Is To
   Beware Of The Pharisees. 65

8  Shall We Rend The Robe Of Jesus
   Though It Be Only A Jot Or Tittle? 75

9  The Jewish Engagement
   Is Not A Marriage. 91

10 Are You Married Or Engaged
   To Jesus? 105

11 Was It Fornication Or Adultery? 117

12 Let's Go Fishing: Specifically,
   Generically, And Proximately. 145

13 A Grammatical Idiosyncrasy Is
   Embedded In Matthew 19:9. 179

# CONTENTS

14 When ... is
A Marriage Consummated? 199

15 Shall We "Re-turn" To Covenant? 225

16 For What Cause? 257

17 What Is A Divorce? 279

18 What <u>Kind</u> Of Wife
Is An Exception? 289

19 There Is A Unique Biblical Blessing
For Those Who Have Been
"Put-away"! 299

20 Desertion Is Not Dissolution.
It's A Call To War. 313

21 Paul's Teachings Are
Taken Out Of Context. 331

22 Come Now, And Let Us
Reason Together ... 353

Scripture Bibliography 385

### Extra Points Of Interest

*William Tyndale (1494-1536) was murdered for translating the New Testament into English. 6*

*God's Word hasn't changed but church doctrine has. 14*

*Hebrew words and expressions are translated for New Testament Gentile audiences. 24*

*Quick Guide Test to Check Bibles for Translation errors. 144*

*God's Word is not bound-copyrighted. 178*

*NIV, like all new versions, must change thousands of God's words with each new version. 256*

# Acknowledgments

To acknowledge all those who had a part in helping with this book is challenging as many individuals helped in a variety of ways.

First, I must acknowledge my LORD and Saviour Jesus Christ. By His Holy Spirit, He has taught me through His Word and through providential circumstances many of the topics covered in this book. From a human perspective, God put in my pathway several wonderful sisters and brothers in the LORD who were needed to help with this huge project. Among them are those who have been patient with my constant writing and rewriting as they edited and re-edited chapters: Gary Ciesla and Ann Nixon. (Ann, additionally, looked up every King James Scripture many times and hand collated the Scripture Bibliography.) Their "long suffering" with me has surely been a labor of love. Dr. D. W. Waite, Pastor and founder of *Bible for Today*, has been both my friend and teacher for 16 years. No matter the question, especially the many about Hebrew and Greek, he has always responded promptly and with much patience. His many publications on Bible versions and the interpretation of manuscripts have been a wonderful resource. I'm grateful for Pastor Fresia's encouragement to embark on this project. Thanks to Elaine Newman whose many hours of computer work were a blessing and to my friend Judy Shannon for my many "911" phone calls for grammar questions; to my friend Kim Fratrik of $2^{nd}$ Cup Studio for design inspiration for the cover, and to Professor Victoria Ackerman my Photoshop instructor for her help with designing and executing the cover.

I could not end this page without expressing my gratitude to the LORD for my covenant husband of almost half a century and the additional blessings of our children. Both he and our children have been major influences in sandpapering some of my rough edges. They also provided me with a point of view to write this book—that of experiencing those many challenges and blessings of living out God's perspective on marriage. *I have no greater joy than to hear that my children walk in truth.* 3 John 1:4

# Foreword

Divorce and "re-marriage" are so readily accepted in most of our churches, and in society at large, that we have almost completely lost sight of God's view of marriage. Divorce is rampant. There is a worldwide epidemic of destruction in individual lives stemming from the breakup of families. Thus, it's time for every person to take an active part in building strong families. There is, however, a missing link. Most do not understand marriage from God's perspective. As a result, the family, as God designed it, is quickly disappearing. We must all take part in turning this trend around, but that is difficult when most people don't understand what God has to say about marriage and divorce. That's why a teaching of the Word of God on this issue must be Biblically and thoroughly presented.

**For whom is this book written?**

- For pastors,
- For youth,
- For single people,
- For married people,
- For divorced people.

1. For pastors: Pastors are charged to keep watch over their congregations; to teach and equip; to be watchmen on the walls to warn and rebuke when sin is in the lives of their parishioners. They regularly meet with people who

face issues regarding marriage and broken relationships, but is their counsel Biblical?

2. For young people: Young people must understand that dating is a serious matter which must be approached with great care. The natural and physical attraction that young men and women feel toward each other can, if the couple is not careful, get out of control. It's important that young people are taught that fornication is a serious sin in the eyes of God. They must also learn that marriage is a serious lifelong commitment, not a temporary living arrangement to fulfill sexual desires or to escape an unpleasant home environment.

3. For single adults: Paul has a message for those who are single:

*… He that is unmarried careth for the things that belong to the Lord, how he may please the Lord.* 1 Corinthians 7:32 And for older widows: *The aged women likewise, that they be in behaviour as becometh holiness … That they may teach the young women to be sober, to love their husbands, to love their children.* Titus 2:3-4

Widows and single adults must also understand God's perspective on marriage so they will not only live according to His guidelines but teach and guide others in their understanding of what the LORD has recorded in the Bible about marriage.

4. For married couples: Married couples must make whatever adjustments are needed in order to strengthen their love for one another; to put no limits or numbers on forgiving one another, and to not turn in for the night when there are still issues between them. They must learn how to live together in love and to model that for their children as well as for all of society. Children learn from what they see and experience. Parents must be the Biblical example of God's perspective on marriage: one man for one woman until death they do part. Marriage is a reflection of Christ's love for the church. Divorce is not an option just because there may be strains in the relationship.

5. For the divorced: This book is especially important for this growing class of people. They may have friends and relatives who have

given them advice, but it's likely that few who have offered the advice are equipped with accurate facts from the Bible on marriage and divorce. Those who have separated from or divorced their one-flesh living spouse must not date. If anyone reading this book doesn't understand why, the grave importance of this issue should give all the more reason to study the Word of God very carefully and continue to read this entire text. We are always ready to pray with you and to answer individual questions. Write to us at Restoration Of The Family, PO Box 621342, Oviedo, FL 32762-1342, or contact us through our website: www.RestorationOfTheFamily.org.

Marriage and divorce are issues that can become a matter of spiritual life or death. It's not an option for Christians to "agree to disagree" on such important issues as marriage and divorce: *Can two walk together, except they be agreed?* Amos 3:3 Marriage is what Scripture teaches is the earthly representation of Christ and His church and is something everyone should hold in high regard. Anyone who cannot share the Scriptures to explain why marriage and divorce can become a matter of spiritual life or death, why it is that God hates divorce, and why He does not recognize "re-marriage" as a valid marriage needs to carefully study this book.

---

*Study* to shew thyself approved unto God,
a *workman*
that needeth not to be ashamed,
rightly dividing the word of truth.
2 Timothy 2:15

---

# Introduction

Why are more marriages ending in divorce today? What has happened? Is God's Word unclear on this issue? Has His Word changed over the centuries, and has His design for marriage been modified? There appears to be tragic, growing beliefs that God's Word has changed and what was recorded in the past needs to be updated.

There are two primary catalysts feeding these changing beliefs—especially since the 1900s. The change started (and continues) within the church. The organizational church has gradually changed its standards concerning divorce and "re-marriage" to reflect what is happening in society. A historical overview of these documented changes to church doctrines on marriage and divorce, **from church archives** is discussed in *It's A Matter of Life or Death: Wrong Thinking About Marriage Leads to Destruction*. This book is available from Restoration of the Family, PO Box 621342, Oviedo, FL 32762. A summary of this sad decline in church doctrine is given on page 14.

Secondly, man has tried to restructure the Bible to mirror contemporary lifestyles. Thus, we have had hundreds of different Bibles with varying versions of God's Word from which people have studied and derived their theological beliefs. Most of these revised Bibles reflect changing beliefs, language patterns, and lifestyles of society. That's a mistake because these changes typically mirror disintegrating present-day lifestyles. Even more important is the fact that it is a very serious sin against God to change His written Word (what is included in the Bible) or to teach doctrine that opposes Scripture. See Deuteronomy 4:2, Proverbs 30:6, and Revelation 22:18-19, et. al.

Some of what may be driving the above changes is that the church isn't willing to pay the price to take a hard line on what the Scriptures say about marriage, divorce, and "re-marriage." That's because these topics have become very controversial, unpopular subjects to address Biblically. Compromise within the church may or may not be the result of fear of losing members and tithes, or it may or may not be ignorance of what the Scriptures teach. Yet, there is always a high price spiritually to pay for compromise. That is especially true now, and it will no doubt continue to be so in the future.

*So thou, O son of man, I have set thee a watchman unto the house of Israel; therefore thou shalt hear the word at my mouth, and warn them from me. When I say unto the wicked, O wicked man, thou shalt surely die; if thou dost not speak to warn the wicked from his way, that wicked man shall die in his iniquity; but his blood will I require at thine hand. Nevertheless, if thou warn the wicked of his way to turn from it; if he do not turn from his way, he shall die in his iniquity; but thou hast delivered thy soul.* Ezekiel 33:7-9

These are not new matters. The Truth, as God has it recorded, has been difficult for many to receive. In fact, Jesus talked straight forwardly with His disciples concerning His teachings that many reject. That's why the Scriptures which offend many are avoided or often replaced with man-made loopholes:

*Many therefore of his disciples, when they had heard this, said, This is an* **hard saying***; who can hear it? When Jesus knew in himself that his disciples murmured at it, he said unto them,* <u>*Doth this offend you*</u>*?* John 6:60-61

However, these same disciples, after hearing Jesus' teaching about the indissoluble nature of marriage as recorded in Matthew 19:1-9, responded with a reverential fear of anyone taking marriage lightly:
*His disciples say unto him, If the case of the man be so with his wife, it is not good to marry. But he* [Jesus] *said unto them, All men cannot receive this saying, save they to whom it is given.* Matthew 19:10-11

But what should be happening today in response to those "hard sayings" taught by Jesus? Hard sayings or not, those who have been called to teach, preach, and witness are to teach the fullness of the Scriptures—*in season and out of season*:

*Preach the word; be instant in season, out of season* [whether popular or unpopular]; *reprove, rebuke, exhort with all longsuffering and doctrine. For the time will come when they will not endure sound doctrine; but after their own lusts shall they heap to themselves teachers, having itching ears; And they shall turn away their ears from the truth, and shall be turned unto fables.* 2 Timothy 4:2-4

However, instead of accepting and teaching the simple facts that God so clearly presents on marriage and divorce, the church calls for conferences, for discussions and analytical studies. Leaders try to find a way to interpret the Scriptures to satisfy some loophole that would allow the divorce and "re-marriage" of divorced persons. They focus their efforts on pages of research based on what the opinions of others have been throughout the ages. They look to those who are experts in Hebrew and Greek to tell them what they feel the languages underlying the English translations REALLY say.

> Churches call for conferences instead of accepting the clearly written Word of God.

Ironically, or perhaps, hypocritically, most Christians take a hard line on the sin of homosexuality (although that, too, is quickly changing) even though there are far fewer clear, repetitive Scriptures on this sin versus the many Scriptures on marriage between one man and one woman. That doesn't mean such wrongful relationships between two males or two females are any less serious to God than are adulterous ones. Yet, millions worldwide sit comfortably in congregations, and others hold leadership positions while they and those sitting in the pews are also Biblically living in a lifestyle that God says is adultery. Most call these relationships the socially acceptable term *"re-marriage."* "Re-marriage," however, is a form of bigamy or polygamy. That's because someone has married a second spouse while he has a one-flesh spouse who is living but from whom he has been granted a legal divorce. ("Re-marriage," *marital adultery*, and *adulterous "marriage"* are used as synonymous terms in this book.)

Many in the church have tip-toed around broken marital relationships trying not to offend those so affected or involved. Leadership seems to believe that God can cure an alcoholic; God can cure a drug addict; God can take away a prostitute's desire, but if there has been a marital problem that leads to divorce, that becomes a different issue. They wrongly conclude God wouldn't expect a young divorced wife to go through life without "another" husband to live with her, nor would God expect a divorced husband to continue to live alone the rest of his life. Oh woe!

> Churches feel God can cure a drug addict, but He doesn't have the power to heal marital relationships.

## Is a conference necessary?

Not only is God's perspective on marriage and divorce repetitively given in the Bible, it is given in very simplified terms.

*And they twain shall be one flesh: so then they are <u>no more</u> twain, but one flesh. What therefore God hath joined together, <u>let not</u> man put asunder.* Mark 10:8-9

*Wherefore they are no more twain, but one flesh. What therefore God hath joined together, let not man put asunder.* Matthew 19:6

Many say they cannot understand the Bible. It's true there are passages that require additional study and sometimes outside historical and geographical research. However, basic doctrines, especially those on marriage and divorce, are clearly presented. Those who seriously study the Word and learn <u>how</u> to study the Bible contextually, with the guidance of the Holy Spirit, will understand Biblically sound doctrine. What most fail to do is to spend quality and quantity time reading and studying <u>from the Bible</u>.

You may be surprised to learn that according to two top readability standards, the F-K: Flesch-Kincaid Reading Index and the GFI: Gunning's Fog Indexes, the King James Bible's grade level readability was found to be as low as from grade 6.20 to grade 8.63 When tested against several other versions, the King James Bible, indicated a greater readability level than any of the other modern Bible versions that were thoroughly examined. This has been verified by a comparative computational study done by D. A. Waite, Jr. His findings have been published in a booklet, "The Comparative Readability of the Authorized Version." This is available from The Bible for Today, 900 Park Avenue, Collingswood, NJ 08108.

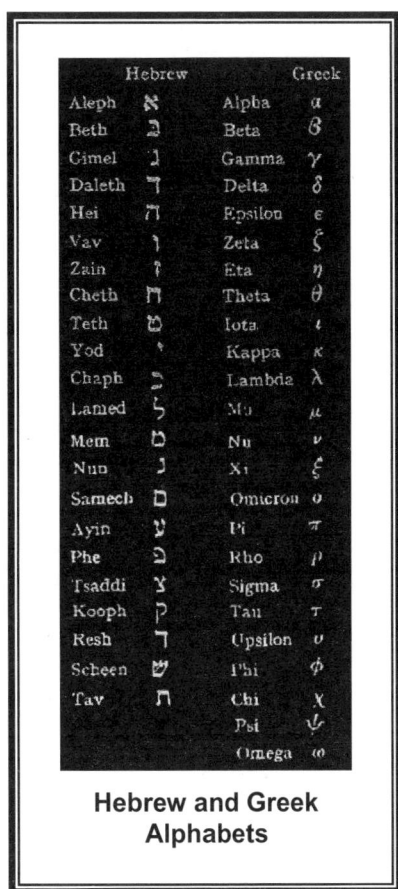

**Hebrew and Greek Alphabets**

So, should it be necessary to have a conference to understand what the words *no more twain* and *let not man put asunder* mean? Even though the grammar isn't correct, a two-year old can understand what is meant when a parent says, "Don't do that no more." Likewise, do we need a linguistic expert to explain the underlying Greek to understand that God clearly says to *not divorce* because they are *no more twain* (two)?

### But the Greek really says ...

Christians are also being led to believe that they cannot understand, in English, what God "really" means. Have we, in principle, reverted to the "church age" when Bibles weren't as readily available in the common language, and thus most had to rely on what clergy told them the Scriptures said? That practice is being infused today when we are made to believe that there is a need to examine the Hebrew or Greek languages that underlie the Bible in order to correctly interpret God's holy, infallible book.

Hebrew and Greek are languages few Christians can read, and a very small percentage of people have these texts available to examine for themselves. It's not uncommon to hear pastors say, "The Greek really says …" "This is what God really means." Thus, they dull the senses of people making them think they cannot understand the words in the Bible without an interpreter who has knowledge of Hebrew and Greek, especially when the topic of marriage and divorce is at issue.

Please don't take this out of context. I'm not saying there is no place for those who are learned in these underlying languages. I respect and am thankful for several theologians with this kind of expertise who have helped me to understand some of the nuances of these languages as they apply to reinforcing what has been translated into the English language for the Word of God. However, there is a time and place for such studies, and that is a topic which will be discussed further in this book. The point that is being made is that it isn't necessary to know anything about these languages, foreign to most, to correctly understand God's perspective on marriage and divorce from a Bible *that has been accurately translated*. However, it is vital for Christians to *develop* skills to assess the accuracy of their Bible. This is because there are so many Bibles on the market, all of which claim to be the best, the most accurate, from the best manuscripts, the easiest to read.

The authors of new Bible versions have sold them to the masses through multi-million dollar advertising schemes. They tell their potential buyers that their "latest and greatest" Bible is translated from the oldest and best manuscripts and tout their Bibles as the most accurate translation of the underlying Hebrew or Greek text. Many blatantly proclaim that their Bible has updated God's "archaic" language, or that their Bible is easier to read. (One must be very careful about saying that the words of God are archaic.) They talk of doctrinal errors based on mysterious, often unnamed, manuscripts and those to which readers have no access to verify.

> One must be very careful about saying that the words of God are archaic.

So what do we have? Confusion! Yes, we have confusion:
- Confusion about unnamed, unavailable manuscripts.
- Confusion about what the Hebrew and Greek really say about marriage and divorce.

- Confusion among pastors and laypeople alike regarding their beliefs on marriage and divorce.
- Confusion on which Bible is really God's Word.

## Every person needs to know how to evaluate the doctrinal accuracy of the Bible.

When the apostle Paul wrote many of the books of the New Testament, he, too, was also dealing with "other versions" of God's Word. In fact, he gave serious warnings against such apostate writings and expressed his concern that even those he had taught might be pulled into the false doctrines of the other versions:

*But I fear, lest by any means, as the serpent beguiled Eve through his subtilty, so your minds should be corrupted from the simplicity that is in Christ. For if he that cometh preacheth another Jesus, whom we have not preached, or if ye receive another spirit, which ye have not received, or another gospel, which ye have not accepted, ye might well bear with him.* 2 Corinthians 11:3-4

*I marvel that ye are so soon removed from him that called you into the grace of Christ unto another gospel: Which is not another; but there be some that trouble you, and would pervert the gospel of Christ.* Galatians 1:6-7

This book is not a conventional text on marriage and divorce. It's one that has a different purpose. That purpose is to TEACH the reader HOW to study the Word so he can determine correct doctrine. You've heard the saying: "Give a man a fish, and he eats for a day; teach a man HOW to fish, and he will eat for a lifetime."

That's the principle behind this book. If the principles introduced are studied and followed, readers will be able to analyze any new version that comes on the market to determine its doctrinal accuracy—at least on marriage and divorce—and without any further reference to the unfamiliar underlying languages. That should be ample reason to carefully complete the <u>study</u> of each chapter in this book. I urge you not to skip any chapter. There are building blocks within each chapter that may not seem important, but they lay the groundwork for what lies ahead in the next chapters.

The structure of this text is such that it should be read in the order in which it has been presented. There are important building blocks that carry over from one chapter to the next. I have 50 years of teaching experience, 40 of those involve ministry-related teachings from which I draw as a resource for principles of learning used in this text. But, most of all, I draw upon the LORD's personal training and Biblical examples which will likely become obvious as you move through this book.

> You can learn principles to assess the accuracy of any Bible.

There is a development of Biblical principles, layer upon layer, but there is also **much** repetition. Both are there for a purpose:

*Whom shall he teach knowledge? and whom shall he make to understand doctrine? them that are weaned from the milk, and drawn from the breasts. For precept must be upon precept, precept upon precept; line upon line, line upon line; here a little, and there a little:* Isaiah 28:9-10

Scriptures and their verses are formatted with *italics* and a slightly smaller font following this format: *Jesus wept.* John 11:35 When there may be confusion about a word within a Scripture, an explanation is given in [brackets] within the verse.

*... Moses **because** of the hardness of **your** hearts suffered* [allowed] *you to put away your wives: but from the beginning it was not so.* Matthew 19:8

> In this text many references are made to the *Word* and the *word*. *Word* with a capital "W" refers to the entire Bible: The Word of God never changes. The *word* with a small "w" refers to individual words within the Bible (or to other words in this text). For example, the words *fornication* and *adultery* are misunderstood by many Christians.

I'm excited to teach and hope that you share that excitement to learn.

*Judith Brumbaugh* MHE, MBA

# 1

# *It's Necessary To Study Loopholes.*

Today, the marriage-covenant could almost be classified as an endangered species. We're on a fast track of throw-away marriages and easy divorces. We never know when we will hear of the tragedy that another couple is filing for a divorce. Most of us in our own immediate families have someone involved in a divorce-"re-marriage" situation. Surely it's important that the church and all Christians begin to speak clearly, and in one accord, on what the Bible has to say about divorce and "re-marriage." Everyone should be equipped to be a part of what the Apostle Paul described as the ministry of reconciliation:

*And all things are of God, who hath reconciled us to himself by Jesus Christ, and hath given to us the ministry of reconciliation.* 2 Corinthians 5:18

That is, whenever we learn of a marriage that appears headed for divorce, we should be equipped and willing to tirelessly encourage the couple towards forgiveness and reconciliation by teaching them what God says about marriage and divorce. However, there is so much diversity of thought on marriage and divorce and many unbiblical teachings feeding this diversity. This must be addressed by taking a serious look at Bible passages which deal with marriage and divorce. It's God Word that must be our standard, and it is that standard for which God ultimately holds us responsible.

This book examines and responds to what many people call *loopholes*. They are using these loopholes to explain what they feel is a reason for their divorce and "re-marriage." God's Word, however, teaches that marriage is binding as long as both shall live (1 Corinthians 7:39); that man should not try to sever the marriage bond (Mark 10:10-12); and that two persons joined in marriage are supernaturally joined until death in what God says is a one-flesh joining (Genesis 2:21-24).

## What is a loophole?

A loophole is an ambiguity or exception in a system, such as a law, that is used to circumvent or otherwise avert the intent—implied or explicitly stated—of the law (paraphrased from *Black's Law Dictionary*). That's what is happening with God's Word—His book of laws. **Do you believe that God's Word is a law book—and one that we are to follow?** Psalm 119, for example, is one of the books of the Bible in which we're taught, contextually and directly, that the Bible is God's law book. If you read Psalm 119, you will see the following references: thy (God's) law 25 times, thy (God's) precepts 21 times,

## Chapter 1

thy (God's) commandments 22 times, thy (God's) testimonies 22 times, thy (God's) judgments 22 times. Sadly, man is on an endless journey to search for and strategically use loopholes to try to avert God's law with a variety of unbiblical doctrines, especially with marriage and divorce.

There is a worksheet on the following two pages that lists several commonly used loopholes regarding marriage, divorce, and "re-marriage." These will be covered in this book. Take time to think through and respond to the statements given on this worksheet about each loophole. **Please, this is one of the most important exercises in which you can invest your time.** Set aside the time to complete it. *It is vital to your understanding of what lies ahead in this book and for how you may, through the Scriptures, understand God's perspective on marriage and divorce.* Before you begin, make a copy of the next two pages so you will have a duplicate to complete once you finish your study of this book with which you can compare. **At least minimally circle (L), (E), or (N) at the end of each numbered loophole.**

Which do you believe describes each numbered statement in the left column: (L) a Biblical loophole for divorce and "re-marriage," (E) an exception given by God which sets aside His one man for one woman until death standard, or (N) neither? Why do you believe or don't believe (L), (E), or (N)? Is your belief based on specific Scriptures (S), or is it adapted from opinions of others, or from sermons you have heard (O)? Circle (S) or (O) in the second column for Scripture or opinion. Can you defend your belief by listing specific verses in the third column? Once you finish reading this book, return to this chart and compare your answers to see if you have learned anything new that may change what you initially wrote.

| Worksheet to analyze your beliefs on marriage and divorce. | | |
| --- | --- | --- |
| Circle (L) if you feel this is a loophole, (E) if you feel it is an exception given in the Bible, or (N) if neither loophole or exception applies. | Scripture OR Opinion | List verse or verses. |
| 1. God gives a loophole to divorce and "re-marry." (L) (E) (N) | S   O | |
| 2. Matthew 19:9 is an exception included so that spouses can divorce and "re-marry." (L) (E) (N) | S   O | |
| 3. The exception clause in Matthew 19:9 says, "except for adultery." (L) (E) (N) | S   O | |
| 4. The exception clause in Matthew 19:9 says, "except for marital unfaithfulness." (L) (E) (N) | S   O | |
| 5. The exception clause in Matthew 19:9 says, "except for sexual immorality." (L) (E) (N) | S   O | |
| 6. The exception clause in Matthew 19:9 says, "except for immorality." (L) (E) (N) | S   O | |
| 7. A marriage entered into before a person is saved is not viewed as permanent as a marriage created after a person is saved. (L) (E) (N) | S   O | |
| 8. God allows divorce for abandonment, physical cruelty, or mental cruelty. (L) (E) (N) | S   O | |
| 9. A marriage is only valid after it is physically consummated. (L) (E) (N) | S   O | |
| 10. A person who is divorced from a covenant-marriage can repent of the first marriage and then be free to marry another spouse. (L) (E) (N) | S   O | |
| 11. If an unbeliever deserts the marriage, God says the believer is no longer bound to that person. (L) (E) (N) | S   O | |
| 12. Because of God's grace, a saved person who commits the sins listed in Galatians 5:19-20 and 1 Corinthians 6:9-10 **will** inherit the kingdom of God; that is, even though he is living in a lifestyle of sin, including fornication, adultery, sodomy, drunkenness, etc., he is saved. (L) (E) (N) | S   O | |

| | | |
|---|---|---|
| 13. Once a person is divorced, he cannot return to that spouse. (L) (E) (N) | S | O |
| 14. If God didn't mean for people to divorce, He would not have said, "Let not man put asunder." Therefore, it's okay to divorce. (L) (E) (N) | S | O |
| 15. God does not expect the innocent party to live the rest of his life alone. (L) (E) (N) | S | O |
| 16. Standards on marriage and divorce for men and women are different. God allows men to "re-marry" but not women because Romans 7:2-3 only addresses women who put away their spouses and marry another. (L) (E) (N) | S | O |
| 17. Prayers over a divorced person can wash away the sin of adultery and make him or her "clean" to marry again. (L) (E) (N) | S | O |
| 18. When I "re-married," I made a promise under an oath to God which must be kept. (L) (E) (N) | S | O |
| 19. God approves of "re-marriage" because He allowed Moses to approve of divorce. (L) (E) (N) | S | O |
| 20. A divorce dissolves a marriage. (L) (E) (N) | S | O |
| 21. Adultery dissolves the marriage-covenant. (L) (E) (N) | S | O |

Keep the definitions below of *loophole* and *"re-marriage"* as a handy reference as you study this text:

A **loophole** is an ambiguity or exception in a system, such as a law, that is used to circumvent or otherwise avoid the intent—implied or explicitly stated—of the law.

**"Re-marriage" with quotations marks** refers to someone who has divorced his one-flesh spouse and married another person while his covenant spouse is alive.

## Extra Points of Interest

### William Tyndale (1494—1536) was murdered for translating the New Testament into English.

It's difficult for most who read this book to imagine not having free access to a Bible in their native language. However, for many years, that was not the case. The ruling church held, tightly fisted, the Scriptures in languages only they could read. Laity was held in bondage able to hear only what clergy told them was contained in the Holy writ. However, what clergy taught was corrupted doctrine and reflected their hypocritical and ungodly lifestyles. Even so, there was a godly priest William Tyndale who was proficient in seven different languages including Hebrew, Greek, and Latin who saw first-hand these ecclesiastical abuses. He also knew God holds each person accountable for what is in the Bible and that every person must study the Word for himself. His burning desire was to provide a translation every person could read: "that the poor might also read and see the simple, plain Word of God." Tyndale believed that *All Scripture is inspired by God* ... 2 Timothy 3:16-17, and it should not be changed by man—the practice of clergy of his day. Thus, he began the arduous work of translating the Bible into an early modern English text the common man could read. He drew his New Testament translation from a Greek text collated by the scholar Desiderius Erasmus. Erasmus' collation was the underpinnings for what later came to be called the Textus Receptus. Both the Textus Receptus and Tyndale's early modern English Hebrew and Greek syntax and idioms were significant resources used by the 47 scholars (with input from hundreds of laymen, priests, and preachers who knew Greek and/or Hebrew) who put together the translation named the King James Bible. (Interestingly, Tyndale also wrote *The Practyse of Praelates* opposing Henry VIII's divorce because it went against Scripture.)

Missing above, however, is the great peril under which Tydale and untold others suffered to bring to you and me a Bible we can read in our common language. (See also John Foxe's *Book of Martyrs*.) In Tyndale's England, it was a death-penalty offense to translate the Bible into the native tongue, a ban vigorously enforced by the church. The only Bible version authorized was Jerome's corrupt Latin Vulgate. These prohibitions, however, did not deter Tyndale. He completed his New Testament translation; however, his Old Testament work was aborted when he was imprisoned after being betrayed by a friend and incarcerated for almost two years enduring horrific physical and mental persecutions. He was unfairly tried and convicted of heresy and treason and put to death by strangulation and his body burned at the stake. His works and views were judged heretical by both the Catholic Church and later by the Church of England, and his Bible translation was banned then and for 125 years after his death with the death sentence even for those who possessed, read, or taught from a Tyndale Bible. **His CRIME**: He placed God's Word in the hands of the English-speaking world so they could read it for themselves. What is the price you pay to read the Bible in English?

# 2

# *Use Biblical Guidelines To Study And Interpret Scriptures.*

This may seem like a boring and unnecessary topic; however, this is a book designed to **teach** principles to help in the correct interpretation of God's Word on topics that are probably the most debated of all Biblical doctrines: marriage and divorce. Those who learn to apply these guidelines will have tools, or what could be called the weapons of spiritual warfare, to fight against Biblical deception. Those who learn and apply these guidelines to their study of God's Word will not be thrown back and forth wavering between this and that teaching, or between this and that Bible, or between this and that Hebrew and Greek expert. Applying Biblical

## Use Biblical Guidelines To Study And Interpret Scriptures.

guidelines should be considered not just when studying about marriage and divorce, but whenever any topic in the Bible is studied:

*But let him ask in faith, nothing wavering. For he that wavereth is like a wave of the sea driven with the wind and tossed. For let not that man think that he shall receive any thing of the Lord.* James 1:6-7

Here are some important Biblical guidelines that will be used throughout this study:

1. Compare Scriptures with Scriptures, especially when there are parallel Scriptures or passages—those dealing with like or related topics.
2. Investigate differences in verses and in the wording of similar teachings. Look for Scriptural clues and reasons for these differences.
3. Consider those who are speaking, the audience spoken to, and the reason for the conversation or related event.
4. Consider the culture and idiomatic expressions surrounding the teaching.
5. Beware of <u>assumed</u> doctrine <u>created</u> from a single verse if it conflicts with other related Scriptures.
6. Carefully consider the context—what the author is addressing as indicated by surrounding or parallel Scriptures (those on the same topic). Most words have many meanings. Be sure the definition chosen fits the specific circumstance.
7. Apply consistent rules of grammar which line up with context and reflect the cultural language.
8. Cross reference words with the aid of a concordance to see how the given word is used in both the Old and New Testaments. It's vital to rely upon the *Bible's internal dictionary* (how words are used throughout the Bible) rather than outside resources such as Webster's Dictionary or Strong's Concordance. Even though these reference tools can be helpful, the final decisions for interpretation of Scripture must be based on consistent, Scripturally based doctrine. If the definition of a word makes a verse inconsistent with other Scriptures, then it's the wrong definition.

The essence of the last three guidelines is context, context, context. You will read a lot about context in this book. Therefore, two examples follow to emphasize the importance of this concept which is often neglected in Bible teachings. The first example is based on a personal experience; the second is taken directly from Scripture.

**Personal experience**: I have taken mission trips to Jamaica. Suppose I told you that I rode my bike from Florida to Jamaica in the West Indies. Would you believe me? Of course you wouldn't because there's a huge body of water separating the coast of the United States and the island nation of Jamaica. Your contextual and geographical knowledge tell you I either flew on an airplane or rode on a ship. That's the importance of context.

**Scriptural example**: You've probably heard people use Scriptures out of context. The following example is extreme and implausible, but it illustrates an important principle about context that must be observed.

*And he* [Judas] *cast down the pieces of silver in the temple, and departed, and went and hanged himself. And ... do ye also ...* Matthew 27:5; Luke 6:31

The two Scriptures in their entirety are as follows:
*And he [Judas] cast down the pieces of silver in the temple, and departed, and went and hanged himself.* Matthew 27:5

*And as ye would that men should do to you, do ye also to them likewise.* Luke 6:31

It's obvious what the error is in the first set of Scriptures. Two verses are combined, but Luke 6:31 is quoted out of context. What has been wrongly combined gives a totally false, unbiblical message, even though Scripture has been quoted. While this example seems quite extreme, it illustrates something people do regularly in the study of God's Word—they quote Scriptures out of context.

Most understand the importance of context in everyday applications; however, when it comes to Bible study, this important principle is often either forgotten or inadvertently misapplied. Proper contextual application is often not used, especially when people study marriage and divorce. This lack of proper contextual application frequently happens when one or both spouses have "re-married," or they are seeking to marry another while they have a living one-flesh spouse.

Here's a common remark that is given, even by committed Christian believers: *David committed adultery,* and *he was a man after God's own heart.* Both of those clauses contain statements that are true. David committed adultery, and David was called a man after God's own heart, and these statements can be proven Scripturally. However, this is a prime example of taking Biblical Truths and applying them out of context. Yes, David *was* a man after God's own heart, but he *was not* a man after God's own heart *when* he sinned against God by committing adultery AND murder. It was when his heart turned back to the LORD, in repentance and faith, that David had the attributes that would be characteristic of a person who has a heart after God's own heart. No one is a person after God's heart who is living in rebellion to the LORD. God hates sin. Sin separates us from God.

In contrast to the practice of linking David's adultery with righteousness, I have never, in forty years of family ministry, heard anyone say, "David murdered, and he was a man after God's own heart." It's always the adultery example.

## God's timing in the lives of men was evident in David's life.

God shows patience with man's rebellion. When the time was ripe for David's repentance, the LORD sent a messenger, the prophet Nathan, to David. The Spirit of the LORD was likely working within the soul of David to awaken him to the abhorrent nature of what he had done and had so wickedly covered up. (Study Psalm 32:3-4.) It was after an indeterminate period of time when Nathan confronted David about his sin that his soul was pricked: *And the LORD sent Nathan ...* 2 Samuel 12:1

It was then that we read David turned his hatred and lust to a grieving heart and repentance. Some of his cries of repentance are heard through the Psalms he penned after he returned to the LORD, especially Psalm 51. David poured out his remorse in pleading with the LORD to have mercy upon him; to blot out his sin; to wash him throughly from his iniquity; to cleanse him from his sin: *For I* [the Psalmist, assumed to be David] *acknowledge my transgressions: and my sin is ever before me.* Psalm 51:3 David, however, could not erase the horrific things he had done, even though he had repented.

I hope that no one is so deceived that he may even consider murder or adultery by following in the same path as David trod. David surely did not get away with adultery, as some misguided people sadly remark. Those who think he did would do well to study all of 2 Samuel, Chapters 11 and 12. See 2 Samuel 12:9-12 below:

> David wasn't a man after God's own heart when he was consumed with lust, lies, and hatred.

*Wherefore hast thou despised the commandment of the LORD, to do evil in his sight? thou hast killed Uriah the Hittite with the sword, and hast taken his wife to be thy wife, and hast slain him with the sword of the children of Ammon. Now therefore **the sword shall never depart from thine house**; because thou hast despised me, and hast taken the wife of Uriah the Hittite to be thy wife. Thus saith the LORD, Behold, I will raise up evil against thee out of thine own house, and I will take thy wives before thine eyes, and give them unto thy neighbour, and he shall lie with thy wives in the sight of this sun. **For thou didst it secretly: but I** [God] **will do this thing before all Israel, and before the sun.***

> David wasn't a man after God's heart when he committed adultery and murdered.

> David sowed to the wind and reaped the whirlwind.

The lives of David and his family were marked with tragedy from that time on. He and his children were guilty of rape, murder, incest, hatred, and greed. Even on David's deathbed, one of his sons, whom *he had neglected to discipline* in earlier years, tried to illegally take the throne from his own father.

> Parents who practice ungodliness or who do not discipline their children may reap a harvest of disaster.

How, may I ask, could anyone so wrongly think that David "got away with adultery"? Let us pray that this egregious contextual error, misspoken by so many—that David got away with adultery—that he committed adultery and was, *concurrently,* a man after God's own heart, would never be uttered again by faith-abiding followers of Jesus Christ. May we, instead, point those who do not understand to the Scriptures such as those given above which chronicle the tragic events in the lives of David and his children.

New Testament believers should know there is no grace that covers unrepentant sin. There were, however, things done in the Old Testament that weren't seemingly judged as they are today. There were many practices in the Old Testament that are no longer for today, such as the ceremonial law, the animal sacrifices, concubines, etc. Acts 17:30 is an important Scripture that must be factored in when we lack understanding of how God dealt with Old Testament sins. We must know that God is a God of justice, and we do not understand the whole picture from God's point of view from the beginning to the end of most things. That's why we must not judge Biblical matters by our limited understanding but to trust in the Lord (the written Word of God): *And the times of this ignorance God winked at; but now commandeth all men every where to repent.* Acts 17:30 However, it was mentioned on page seven, the importance of being able "to fight against Biblical deception." *(For the weapons of our warfare are not carnal, but mighty through God to the pulling down of strong holds;) Casting down imaginations, and every high thing that exalteth itself against the knowledge of God* ... 2 Corinthians 10:4-5 It's vital for every believer to be equipped with these weapons. Study Ephesians 6:10-18.

## God's Word hasn't changed, but church doctrine has.

The following is an abbreviated church history on marriage and divorce from the archives of a major denomination to show how this denomination, and most others, has changed its teachings and beliefs on marriage. This excerpt is quoted from *It's A Matter of Life or Death; Wrong Thinking about Marriage Leads to Destruction;* Judith Brumbaugh: Restoration of the Family, PO Box 621342, Oviedo, FL 32762.

### Rules Relating to Marriage

**Up to 1892:** There was no mention of divorce: Those married in the church must be saved. Second Corinthians 6:14 was quoted in this section: *Be ye not unequally yoked together with unbelievers: for what fellowship hath righteousness with unrighteousness? and what communion hath light with darkness?* Parents must give consent to marry. No clergy could perform a marriage ceremony for a divorced person.

**1892:** This was the first mention of approval of divorce: "Divorce for adultery is lawful ... No minister is to solemnize any marriage in any case where there is a divorced wife or living husband ... but the 'innocent' party, if adulterous behavior of a mate had been proven, is permitted to marry a second partner." Reference again is made to 2 Corinthians 6:14, and parents must give consent for the marriage.

**1900:** The Scripture reference to 2 Corinthians 6:14 was omitted as well as consent of parents needed before their children could marry.

**1940:** The "innocent party" exemption was expanded to include other vicious acts which "invalidated the marriage vow," including mental or physical cruelty.

**1960:** The adultery exception was removed. The following was added: "In view of the seriousness with which the Scriptures and church regard divorce, clergymen can marry one-flesh spouses to other mates if the divorced person is 'sufficiently aware' of the factors leading to the failure of the previous marriage and the divorced person intends to make a second marriage "truly Christian.'"

**1976:** Basically all prohibitions were removed: "When partners after thoughtful consideration and counsel are estranged beyond reconciliation, the church recognizes the right of divorced person to marry."

# 3

# *There's Nothing New Under The Sun!*

Easy divorce and finding excuses for divorce are nothing new. Putting away and marrying another were also commonly committed sins when the Bible was written. Sadly, the Pharisees, who were the religious leaders and experts in the Old Testament law, were also the ones who tried to twist the Scriptures to find loopholes for "putting away" (divorcing) their wives. Ironically, they were blinded by their knowledge of the Scriptures. They knew all <u>about</u> God, but they did not <u>know</u> God. They did not recognize that it was God in the flesh (Jesus) Who was standing in front of them and Whom they tried to maneuver into approving of divorce with their subtle, craftily constructed questions. Study two of their recorded questions below:

*The Pharisees also came unto him [Jesus], <u>tempting</u> him, and saying unto him, Is it <u>lawful</u> for a man to put away his wife for every [any] cause?* Matthew 19:3

*They say unto him, Why did Moses then command to give a writing of divorcement, and to put her away?* Matthew 19:7

These experts in Old Testament law already knew the answers to the questions they asked Jesus. He, unlike most of us, didn't debate their misleading questions. They were questions taken out of context and framed, as attorneys sometimes do, to force an answer they wanted instead of permitting the "respondent" to answer in a way that would express Truth. Jesus, of course, was fully aware they knew the Scriptural answer to their questions.

> Jesus taught by example. He didn't debate about sin. He asked questions and quoted Scripture.

Instead of debating with these religious leaders, Jesus tried to teach them—or more likely—tried to convict them—by quoting the Word. This was the pattern He used so often. He quoted the Word and gave Biblical examples. These are principles each of us should learn and use. In His reply, Jesus (1) asked a rhetorical question—one for which the answer was evident and to which He wasn't looking for an answer: *Have ye not read ...?* Matthew 19:4 He then (2) quoted Scripture to answer His rhetorical question.

That Scripture from which Jesus quoted is from the first book of the Old Testament, Genesis. **Don't miss the extreme importance of not just *what* Jesus quoted but *from where* He quoted.** Genesis is part of what is called the *Torah*. The Torah is considered Judaism's most important text by the Jews—these Pharisees. It's the comprehensive term for the substance of Judaism. The Torah includes the first five books of the Old Testament: Genesis, Exodus, Leviticus, Numbers, and Deuteronomy. But don't you just chuckle at Jesus' question and how He, in turn, "lawyered" his rhetorical question? It was "clothed" in the very text, their favored Torah, in which the Pharisees were experts but ironically <u>blinded by their own expertise</u>:

*And he answered and said unto them, **Have ye not read**, that he which made them <u>at the beginning</u> made them male and female, And said, For this cause shall a man leave father and mother, and shall cleave to his wife: and they twain shall be one flesh? Wherefore they are no more twain, but one flesh. What therefore God hath joined together, let not man put asunder.*
Matthew 19:4-6

It's important to bear in mind that Jesus wasn't asking the question (*Have ye not read ...?*) because He didn't know the answer. He is all knowing. He certainly knew that not only did the Pharisees know what was recorded in Genesis about God's "law of marriage," but they were prideful about their knowledge of Scripture. In His reply to the Pharisees, Jesus answered them by quoting from Genesis 2:24. This is a parallel, closely related, important Scripture:

| Jesus knew the Pharisees had "read" and that they knew what the Old Testament said from which He quoted. ||
|---|---|
| *Therefore shall a man leave his father and his mother, and shall cleave unto his wife: and they shall be **one flesh**.* Genesis 2:24 | *And said, For this cause shall a man leave father and mother, and shall cleave to his wife: and they twain shall be **one flesh**?* Matthew 19:5 |

Genesis 2:24 is God's clear picture of the indissoluble nature of a **one-flesh** marriage. It is His original, universal, and ONLY plan for

marriage: one man for one woman until one of the two is removed physically from this earth through death. God's intent for marriage has not changed, nor will it ever change:

> *For ever, O LORD, thy word is settled in heaven.*
> Psalm 119:89

At the beginning of this chapter, it was mentioned that unscriptural marriages and divorces are not a new invention of modern man. These were a problem when Jesus walked this earth and even when Moses led the Israelites out of Egypt. That's why Jesus and the New Testament writers have so much to say about these topics, and it's why we're told Moses tried to "manage" or deal with the sin of his people divorcing and marrying multiple wives or husbands:

*They* [Pharisees] *say unto him* [Jesus], *Why did Moses then command to give a writing of divorcement, and to put her away?* Matthew 19:7

Again, the Pharisees knew the answer, but they had hardened hearts and refused to accept the Word of God; or perhaps it was that they could not "hear" (understand) because of their hardened hearts.

*... Moses **because** of the <u>hardness</u> of **your** hearts suffered* [allowed] *you to put away your wives: but from the beginning it was not so.* Matthew 19:8

Let's put this in perspective so confusion over Moses' allowing for divorce will be clarified. Look at it from the perspective of Jesus. He said it was because the people whom Moses was trying to lead had hearts which were hardened; Jesus further set the record straight; it was Moses, not He, who "allowed" it.

This "allowing for divorce" may be a relevant warning to those today who also say, with the wrong heart attitude, "Moses allowed for divorce." Do they not also, perhaps by implication, have hardened hearts as did the Pharisees?

Think on this. Consider how many divorces take place in the United States: **more than one million each year**. Now <u>who</u> do you think has "allowed" this to happen?

> Moses "allowed" divorce. Jesus "allows" what He hates: over one million divorces every year!

Man has legalized, taken part in, and promoted divorce actions, but God has "allowed" these. The LORD also "allows" man to murder and commit other sins. That's part of the complex picture of free will. However, the question and focus should be, "Does God *approve* of these sins?" No, he does not, and as a matter of Scripture, He hates sin and especially that of divorce:

*For the LORD, the God of Israel, saith that he **hateth** putting away: for one covereth violence with his garment, saith the LORD of hosts: therefore take heed to your spirit, that ye **deal not treacherously**.* Malachi 2:16

Out of His love and concern for our good, God is saying: "Don't divorce your covenant spouse." Man, however, is not a puppet. He has the option to choose to remain faithful, "for better or for worse," or to violate his marital-lifetime commitment to his one-flesh spouse. It's God's love that "allows" us to choose sin or righteousness.

> God's love allows us to "yield to whom we want to obey."

*Know ye not, that to whom <u>ye yield yourselves</u> servants to obey, his servants ye are to whom ye obey; whether of sin unto death, or of obedience unto righteousness?* Romans 6:16

It's important to understand:
- Neither Jesus nor His inerrant Scriptures (the Word) change because of the passage of time or sin on someone's part.
- The universal <u>application</u> of Scripture doesn't change regardless of someone's circumstances, heritage, age, or political standing. Jesus is no respecter of persons.
- The Word, the Holy Spirit, and God will always agree.
- God, Jesus (the Word), the Holy Spirit, and the Holy Ghost, are One: the Godhead. The Godhead gives messages that are always consistent with the written Word—the Bible.
- Jesus will not overlook adultery: ... *whoremongers and adulterers God will judge.* Hebrews 13:4

## What does God allow?

God is revealed in three different ways: God the Father, God the Son [also the Word], and God the Holy Ghost. These three are One and **always** agree. They are corporately expressed in the New Testament as the Godhead: Acts 14:29, Romans 1:20, and Colossians 2:9. It's very important to understand what it means to say these three will never disagree. This is because there are many who say they "hear" messages "in their spirit" or are given "a word of knowledge" from others; yet, these "messages" do not line up with Scripture. If that happens, the "messenger" has not been the Holy Spirit. The Holy Spirit will never give a message which conflicts with the written Word, assuming the Bible used does not contain doctrinal error. This point is made because some people will say God told them to divorce their covenant spouse, or that God told them He will bring them another spouse when they already have a living, one-flesh spouse.

*For there are three that bear record in heaven, the Father, the Word, and the Holy Ghost: and these three are one. And there are three that bear witness in*

*earth, the spirit, and the water, and the blood: and these three agree in one.*
1 John 5:7-8

<u>*Jesus Christ*</u> *the same yesterday, and to day, and for ever.* Hebrews 13:8. *In the beginning <u>was the Word</u>, and the Word was with God, and the Word was God. ... And the Word was made flesh [Jesus], and dwelt among us ...* John 1:1,14

*... for <u>thou hast magnified thy word above all thy name</u>.* Psalm 138:2

Neither God, His Word, nor His Spirit will ever give instructions that lead to the ending of His supernatural, invisible, permanent, one-flesh joining—marriage—other than what is written in the Bible. What is written in the Word is clear. It's only the physical death of one of the spouses that dissolves a covenant-marriage. Again, God will not tell us one thing by His Spirit and give a conflicting message in His Scripture about marriage—or any other doctrine:

*The wife is bound by the law as long as her husband liveth; but if her husband be dead, she is at liberty to be married to whom she will; only in the Lord.* 1 Corinthians 7:39

## It's not a "re-marriage."

**We camouflage adultery.**

Man tries to camouflage what God says He hates in one way by calling the sin of adultery what it isn't, "re-marriage." Looking at adultery through the lenses of "re-marriage" doesn't carry with it, for most who use this term, the implication of a sinful lifestyle. If those same people were called adulterers and adulteresses—the terms God uses—they might begin to see their lifestyle as God sees it.

The prefix "re" means to repeat with the same criteria. For example, if a person re-enters a room, he must have been in that SAME room previously. Likewise, if a person were to Biblically re-marry, he would marry the same person a second time. We don't know if the man at the left is entering the room for the first time or is re-entering a room he has been in before. Also on the door panels are two different "views" of marriage: (1) God's: Covenant, Re-marriage; (2) Man's: Adultery, "Re-marriage."

**You can't re-enter a room you have never entered previously.**

God never uses the term "re-marriage." It's people in the world who have turned the term into a euphemism by saying someone is "re-married." It's what has become politically correct and socially acceptable—according to the standards of society. The LORD labels everyone who divorces a one-flesh spouse and marries another person an *adulterer* because that person is committing adultery. That's why, when "re-marriage" means adultery, it is always enclosed in quotes in this text.

## Chapter 3

Many people measure feelings and success as parameters to evaluate the validity of a marriage. While many adulterers and adulteresses are successful in the world and may feel fulfilled, happy, and blessed, a marriage isn't created on feelings and success. It's based on a joining by God. It's <u>WHAT</u> God hath joined together. Another important aspect to be assessed is why anyone would do something God hates and says will keep him out of the Kingdom of God—"re-marriage":

*For the LORD, the God of Israel, saith that he hateth putting away: for one covereth violence with his garment, saith the LORD of hosts: therefore take heed to your spirit, that ye deal not treacherously.* Malachi 2:16

*The heart is deceitful above all things, and desperately wicked: who can know it? I the LORD search the heart, I try the reins, even to give every man according to his ways, and according to the **fruit of his doings**.* Jeremiah 17:9-10

Some who read this text may not realize that adultery is one of several sins listed in Galatians 5:19-21 and 1 Corinthians 6:9-10 that keeps those who do not repent from it from inheriting the Kingdom of God. Their lack of understanding may be in part because many of God's words have been removed through modern Bible translations. In the chapters ahead, many of these omissions will be discussed as well as why the removal of these words is spiritually perilous.

*Now the works of the flesh are manifest, which are these; Adultery, fornication, uncleanness ... as I have also told you in time past, that they which do such things shall not inherit the kingdom of God.* Galatians 5:19-21

*Know ye not that the unrighteous shall not inherit the kingdom of God? Be not deceived: neither fornicators, nor idolaters, nor adulterers, nor effeminate, nor abusers of themselves with mankind, Nor thieves, nor covetous, nor drunkards, nor revilers, nor extortioners, shall inherit the kingdom of God.* 1 Corinthians 6:9-10

## Hebrew words and expressions are translated for New Testament Gentile audiences.

You may have heard it said, as have I for many years, that Matthew wrote his gospel to the Jews as did most of the New Testament writers. Could it be that there is evidence to shift that belief to be a bit broader? Even though the Jews, including the disciples, often didn't understand the teachings of Jesus, He, on several occasions, ascribed their lack of understanding to a different level of comprehension: *And he said unto them, How is it that ye do not understand?* Mark 8:21

The New Testament writings give us a look into Jewish customs, expressions, beliefs, and thinking. It was written by people who had a strong Hebrew background; yet, **it was also written for a Greek-speaking culture who didn't understand the Jewish customs or the Hebrew language.** There are, for example, some 80 references to the Jews in Acts and 68 in the Gospel of John so perhaps it would be more intuitive to say that the New Testament is about the Jews but not written wholly specifically to the Jews. For example if an author is writing TO a group of people, he wouldn't normally make statements such as the following—many more of which are found throughout the New Testament: *And this is the record of John, when the Jews sent priests and Levites from Jerusalem ...* John 1:19 *Much people of the Jews therefore knew that he was there ...* John 12:9 *Now the feast of unleavened bread drew nigh, which is called the Passover.* Luke 22:1 Surely, no Jew needs to have explained to him that the *feast of unleavened bread* was the *Passover*!

On page 265 (second paragraph), there is an expression I have specifically written as a "play" on Jewish expressions: "which being interpreted is." This expression is so written to emphasize how there are like embedded Jewish idioms that "silently" explain terms to readers they normally might not understand and which emphasize the Hebrew influence within the writings of the New Testament. These terms are ones the Jews would have understood, but Gentiles then and today likely would not: *...**Emmanuel**, which being interpreted is, God with us.* Matthew 1:23; *... **Messias**, which is, being interpreted, the Christ.* John 1:41; *... which is called in the Hebrew tongue **Bethesda**, having five porches.* John 5:2; *... called the place of a skull, which is called in the Hebrew **Golgotha**.* John 19:17; *... a place that is called the Pavement, but in the Hebrew, **Gabbatha**.* John 19:13 *... **Eloi, Eloi, lama sabachthani**? which is, being interpreted, My God, my God, why hast thou forsaken me?* Mark 15:34

# 4

# Let's Begin At The Beginning: A Very Good Place To Start!

All questions and discussions about marriage should start and end with the Bible. Ironically, many who rarely seriously study the Bible seem to have an uncanny ability to defend, with seeming accuracy, Scriptures which they feel provide loopholes. This is especially true when they, a family member, or a close friend are involved in the issue of "re-marriage." God's unwavering standard of marriage—one man for one woman until death parts them—becomes something "their God" would not expect. Who are we to believe? There are so many varying teachings and teachers who seem so authoritative. Teachers and pastors have college degrees; they know Hebrew and Greek; many lecture with charisma that almost charms audiences into a stupor. There are many versions of the Bible, all with varying translations proclaiming they translate from the best and oldest manuscripts. But what makes them the best, and is the oldest the best just because it may be the oldest?

God presents marriage and divorce for us in simple words that even a child can understand: ... *They shall be one flesh. ... What therefore God hath joined together, let not man put asunder.* Genesis 2:24; Mark 10:9 Yet, man has made the "simplicity of the gospel" very complex. Paul states it so contemporarily. It's what is happening today:

*But I fear, lest by any means, as the serpent beguiled Eve through his subtilty, so your minds should be corrupted from the **simplicity** that is in Christ. For if he that cometh preacheth another Jesus, whom we have not preached, or if ye receive another spirit, which ye have not received, or another gospel, which ye have not accepted, ye might well bear with him.*
2 Corinthians 11:3-4

## What was the principle Jesus was giving for every person to understand ... *from the beginning*?

When Jesus spoke to the Pharisees about the hardheartedness of the Old Testament spouses who had "re-married," He also stated that His

"law of marriage" had not changed. It was the same as what He created in the garden of Eden for all generations—the picture of the indissolubility of a one-flesh marriage. There was no way for Adam to put Eve away or for Eve to put away Adam because they were one flesh—until death:

*And the rib, which the LORD God had taken from man, made he a woman and brought her unto the man. And Adam said, This is now bone of my bones, and flesh of my flesh: she shall be called Woman, **because she was taken out of Man**. Therefore* [in a like manner] *shall a man leave his father and his mother, and shall cleave unto his wife: and they shall be one flesh.* Genesis 2:22-24

## Teachings on marriage should model those of Jesus; they should start at the beginning.

One of the major weaknesses of most studies on marriage and divorce is the fact that few start with a study of God's creation of marriage in the book of Genesis. In all other disciplines, most agree that it's vital to first lay a foundation of basic information before trying to master the advanced concepts. For example, we cannot understand advanced Algebra if we don't have some mastery of basic mathematics. However, when it comes to such an important topic as marriage and divorce, rarely do such discussions start with Genesis 2:22-24, nor do they even include a review of these formative Scriptures.

> All discussions on marriage should follow Jesus' example and include a study of Genesis 2:22-24.

Without this basic foundation, when man tries to authoritatively discuss verses so dependent upon the Genesis account of marriage, he becomes enmeshed in everything except the Scriptures themselves. He considers what man thinks, or he enters into complex discussions regarding the underlying Greek words and grammar. He draws unwarranted focus to obscure manuscripts. Did Jesus do this? No, His teaching model given in both Matthew 19 and Mark 10 was to *refer to the Scriptures* on the nature of marriage.

Jesus, for example, specifically referred the Pharisees to the BEGINNING OF SCRIPTURE, the creation of marriage as it was recorded in Genesis. On each of those occasions, notice the audience Jesus was addressing. It was the religious "experts" of His day:

*And he answered and said unto them* [Pharisees]*, Have ye not read, that he which made them at the <u>beginning</u> made them male and female.* Matthew 19:4*; But from the <u>beginning</u> of the creation God made them male and female.* Mark 10:6 *He saith unto them, Moses because of the hardness of your hearts suffered you to put away your wives: but from the <u>beginning</u> it was not so.* Matthew 19:8

It wasn't that they hadn't read those Scriptures. It was that they refused to accept the clear visual of marriage that God had established in Genesis. Perhaps this was because they were people-pleasers; or, maybe they, too, were divorcing and marrying multiple spouses:

*He saith unto them, Moses because of the hardness of <u>**your**</u> hearts suffered <u>**you**</u> to put away your wives: but from the beginning it was not so.* Matthew 19:8

The Scriptures must be the **basis** for decision-making on Scriptural matters. Decisions should not be based on sources outside the Word of God; not this or that renowned teacher or Hebrew/Greek expert; not on Hillel, or Shammai, or the vast list of "church fathers"—but on God's preserved Word. Other teachings can add background information, but such references should not be used to alter what the Word of God teaches. God needs no one to affirm what He has preserved through His Scripture.

That's what will be taught in this text. The final analysis of Biblical discussions will come from the Scriptures as they are recorded in the

English text. God gives more than enough proof in His authoritative Scriptures which have been translated into our common language:

| All discussions of marriage, divorce and "re-marriage" must begin with the creation of marriage in Genesis. | | |
|---|---|---|
| Genesis 2:21-24 | Matthew 19:4-6 | Mark 10:6-9 |
| *And the LORD God caused a deep sleep to fall upon Adam and he slept: and he took one of his ribs, and closed up the flesh instead thereof;* | *And he [Jesus] answered and said unto them,* **Have ye not read***, that he which made them at the* **beginning** *made them male and female,* | *But* **from the beginning** *of the creation God made them male and female.* |
| *And the rib, which the LORD God had taken from man, made he a woman, and brought her unto the man.* | *And said, For this cause shall a man leave father and mother, and shall cleave to his wife: and they twain shall be one flesh?* | *For this cause shall a man leave his father and mother, and cleave to his wife;* |
| *And Adam said, This is now bone of my bones, and flesh of my flesh: she shall be called Woman, because she was taken out of Man.* | | *And they twain shall be one flesh: so then they are no more twain, but one flesh.* |
| *Therefore shall a man leave his father and his mother, and shall cleave unto his wife: and they shall be one flesh.* | *Wherefore they are no more twain, but one flesh. What therefore God hath joined together, let not man put asunder.* | *What therefore God hath joined together, let not man put asunder.* |

The Genesis account of the creation of marriage is succinctly and simply given, but man has made the interpretation of this miracle so complex. First, there was man (Adam). He was formed from the dust of the ground. Then woman (Eve) was created, not from the dust of the earth, but from the rib of Adam. Adam didn't see this take place; he was asleep. From the Biblical record, it appears that after God took the rib from Adam, He either created Eve in another location in the garden, or He took her around the garden before God awakened Adam from his sleep. We're told that God **brought** Eve to Adam.

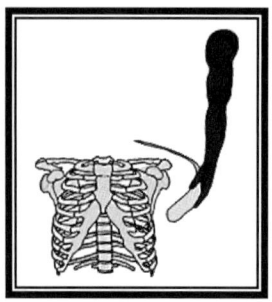 

***And** the rib, which the LORD God had taken from man, made he a woman, **<u>and brought her</u>** unto the man.* Genesis 2:22

## Every word of God is pure, even every *and*.

God has a plan and purpose for every word in the Bible. There are no accidents on His behalf—even for a word most people don't study—*and*. This three-letter conjunction has broad applications in the Bible that go beyond what many have been taught. *And* is used as a connective which joins thoughts and actions; however, especially in the Bible, *and* is also used as a signpost to indicate indeterminate periods of time. That's the aspect of *and* that many gloss over. There is also an important idiosyncrasy of Biblical language structure. *And* is a common word used to start many verses in the Bible. Most grammarians frown on the practice of starting sentences with *and,* but God makes a regular practice of doing so. Most of the verses in the first several chapters of Genesis start with the word *and*. Study an example on the next page from Genesis 1:1-7:

Chapter 4

> ***And* has many important functions that may be overlooked.**
> Genesis 1:1-7
>
> *1:1 In the beginning God created the Heaven **and** the earth.*
>
> *2 **And** the earth was without form, and void; **and** darkness was upon the face of the deep. **And** the Spirit of God moved upon the face of the waters.*
>
> *3 **And** God said, Let there be light: **and** there was light.*
>
> *4 **And** God saw the light, that it was good: **and** God divided the light from the darkness.*
>
> *5 **And** God called the light Day, **and** the darkness he called Night. **And** the evening **and** the morning were the first day.*
>
> *6 **And** God said, Let there be a firmament in the midst of the waters, **and** let it divide the waters from the waters.*
>
> *7 **And** God made the firmament, **and** divided the waters which were under the firmament from the waters which were above the firmament: **and** it was so.*

Starting a sentence with the word *and* is a pattern that runs throughout the Bible. As mentioned above, this important word serves several purposes. It is used as a connective joining thoughts and actions, but more importantly for this study, it is also a signpost to indicate indeterminate periods of <u>time</u>. That is likely a new concept for many readers but one that should be noticed. Study, from your Bible, the tragic story of David's falling prey to lust and murder in 2 Samuel 11. Circle each time *and* begins a verse, and notice the many times that this conjunction is an indicator of an indeterminate period of time.

To gain a greater appreciation for the word *and* being used as a sign to represent an unknown period of time, look in your Bible again. Focus on the first two chapters of Genesis. Can you guess how many times the word *and* is used to begin the verses and clauses in these first two chapters? The answer is ... 154 times! Whether at the beginning of a verse or within a verse, *and* can be a key to let the reader know that this is an undefined period of time. Few readers are aware of this Biblical internal time clock that God has had ticking silently throughout all ages and how, in the Bible, the word *and* is often used to indicate God's silent clock. Man is deceived when he thinks he controls time.

Man thinks he controls time. It's God's time clock that has been ticking.

We know that the LORD could have completed the actions in Genesis 1:1-7 in a nanosecond, a billionth of a second, or less. He doesn't tell us how long it took. What we do know is that God included 154 *and* "signs" for some reason in the first two chapters of Genesis. His words are not an accident.

This unconventional use of the word *and* should help us to pause, take notice, and be reminded that reading the Bible is not something we should do in a quick and carefree manner. Every word has a purpose.

## Chapter 4
## How long did it take God to create woman?

When we see the word *and*, especially at the beginning of a sentence, it is often an indicator of an action. We rarely know the time frame or the possible concurring unrecorded events for that action. We only know those acts are for an unspecified length of time:

*<u>And</u> the rib, which the LORD God had taken from man, made he a woman, <u>and</u> brought her unto the man.* Genesis 2:22

Likewise with God's creation of man and woman, we are not told how long it took to create man, nor how long it took to create Eve from the rib of Adam. Additionally, we're not told how much time elapsed, or what took place in the interim between the point at which God created Eve from the rib of Adam **and** when He brought her unto the man (Adam). This is part of the "veiled" mystery of the Scripture—something God has chosen not to reveal.

Even so, the two *ands* in Genesis 2:22 should now make you stop and think about a potential time lapse **and** what may have happened during that time. *Ands* can provide additional insight into the picture God presents in Genesis 2:21-24. Jesus quoted from this passage in three New Testament Scriptures to define marriage: Matthew 19:4-5, 19:8, and Mark 10:6-9. The Genesis account can serve as the LORD's visual for the kind of bond He creates when two people are made one flesh. These "picturesque" Scriptures help to show the indissoluble nature of a man and a woman after God joins them into a one-flesh creation. Study additional examples on the next page of *and* used as a connective and to indicate an indeterminate period of time.

| *And* is a small but powerful word. It joins not only thoughts and actions but also bridges gaps of indeterminate time. ||
|---|---|
| Joining actions | Joining time |
| *Whosoever putteth away his wife, **and** marrieth another, committeth adultery: **and** whosoever marrieth her that is put away from her husband committeth adultery.* Luke 16:18 | ***And** the earth was without form, and void; **and** darkness was upon the face of the deep. **And** the Spirit of God moved upon the face of the waters.* Genesis 1:2 |

The following are sequential actions, but they are not simultaneous. Perhaps you hadn't considered this important signpost and usage of *and*:

- **And** Adam gave names to all cattle.
- **And** the LORD God caused a deep sleep to fall upon Adam.
- **And** he slept.
- **And** he took one of his ribs.
- **And** closed up the flesh instead thereof.
- **And** the rib, which the LORD God had taken from man, made he a woman.
- **And** brought her unto the man. Genesis 2:20-22

Again, what potentially happened between the time when God took the rib from Adam **and** brought Eve to him? Where did God go? Could it be that the LORD showed Eve the garden? The garden was immense. It was there that Adam named all the cattle, the fowl of the air, and every beast of the field. Within this massive perfect garden ... *God planted ... every tree that is pleasant to the sight, and good for food; the tree of life also in the midst of the garden, and the tree of knowledge of good and evil.* Genesis 2:8-9 The garden seemingly was enclosed and had just one entrance—at least after the point at which man and woman were evicted from the garden because of their sin against God. The LORD

*... placed at the east of the garden of Eden Cherubims, and a flaming sword which turned every way, to keep the way of the tree of life.* Genesis 3:24

## Think of words as containers, containers for multiple meanings and usages.

Words convey multiple concepts. There is a purpose for the inclusion of each word, no matter how large or small. The word *set*, for example, has 464 definitions in the Oxford English Dictionary. *Run* has 396 definitions. The word *wine* has many different applications in the Bible ranging from the pure juice extracted from the grape to a state which can cause drunkenness. So it's vital to apply the correct contextual application of words, knowing they have so many different shades of meanings.

That's why it's important to read the Bible differently than one might scan a newspaper, or speed-read a novel. Thus *God* (1) *caused a deep sleep to come upon Adam AND Adam slept AND* (2) *he took one of his ribs AND* (3) *closed up the flesh instead thereof; AND the rib, which the LORD God had taken from man,* (4) *made he a woman, AND* (5) *brought her unto the man.* Genesis 2:21-22 It was after these events that God joined together, from two totally independent people, something original and very precious. WHAT it is that God joins together, we're not told; but He calls it one flesh. What we do know is that God's joining is so complete that it cannot be reversed by any act of man: ... *they are **no more** twain, but one flesh.* Mark 10:8 We also learn from Scripture that God considers any other type of marital joining a sin against Him which He names *adultery*.

## The word adulterate provides special insight to understand the nature of Adultery.

Why might the LORD have chosen the words *adulterer* or *adulteress* for someone who marries or is married to a person who has a living one-flesh spouse? It's because it is not the real thing, from God's perspective. There is something which doesn't belong—a "foreign substance." You may have heard it said that God looks on the heart. In other words, He sees more than just what's on the surface. That's a principle that can be applied by taking an unconventional look at the "heart" of the noun *adultery*. The root word from which adultery comes is derived from the Latin verb *adulterium* or adulterate. Here are some definitions and synonyms for adulterate: to corrupt, debase, make impure by adding a foreign or inferior substance, often by replacing valuable ingredients with inferior ones; to contaminate or depreciate; to make impure or inferior by adding alien or less desirable materials; altered; adulterer, adulteress.

A one-flesh marriage is very different from an adulterous "marriage." God creates the former; man creates the latter. God calls those joined by Him in a one-flesh marriage *husband* and *wife*. He calls those joined by man *adulterers* (husbands) and *adulteresses* (wives). Please understand that these Biblical terms are difficult to write knowing they offend many. To offend a reader is not the purpose of using these Biblical terms. The purpose is to help those who haven't understood or read these Scriptures to study for themselves and pray for enlightenment from the Word of God.

# 5

# *Biblical Guidelines To Scripture Interpretation Become Very Important.*

Y ou may or may not have realized it, but what was taught in Chapter 4 made use of two of the important Bible study guidelines listed in Chapter 2 on page eight—context and word usage. Each of the guidelines holds an important key to correct interpretation of Scripture. However, they are especially important with the study of Matthew 19:9. Matthew 19:9 is a verse which will be the subject of several chapters as well as another parallel verse in Matthew's gospel, Matthew 5:32. Review page eight to see if you know how each of the nine guidelines listed there might apply to this chapter. Make a note of those you feel have an impact on the interpretation of the power-packed statement that Jesus made as recorded in Matthew 19:9:

*And I say unto you, Whosoever shall put away his wife, except it be for fornication, and shall marry another, committeth adultery: and whoso marrieth her which is put away doth commit adultery.* Matthew 19:9

You might think that *power packed* is an extreme expression. However, Matthew 19:9 has become the most hotly debated Scripture on divorce used by Christians and non-Christians today. This is my personal, strongly held belief because, in my 40 years of ministry, Matthew 19:9 has been the focal point for those who search the Bible looking for a loophole to justify divorce and "re-marriage." Yet, do you really think that Jesus didn't know the wording in Matthew 19:9 would be hotly debated, even though similar wording is uniquely given in another instance within this same gospel? It's also the primary verse misinterpreted by many pastors and ministries. This pattern of misapplying Matthew 19:9 has been increasing as the proliferation of new versions of the Bible has also increased. These versions have a common pattern of inserting words to justify the sin of adultery; and, as will be shown in later chapters, many of these paraphrased words are not in the underlying texts from which the authors of these Bibles are translating.

One of the guidelines for accurate Bible study is to compare parallel Scriptures and passages. As mentioned above, Matthew 5:32 is a parallel Scripture to Matthew 19:9, but there's also a parallel passage given in the book of Mark (10:4-12). Why are these addressed as parallel Scriptures? It's because they not only address putting away a wife but also state the danger of what often follows in the lives of one or both spouses who are involved in a divorce proceeding. They often "re-marry" another person; even though, according to God's "law of marriage," they are still one flesh with their original spouse.

Jesus' concluding remarks, in each of these Scriptures, Matthew 5:32, 19:9, and Mark 10:4-12, serve as a reminder of the danger of adultery that is tied to "re-marriages." That's why we must continue to help others to seek answers within the Scripture so they will know, from the Word of God, why "re-marriage" is not the kind of marriage that God defines as one-flesh, but as adultery. Many who read this book may not accept the presented Scriptural proofs. They don't see the sharing of these Scriptures as what it is meant to be—a lifeline. It's not a matter of being unkind when these Truths are shared. It's a matter of loving people enough to help them avoid eternal disaster:

*And of some have compassion, making a difference: And others save with fear, pulling them out of the fire; hating even the garment spotted by the flesh.* Jude 1:22-23

Each person, however, has been given the right by the LORD to exercise his own free-will choice. This is nothing new. God's chosen people, the Israelites were also given a like choice when Joshua told them to choose whether they wanted to serve the pagan gods with whom they had become fond or to serve the LORD:

*And if it seem evil unto you to serve the LORD, <u>choose you</u> this day whom ye will serve; whether the gods which your fathers served that were on the other side of the flood, or the gods of the Amorites, in whose land ye dwell: but as for me and my house, we will serve the LORD.* Joshua 24:15

Biblical Guidelines To Scripture Interpretation Become Very Important.

## Compare Scripture with Scripture.

Three parallel Scripture passages are given below. The gospels of Matthew and Mark are much alike in context; however, there are some important differences pertinent to this study. For example, what information is included in Matthew 5:32 and 19:9 that is not included in Mark 10:11-12? The words printed below in **bold** text illustrate the significant differences between the verses. These differences are not textual errors or scribal additions or deletions; they represent cultural differences between the Jews and Gentiles that are an integral part of the Word of God. Who were the main audiences in each passage given below and what was the purpose of the conversation in each?

| Jesus warns against putting away in three parallel passages. In two of these, both in Matthew, He gives the exception. | | |
|---|---|---|
| Matthew 5:32 | Matthew 19:9 | Mark 10:11-12 |
| *But I say unto you, That whosoever shall put away his wife,* ***saving for the cause of fornication****, causeth her to commit adultery: and whosoever shall marry her that is divorced committeth adultery.* | *And I say unto you, Whosoever shall put away his wife,* ***except it be for fornication****, and shall marry another, committeth adultery: and whoso marrieth her which is put away doth commit adultery.* | *And he saith unto them, Whosoever shall put away his wife, and marry another, committeth adultery against her. And if a woman shall put away her husband, and be married to another, she committeth adultery.* |

If you reviewed the guideline list on page eight, you may recognize how several of those guidelines are illustrated above: compare Scriptures, especially parallel ones; investigate differences in the wording of similar teachings; consider the audience and cultural influences. Matthew 5:32 and 19:9 include the words *saving for the cause of fornication* and *except it be for fornication*, what most call the exception clauses. Mark, however, seemingly recording the same information, did not record those words.

## The Jewish engagement language must be properly interpreted.

Biblical guideline four on page eight lists the importance of considering the culture and idiomatic expressions surrounding the teaching. The Bible is written for everyone; however, different books of the Bible have different styles and emphases. Even though Mark and Matthew included many of the same topics, as you saw above, there are some noticeable differences between their contents. Matthew, a Jewish tax collector, wrote his gospel with a perspective to address several issues unique to the Jewish culture. One such issue that is especially important to the correct interpretation of Matthew's writings is the engagement language included not only in Matthew 5:32 and 19:9 but in several other passages throughout the Bible. It wasn't that Gentiles didn't also have engagements, but it's the Jewish *engagement language* and espousal practices included in Matthew that must be grasped by readers if the correct interpretations of Matthew's teachings are to be understood.

Jewish engagements are called *espousals* in the New Testament and usually *betrothals* in the Old Testament. Because of a lack of knowledge of the Jewish engagement language, most people who refer to the Matthew 19:9 exception clause start off in the wrong direction.

They also do so because they often appeal to it for the wrong reason. They are coming to a Jewish kosher deli looking to buy a ham or pork sandwich. They will not find what they are seeking. A Jewish kosher deli would never sell ham or pork! Likewise, those looking for Biblical support of divorce and "re-marriage" are looking in the wrong place. They won't find it in

> Those who come to a Jewish kosher deli looking for a ham sandwich will not find what they seek.

God's Word. They miss the cultural clues offered on Matthew's "menu." Yet, it is these missed clues that clarify why Matthew included the exception clause, but other New Testament writers did not.

The Pharisees, like many people today, came to Jesus asking if there were reasons to divorce. Notice, however, they did not ask if it were permissible to "re-marry." (That seems to be a major concurrent question today.) The Pharisees' question in Matthew 19:3 was ... *Is it lawful for a man to put away his wife for every cause?*

Reasons to divorce a one-flesh spouse were totally foreign to the "kosher" *answer* Jesus gave as His response to the Pharisees in Matthew 19:9. Jesus succinctly included two differing contexts in His answer. One was uniquely recorded only in the book of Matthew. The contexts of the response Jesus gave were twofold: one included an exception that could apply to the Jewish espousal; the other was not an exception, but a response that would apply to all covenant marriages. It is the former, *except it be for fornication* (in Matthew 19:9) that is misinterpreted because it is applied out of context. This is the same misused <u>contextual</u> *principle* given in the three examples in Chapter 1. The first one described riding a bike to Jamaica. A second example illustrated combining a Scripture about Judas' suicide with another unrelated verse. A third was the reference to those who incorrectly use David's adultery as an excuse to justify their adultery. Each example showed the importance of not just reading the words but understanding the context.

## The message the LORD gave in Matthew 19:9 was not a new one.

Prior to the confrontation between Jesus and the Pharisees, recorded in Matthew 19:9, Jesus had already spoken publicly on adultery. This was in His *Sermon on the Mount* recorded in Matthew 5:32. This was the SAME basic issue the Pharisees brought to Jesus for Him to address a second time.

The Pharisees were adept at taking God's law from the Old Testament and applying it to situations that God never intended. They applied His laws out of context. They changed it and placed their own man-made commandments and traditions above God's Word:

*Howbeit in vain do they worship me, teaching for doctrines the commandments of men.* Mark 7:7

Jesus, in the *Sermon on the Mount* (Matthew 5-7), was training His disciples as well as correcting unscriptural teachings the people had heard from their religious leaders. He was helping them to refocus on God's unchanged law. Jesus, as part of His teachings in the *Sermon on the Mount*, not only restated the Old Testament commandment, *Thou shalt not commit adultery* (Exodus 20:14), but He also explained the deeper meaning of it. He wasn't setting aside Old Testament law: He was putting it in correct perspective; that is, in its proper context. The context is that sin starts in the heart and usually will be manifest in the flesh—given time; that is, **sin is a heart issue**.

| Matthew 19:9 was not the first time Jesus taught on adultery. ||
|---|---|
| *Ye have heard that it was said by them of* **old** *time* [Old Testament days], *Thou shalt not commit adultery:* Matthew 5:27 | *But I say unto you, That whosoever looketh on a woman to lust after her hath committed adultery with her already in his heart.* Matthew 5:28 |

Jesus tied together the seventh and tenth commandments from the Old Testament, Exodus 20:14 and 17. He also gave a concrete example by which man can measure the broad application of adultery. A person who covets his neighbour's wife has already committed adultery in his heart:

*14 Thou shalt not commit adultery. 17 Thou shalt not covet thy neighbour's house, thou shalt not covet thy neighbour's wife, nor his manservant, nor his maidservant, nor his ox, nor his ass, nor any thing that is thy neighbour's.* Exodus 20:14, 17

*They say unto him, Why did Moses then command to give a writing of divorcement, and to put her away? He saith unto them, Moses because of the hardness of your* **hearts** *suffered you to put away your wives: but from the beginning it was not so.* Matthew 19:7-8

*But every man is tempted, when he is drawn away of his <u>own</u> lust, and enticed. Then when lust hath conceived, it bringeth forth sin: and sin, when it is finished, bringeth forth death. Do not err, my beloved brethren.* James 1:14-16

You may have heard both those who are saved and those who are lost trying to excuse the sin of divorce and "re-marriage" by making a loophole statement: "But Moses allowed divorce." Yet, they miss "hearing" Jesus crying out from the Scriptures: ... *but from the beginning it was not so* ... Man's sinfulness doesn't change the law that God established *in the beginning*. As mentioned in the last chapter, man's adultery was "suffered" (allowed) because the people with whom Moses was dealing had hard hearts—they were lost; they were hardened in their sin. What was and is still debated in Matthew 19:7-9 had already been discussed by Jesus as recorded in Matthew 5:31-32:

| **Jesus' teaching on adultery was not new.** ||
|---|---|
| *It hath been said* [about Moses in the Old Testament], *Whosoever shall put away his wife, let him give her a writing of divorcement.* Matthew 5:31 | *But I say unto you* [today and forever], *That whosoever shall put away his wife, saving for the cause of fornication, causeth her to commit adultery: and whosoever shall marry her that is divorced committeth adultery.* Matthew 5:32 |

## Different audiences have different purposes.

Do you think it was just a coincidence of no consequence that the LORD connected the danger to the soul with that of losing a body part? This is done in the context of speaking of a person who commits adultery, whether the adultery be lust in the heart or manifest through an adulterous "marriage." For example, how serious would it be to pluck out your eye or cut off your hand? Conversely,

> What would it take to have you pluck out your eye or cut off your hand?

how serious would it be to die in an adulterous "marriage"? Study sections from the *Sermon on the Mount* on adultery as given on the next page from Matthew 5:27-28 and 31-32. Then, read the entire passage by including the message in Matthew 5:29-30.

Biblical Guidelines To Scripture Interpretation Become Very Important.

| **Read Matthew 5:27-28 and 5:31-32 (left column). Then, include the contextual message given in verses 29 and 30 (right column).** ||
|---|---|
| *27 Ye have heard that it was said by them of old time, Thou shalt not commit adultery:* <br><br> *28 But I say unto you, That whosoever looketh on a woman to lust after her hath committed adultery with her already in his heart.* | *29 And if thy right eye offend thee, pluck it out, and cast it from thee: for it is profitable for thee that one of thy members should perish, and not that thy whole body should be cast into hell.* |
| *31 It hath been said, Whosoever shall put away his wife, let him give her a writing of divorcement:* <br><br> *32 But I say unto you, That whosoever shall put away his wife, saving for the cause of fornication, causeth her to commit adultery: and whosoever shall marry her that is divorced committeth adultery.* | *30 And if thy right hand offend thee, cut if off, and cast it from thee: for it is profitable for thee that one of thy members should perish, and not that thy whole body should be cast into hell.* |
| The Scriptures on the left are teaching on the same topic—sexual sin. Those on the right focus on the extreme, serious nature of sexual sin. ||

Beware of taking the verses in Matthew 5:29-30 out of context. Focus on the overall message of this passage of Scripture, especially how it connects with the two verses before and the two verses after. Is the LORD saying everyone who is committing adultery should maim his body? No, although it could certainly be argued that the temporary disfigurement of the body, **if it saved the soul, would be preferable to eternal separation from God**. Jesus used figures of

> Beware of taking teaching illustrations out of context.

46

speech to give a strong analogy to show the extreme lengths a person should go to avoid sin. We're not to do harm to our physical body. These figures of speech are intended to teach a principle—the grave eternal consequences of the sin of unrepentant adultery.

The LORD is trying to help everyone understand the depravity of sexual sin, whether it be against one's body or against the marriage-covenant (bed). *Marriage is honourable in all, and the bed undefiled: but whoremongers and adulterers God will judge.* Hebrews 13:4

Sin goes beyond a simple mistake; it becomes a moral and evil transgression of the law of God. Both lusting after another person's spouse and being in an adulterous "marriage" are <u>sins against God</u>, and they are not to be taken lightly. The spiritual "debt" created by sin can be washed away only by the blood of Jesus: IF we repent of that sin; IF we have nothing to do with it; IF we turn entirely from it and to God; IF we separate ourselves from the other party in the adulterous "re-marriage." Then, and only then, will we not die *in* that sin:

*Against thee, thee only, have I* [David] *sinned, and done this evil in thy sight: that thou mightest be justified when thou speakest, and be clear when thou judgest.* Psalm 51:4

*... because thou art his* [Potiphar's] *wife: how then can I* [Joseph] *do this great wickedness, and sin against God?* Genesis 39:9

Unlike the Pharisees in Matthew 19:9, the lay people who heard the words of Jesus seemed touched by the all-inclusive, far-reaching message given in the *Sermon on the Mount*: *And it came to pass, when Jesus had ended these sayings* [the *Sermon on the Mount*], **the people were**

***astonished at his doctrine****: For he taught them as one having **authority, and not as the scribes.*** Matthew 7:28-29 Are you astonished, amazed, and overcome with awe by the teachings of Scripture?

## Look for clues about teachings by studying the audience to whom the teaching is directed.

The message Jesus taught in Matthew 19:9 was included in the *Sermon on the Mount*, but the purpose was different because of the audience He was addressing in each of the two teachings. What were the circumstances surrounding Matthew 19:9? Matthew 19:9 was spoken in a confrontation with the Pharisees. These religious leaders had a different attitude toward the teachings of Jesus than did His disciples and the lay people who were "astonished" at His doctrine in the *Sermon on the Mount*. The Pharisees had their own wicked agenda ... *teaching for doctrines the commandments of men* (Mark 7:7), and they came *tempting* Jesus. Thus, the two teachings, even though similar, had different purposes.

Don't miss this embedded principle or guideline to Biblical interpretation. The purpose for the two teachings differed because the two audiences differed. Consider:

- Those who are speaking.
- The audience spoken to.
- The reason for the conversation or related event.*

*Biblical guideline three from page eight.

# 6

# "ER" Is More Important Than The Emergency Room!

Many look to Matthew's writing for a reason to dissolve a marriage. They, however, are looking at a man-made "tree in the forest" and not at the trees that are growing naturally. That is, they are trying to restructure the words of Jesus, *except it be for fornication* (in Matthew 19:9), to become something they aren't—a loophole to divorce and marry another.

They imply that sin can dissolve God's one-flesh marriage. Jesus, however, gives no "cause" to put away a covenant spouse. He only reinforces that, from the beginning, the indissoluble nature of marriage has never changed. His concluding statements in Matthew 19:9 aren't approving "re-marriage." They are a reminder that everyone who "re-marries" commit***teth*** *adultery*. This is a sin listed in 1 Corinthians 6:9 and Galatians 5:19 with grave consequences. People who commit adultery ... *shall not inherit the kingdom of God*—IF they do not turn from that sinful lifestyle.

Many who are distraught in their marriage become sidetracked trying to find ways to exit it. They neglect to first focus on what marriage is and to make certain that decisions do not violate God's universal "law of marriage." They rarely consider why Jesus inspired Matthew, and only Matthew, to record the exception clause, not only once, but twice in this first gospel of the New Testament.

> The LORD inspired Matthew to record the exception clause, **NOT once, but twice.**

The heart attitude of the Pharisees when they came to Jesus was, perhaps, hidden from the view of many. Could this be the same issue—wrong heart attitude—of those who "come to Jesus" today? They ask with the wrong motive and for the wrong purpose, the wrong question: "How can I get out of a one-flesh marriage?"

*The Pharisees also came unto him* [Jesus], ***tempting*** *him, and saying unto him, Is it lawful for a man to put away his wife for every cause?* Matthew 19:3

The Bible tells us that God created husbands and wives to be an inseparable team, one for another; to subdue the earth; to replenish the earth—in the context of a one-flesh marriage; and they are to reflect a picture of Christ's love for the church. They are, after all, made in the image of God. Therefore, the reason to come to the LORD when serious or minor issues arise between a husband and wife should be:

- For reconciliation of differences.
- To seek ways to strengthen the marital relationship.
- To learn forgiveness and the extent of it, even *until seventy times seven.* Matthew 18:21-22.
- To learn, within the confines of a marriage, to fulfill the kind of love exemplified by the LORD and clearly illustrated in 1 Corinthians 13:4-8 and Ephesians 5:21-33.
- To carefully assess and utilize the gift of the wife being an help meet for the husband and for the husband to accept this gift. *And the LORD God said, It is not good that the man should be alone; I will make him an help meet for him.* Genesis 2:18

## Contextual word studies confirm consistent Biblical doctrines.

Contextual word studies can reveal many underlying treasures of information. A case in point is Genesis 2:18 with the expression *an help meet*. Most Bible authors change the word *help* to some kind of help<u>er</u> or to someone "like him":

- Helper fit for him (ESV, RSV).
- Helper suitable for him (NIV, NASV).
- Helper comparable to him (NKJV).
- Help who is like him (Lamsa*).

*You may or may not be familiar with Lamsa's Bible which he says comes from ancient eastern manuscripts; yet, beware, there is much doctrinal error in his translation.

The examples above may seem like insignificant differences; however, it is God who has given the wife the "title" *help meet*, not help**er**. Does not God know better than man how He wants his *help meet* expressed? Did God say He created a wife who is "suitable" for the husband, or "comparable" to him, or "like" him? No, please carefully read the text. It says ... *I will make an help meet for him.* This is what is recorded in the Hebrew text. It's man-made changes that do not correctly reflect the underlying Hebrew text from which the expression, *an help meet*, is translated.

God created man AND woman in the image of God. *So God created man in his own image, in the image of God created he him; male and female created he them.* Genesis 1:27 Scripture tells the reader that woman is made in the image of God, not in the image of man. She is man's companion and the wife of his covenant: *... she* [is] *thy companion, and the wife of thy covenant.* Malachi 2:14 This *help meet* is described as a *virtuous woman* in Proverbs 31:10. Yet, these characteristics do not diminish that there is to be headship and order in the home. Proverbs 31:12 says, "*She will do him good and not evil all the days of her life.*"

## Hidden internal structure is missed by many.

This next section is included for those who wish to learn a bit more about the miraculous internal structural design of the Bible. This study may seem like too much detail and an unnecessary analysis of words. However, there seems to be a prevailing attitude that many of the words in the King James Bible are archaic or do not reflect the underlying languages as well as do the

> God says His Scripture cannot be broken, and He gives no man permission to change it.

new versions. Hopefully, you will see that those opinions cannot be supported by a rightful analysis of Scripture ... *comparing spiritual things with spiritual.* 1 Corinthians 2:13 Comparing Scripture with Scripture is rarely done. Instead, the focus for proof is often in the quoting of man's opinions based on sources outside the Bible.

The heart attitude for all this word study from *within* the Bible is to help you see for yourself that even little nuances like an *er* on the end of a word can be intertwined in a very complex, internal structure that God says (of His Word) cannot be broken. John 10:35 tells us that ... *scripture cannot be broken.* It's impossible for God to lie; that is, it is impossible for His Word to reflect doctrinal error.

*God is not a man, that he should lie; neither the son of man, that he should repent: hath he said, and shall he not do it? or hath he spoken, and shall he not make it good?* Numbers 23:19

*In hope of eternal life, which God, that cannot lie, promised before the world began; But hath in due times manifested his word through preaching, which is committed unto me according to the commandment of God our Saviour.* Titus 1:2-3

Some would say, "If Scripture cannot be broken, why does man rewrite it into so many different versions?" This statement is like those who ask the question, "If it's impossible for man to put away a wife, why does God warn not to do it?" First, God gives very grave warnings against those who change His Word and to those who put away their spouse and marry another. Secondly, man is deceived when he thinks he can change God's Word or that he can divorce his one-flesh spouse and marry another. Yes, man *can* do both of the above wrongful acts, but he has not changed God or the Word of God; nor has he changed God's one-flesh union. Even though man may rewrite the Bible, God's Word has not changed. And even though man can, in his eyes, divorce a spouse, God's one-flesh union has not changed. That's why I beg you to please study this text—so you will be able to assess when

> Man cannot "change" God's Word nor God's one-flesh union.

words have been supernaturally and contextually translated, placed, and uniquely interlinked—the way the LORD preserved them: 6 *The words of the LORD are pure words: as silver tried in a furnace of earth, purified seven times. 7 **Thou** shalt keep **them**, O LORD, thou shalt preserve them from this generation for ever.* Psalm 12:6-7 Here's how NIV authors change important words: *6 And the words of the LORD are flawless ... 7 O LORD, you will keep us safe and protect us from such people forever.* Psalm 12:6-7 The NIV totally changes what is being kept.

The laborious detail included in this study of *help meet* and other studies that follow throughout this book have several goals. One of those is to help show what is stated above—how miraculously many of the words are uniquely used, have interconnectivity, and are supernaturally chosen and placed. This is something a casual reader will rarely see. Thus many sadly remark: "All Bibles are the same or give the same message." It is hoped that you will understand why that statement is not true.

There are principles in word usage that can be observed by studying how certain words are used in the Bible. This holds true in both the Old and the New Testaments. To illustrate this, *help* and *meet*, as they are used in Genesis 2:18 and 2:20, are examined. That's because there are unique word applications reflected in the underlying Hebrew words from which *an help meet* is translated. These unique uses appear only two times—in Genesis 2:18 and 2:20. That is when they are used in combination, one with the other, to create a title or a way

Chapter 6

to describe the woman God created from the rib of man. God calls this woman *an help meet.*

The word *help* is translated from the Hebrew word *ezer*. *Meet* is translated from a different Hebrew word *neged* which is translated *meet* in Genesis 2:18 and 2:20.

## Ezer (help) has some specific use characteristics.

A contextual study of *help* and *meet* may reveal additional reverence for God's choice of words: *an help meet.* The Hebrew word for *help*,

meet for him. | an help
5048 | 5828
kᵃnegᵃdow | ʽeezer

**God has high esteem for an help meet.**

*ezer*, is translated 21 times in the Bible as *help*. Nineteen of those times, ezer refers to the LORD directly or to the kind of help He wanted to give if the people had accepted His help. Ezer is used two times to name woman as man's wife, his *help meet*. (Ezer is spelled eezer in the Hebrew when there is the article *an* in front of it: "an" help meet.)

There are several different Hebrew words that are translated into the English word *help* depending on how *help* is used in the sentence. Two Hebrew words for help, *ezer* and *azar*, are very closely related. *Azar* is the root from which *ezer* is derived. This is, in principle, what was introduced in Chapter 4 with adulterate and adultery. Adulterate is a verb that encompasses the action which describes what happens when man tries to "join" two people together the LORD says cannot be joined through His covenant of marriage. Man's adultery is an adulteration; it adulterates.

Azar and ezer are alike in principle as are the words *adulterate* and *adultery*, but there are also important differences. Ezer is always translated as *help*. <u>Azar</u> is often translated with a suffix, *er*, such as in the word *help**er***. However, there are some additional differences between these two Hebrew words, especially when ezer is used <u>in combination</u> with the word *meet* to form the name "descriptor" (help meet) that God gives to woman in Genesis 2:18 and 2:20:

- Ezer is translated like a noun, naming something or someone.
- Ezer is never translated into English with the "er" suffix.
- Ezer is a name substitute for, or associated with, God ... *he* [God] *is their help and their shield.* Psalm 115:9 Notice the word is *help* not *help<u>er</u>*.

There appears to be only a slight difference—that in the spelling of the Hebrew words *ezer* and *azar*. Their English counterparts also have two different spellings. Ezer is uniquely only translated *help*. *Azar* is often translated *helper* or *helped*. When *azar* is translated *help*, it is used in the sense of an action, a verb: ... *none shall help him.*

> Words which look alike have important differences.

Daniel 11:45 These slight differences are often glossed over. Even though *azar* and *ezer* are derived one from the other, the *ways* in which they are used in the Bible differ slightly. Those important differences in application are reflected when the LORD has the word *ezer* recorded as part of a descriptive name for woman: *(an) help meet*—not once, but twice:

Chapter 6

> *... I will make him an help meet for him.* Genesis 2:18
> *... there was not found an help meet for him.* Genesis 2:20

This is part of the little details that make a difference to God in the way He wants His words recorded and interpreted. Study the examples in the table below. Relate how the three bullet points on the previous page about *ezer* illustrate ways the Hebrew word *ezer* is translated *help*. It usually refers to God Himself. The only time ezer doesn't refer to God is in Genesis where ezer is used as part of the "noun title" for man's *help meet*. However, don't take this statement out of context. It's not meant that the wife is God. Both man and woman were made in the IMAGE of God. They never become God:

| **The Hebrew word translated *help* usually refers to God, <u>except when it is used for man's help meet in Genesis 2:18 and 2:20.</u>** |
|---|
| *... an help meet for him.* Genesis 2:18, 20* |
| *... and be thou* [LORD] *an help to him from his enemies.* Deuteronomy 33:7 |
| *And the name of the other was Eliezer; for the God of my father, said he, was mine help, and delivered me from the sword of Pharaoh:* Exodus 18:4 |
| *Our soul waiteth for the LORD: he is our help and our shield.* Psalm 33:20 |
| *O house of Aaron, trust in the LORD: he is their help and their shield.* Psalm 115:10 |
| *Ye that fear the LORD, trust in the LORD: he is their help and their shield.* Psalm 115:11 |
| *Our help is in the name of the LORD, who made heaven and earth.* Psalm 124:8 |
| *But I am poor and needy: make haste unto me, O God: thou art my help and my deliverer; O LORD, make no tarrying.* Psalm 70:5 |
| *My help cometh from the LORD, which made heaven and earth.* Psalm 121:2 |
| *O Israel, thou hast destroyed thyself; but in me is thine help.* Hosea 13:9 |
| *God repeats this "noun title" for the woman in Scriptures that are only two verses apart: Genesis 2:18 and Genesis 20. A closely placed repetition is a *sign* which tells the reader: *Take notice.* |

"ER" Is More Important Than The Emergency Room!

## Strong's 5048—*meet*—also has unique characteristics.

Strong's Concordance is a resource dictionary. It is a book much utilized by many Christians. It provides references and information for the Hebrew and Greek words used in the Bible. Even though it is a much-used reference, final decisions on the definition of a word in the Bible must be made by relying upon the context of Scripture. Care must be exercised against blindly accepting man-made conclusions and definitions; whether they be from Strong's Concordance or from any other reference source or dictionary, especially if they bring conflict to Scripture.

As with the word *help*, additional insight can be gained by studying the Hebrew word, *neged* translated *meet* in Genesis 2:18 and 20. Like *ezer* (help), there are also some unique things in the *way meet* is used in Genesis 2:18 and 20. Meet is used 109 times in the Old Testament. It is translated from a variety of different Hebrew words.

*Meet*, like *help* is unique in the way it is used.

However, the only time that meet is translated from a Hebrew word represented by Strong's numeral 5048 is in Genesis 2:18 and 2:20. This is when God names man's wife as *an help meet*. Again, the only time 5048 is translated *meet* is when the LORD names woman who became Adam's wife. And this, as with *help*, is repeated two times— in Genesis 2:18 and in Genesis 2:20. However, the Hebrew word represented by Strong's 5048 is usually translated as a preposition such as *before*, *over*, *against*, *from*, etc. Study the illustration below:

Chapter 6

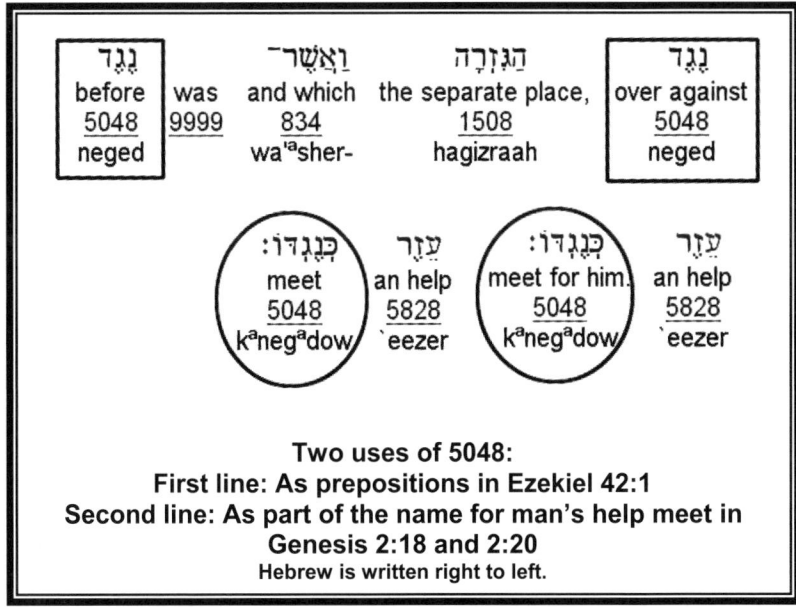

The LORD has a reason for every word in the Bible. He didn't use words to say woman was comparable to man. The word *comparable* is used one time, but based on a totally different Hebrew word 5537:

*The precious sons of Zion, <u>comparable</u> to fine gold, how are they esteemed as earthen pitchers, the work of the hands of the potter!* Lamentations 4:2

## There were 47 highly qualified linguistic translators.

The committee, most of whom gave seven years of their lives to translate the King James Bible, was a unique group of deeply devoted, devout Christians who were skilled grammarians and had developed high levels of linguistic talents. Collectively and individually, they were proficient in many different languages, including not only Hebrew and Greek, but also many cognate languages. They worked alone and then came together in committees to compare and contrast their translations until they came to a consensus. **Never before or since** has such a large group of Biblical experts moved by the Holy Spirit undertaken to work as a team with the task of translating what has become the King James Bible. That's why we have such a credible, consistent, contextual, word-for-word translation in the King James Bible. That was their goal. Review page six.

These scholars accurately translated the Hebrew words for *help* and *meet* in Genesis 2 with their specific applications into English in a way that preserves the meaning given in the underlying Hebrew text. They contextually <u>and</u> linguistically reflected the fact that that *ezer* should not be translated as help*er*, but as help. They recognized the difference between *meet* as a noun and *meet* as a preposition or verb. They faithfully recorded the nuances of context.

> The English must accurately reflect the Hebrew.

The way the LORD has uniquely recorded, through the hands of holy men, not once, but twice, the underlying Hebrew words for both *help* and *meet* reinforces the need for a word-for-word translation. This has been preserved as given in the King James Bible: *an help meet for him.*

## Forget not: He is the Potter; We are the clay!

**Why** were the Hebrew words studied here? It was to show that the words *help* and *meet* are uniquely intertwined within the internal structure of the Bible and should not be changed. Sadly, most scholars and laymen see no problem changing *help* to *helper* in Genesis 2:18

and 2:20. It must be re-emphasized that if God wanted His creation woman to be "cast" *a helper suitable for man*, then He surely had enough of a vocabulary to include specific Hebrew words that would mean *suitable* or *comparable* <u>and</u> would have had the King James translators translate it as such. One of the other fallacies with the man-made image (suitable or comparable) is that perhaps people then could believe there could come a day when she will become *unsuitable* or *no longer comparable* to man! (I say this facetiously.)

Again, the fact that the LORD repeated this expression, *an help meet*, twice should be noteworthy to us so that we aren't tempted to change our position from a vessel being crafted **by** the Potter and change the focus to think that **we are** the Potter. The LORD surely could have chosen different Hebrew words in Genesis 2:18 and 20 so there would be no conflict with the ESV, RSV, NASV, NIV, NKJV, or Lamsa. But, He didn't do that. When these authors explain why they changed God's words to *helper suitable for him*, et al., they may face the same kind of response from the LORD as did Job:

*Where wast thou when I* [God] *laid the foundations of the earth? declare, if thou* [Job] *hast understanding.* Job 38:4

## Why should we FIRST focus on Genesis?

Some might wonder why the repetitive backtracking to Genesis is necessary. First, it's where the LORD first records what a one-flesh marriage is. Secondly, it's important to understand that when God creates a marital union it is something quite spectacular and well beyond that which most of us are capable of understanding or have the ability to express with words. That incomprehensible <u>picture</u> of the creation of woman and her one-flesh joining with man is only given in Genesis. Likewise, the term *help meet* is only given in Genesis <u>and</u> in the context of marriage. The woman is NOT God; but, neither is she a slave or someone merely suitable for man or comparable to man. She is so much more. She is *an help* (ezer) *meet*.

We must not downgrade the image of a wife to a sex object or a subservient slave to her husband. She is the one who stands beside him to *help* with the work that the LORD ordains the "one flesh" team should do—together. There is, however, a positional submissiveness between man and woman, just as there was submissiveness with Jesus to God the Father. God the Father, God the Son, and God the Holy Ghost are One, but they serve different functions.

## God is a God of order.

God is a God of order. He has also designed order in the home. Man serves certain functions, and woman serves others. Yet within their functions God calls both the husband and wife to FIRST be submissive ... *one to another <u>in the fear of God</u>.* Ephesians 5:21 Once the Biblical submission is in place then all the other husband and wife issues can proceed as God designed. Each spouse will take on the *attributes* of the mind of Christ; yet, not literally have THE mind of Christ; that is, they won't have Christ's mind. Neither the husband nor the wife will have any desire to partake in what God hates:

*For the LORD, the God of Israel, saith that he <u>hateth</u> <u>putting away</u> ... take heed to your spirit, that ye deal not treacherously.* Malachi 2:16

## A secular example may help our understanding.

**How many changes to God's Word before we slip off into a state of destruction?**

**Compare the world globe with the Apollo spacecraft off a few degrees and the word *help* off by just two letters.**

As you study this chapter (and others in the book), you may still be thinking that it's not a big deal to change a word such as *help* to *helper*. After all, some might still think, "It's only two letters, *er*." Compare these two letters, "e" and "r," with two degrees in space exploration.

For example, when the spacecraft *Apollo* was returning from the moon, there was concern that "… the spacecraft was coming in too 'shallow;' that is, Apollo 13 was going to skip off the atmosphere and out into space forever."*

*13 Things That Saved Apollo 13, Part 6: Navigating By Earth's Terminator. Nancy Atkinson, April 16, 2010, Universe Today.

The problem with Apollo was **only a couple of degrees** differential in the trajectory of the spacecraft, but there was great concern for such a small difference. Could it be that God's warning not to change His Word is equally as serious? He doesn't want our spaceship to slip over into what will be ... *the fire that never shall be quenched?* Mark 9:43

What's involved in obedience to the LORD's commands? Do we really carefully assess His warnings—and the oft reason given therein for that obedience?

*Ye **shall not** add unto the word which I command you, neither shall ye diminish ought from it, that ye may keep the commandments of the LORD your God which I command you.* Deuteronomy 4:2

God warns that we should not add to or take from the words of Scripture. That's because the Word is by what we are commanded to live. If His commandments and precepts are changed or missing, the resulting message is also changed, and the act of altering the words of God is sin.

When we change two letters—even just one—we are violating God's commands to us. The principle is that once we rebel on what ***seem to us*** to be little matters, **how much more do we think we can change** without altering the image of God and His Word and thereby put ourselves in danger of judgment? All new versions must change thousands of words to obtain a copyright. (See pages 178 and 256.) Recall that the serpent in Genesis 3:4, in essence, only added three letters—ONE WORD—to what God said in Genesis 2:17:

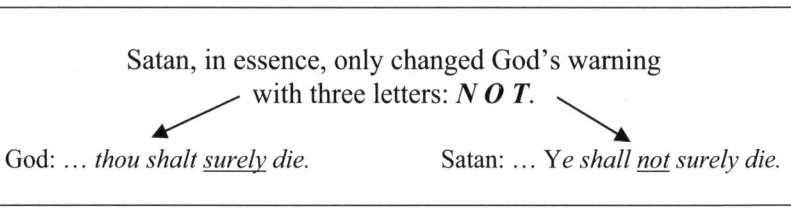

However, with Adam and Eve listening to, and buying into **Satan's version of God's Word**, all of mankind has been affected from there on. Yet, even though *what* Satan said was not what God said, Satan did not change what it was that God said: Adam and Eve were in the transgression. Adam and Eve died!

# 7

# *Jesus' Warning Is To Beware Of The Pharisees.*

The third guideline to help in interpreting Scripture, listed on page eight, is "Consider those who are speaking, the audience spoken to, and the reason for the conversation or related event." The reason for Jesus' conversation in Matthew 19 should be clear from information already presented. The Pharisees came to Jesus to try to find an excuse to divorce their wives. Their attitude and purpose was totally wrong. They came *tempting* Jesus:

| It's the context that tells the reader the purpose for which the Pharisees came to Jesus. Their intent was wicked. ||
|---|---|
| *The Pharisees also came unto him, tempting him, and saying unto him, Is it lawful for a man to put away his wife for every cause?* Matthew 19:3 | *And the Pharisees came to him, and asked him, Is it lawful for a man to put away his wife? tempting him.* Mark 10:2 |

## How wrong is it to "tempt" the LORD?

The Pharisees were just asking Jesus a question. Shouldn't everyone have a right to inquire about those things he doesn't understand? Yes, we should be able to ask questions. However, it's the attitude of our heart that we must examine. The Pharisees already knew the answer to their question: "Is it lawful for a man to put away his wife?" They had read Genesis 2:21-24, and Jesus had taught on this issue in the *Sermon on the Mount*. However, there's something more insidious indicated by the word *tempt* that may have been overlooked. One of the guidelines for interpreting Scripture is to study words contextually. That can include:

- How the word is used in the surrounding verses.
- How the word is used in other verses.
- Who is involved in the passage.
- What is his or their purpose.

## Did they tempt, test, or try?

Think about this question: "What immediately comes to your mind when the words *test* or *try* are mentioned?" It's easy to see that the meaning depends on the context. If you're in a class and the instructor tells you there will be a test tomorrow, you assume you will be tested on class material. If your doctor says he's going to run some tests, you assume these tests have to do with some body function. If you're in a clothing store, you might try on a garment to see if it fits properly, but if you try to explain something, the word *try* takes on a different meaning because of the context.

> The correct meaning of a word must be determined by its context.

Chapter 7

**Satan tempts Jesus.**

What about the word *tempt*? What immediately comes to your mind when this word is mentioned? You probably wouldn't think of a classroom *test*, or a blood *test*, or that you should *try* on a new item of clothing. *Tempt* usually brings to mind a different kind of response. What came to my mind was a tattered book given to me by my grandmother in 1950. It had been given to a grandson by my godly great, great grandmother in 1913 and passed on through the family: *Story of the Gospel and Scenes in Bible Lands*. The image that came to me from this book is pictured above. It illustrates who is called the *tempter* in the Bible.

*And when the <u>tempter</u> [Satan] came to him [Jesus], he said, If thou be the Son of God, command that these stones be made bread.* Matthew 4:3

> The word *tempter* is an important word to study.

The table below lists various ways different Bibles render the underlying Greek for the word *tempter and tempting*. Study the points of similarity and <u>differences</u> between the translations of Matthew 4:3 and 19:3 even though the same Greek root word is being translated.

| προσελθών when came 4334 proselthoón | ὁ the 3588 ho | πειράζων tempter 3985 peirazon | Φαρισαῖοι Pharisees 5330 Farisaioi | πειράζοντες tempting 3985 peirazontes | αὐτὸν him. 846 autón |
|---|---|---|---|---|---|
| Matthew 4:3 *The tempter* [devil] *came to him* [Jesus] ... KJB ... *tempter came* ... ESV, RSV ... *tempter came* ... NIV ... *tempter came* ... NASV, NKJV ... *tempter came* ... ASV | | | Matthew 19:3 *The Pharisees also came unto him, tempting him* ... KJB ... *tested him* ... ESV, RSV ... *to test him* ... NIV ... *testing him* ... NASV, NKJV ... *trying him* ... ASV | | |

Jesus' Warning Is To Beware Of The Pharisees.

All Bibles listed above correctly and contextually translated the underlying Greek word for the noun *tempter* **in Matthew 4:3**. Each of them translated it as *tempter*. The tempter is the devil, Satan. He is evil. His purpose is ... *to steal, and to kill, and to destroy*. John 10:10 Look carefully at the <u>differences</u> among the Bible translations in the right column for Matthew 19:3. These are the verb forms used for tempter—one who is tempting. There is clearly a difference in how the Greek word for *tempting* is translated in Matthew 19:3 in all Bible versions except for the King James Bible. The verb form of the word should reflect the same characteristics as does the noun *tempter*. A *tempter* would be, in this context, one who was maliciously *tempting* God. The word *tempting*, like *tempter*, consistently reveals the wicked character of these religious leaders who were questioning Jesus.

> *Tempt* connects Satan's character with that of the Pharisees.

On previous pages, you were asked to think about what comes to mind when the words *test* or *try* are spoken. Rarely would anyone envision the concept of *tempt* for *test* or *try*. This is because the latter two words usually convey a different meaning, a meaning not related to the word *tempt*.

Every time the underlying Greek word for *tempt* is translated (in the King James Bible), it is consistently translated *tempt*. If someone is tempted, it usually is not for a good purpose. Notice how James gives a vivid additional picture of the contextual meaning of tempt:

*Let no man say when he is tempted, I am **tempted** of God: for God cannot be **tempted** with <u>evil</u>, neither **tempteth** he any man.* James 1:13

Chapter 7

What picture comes to mind for the contextual meaning of *tempt* when you read Matthew 4:3? It should be of someone who is evil. Why do you think the LORD would have repeated the same root word for the act of the Pharisees in coming to Him to ask a question to which they already knew the answer? It was because their intent was of the same insidious nature as that of Satan as given in Matthew 4:3. By studying the word *tempt* readers can see how the meaning of words used in the Bible can be determined within the Bible's internal dictionary. By this is meant that word meanings can be determined by studying how the same word is used in other places in the Bible that might have a similar Biblical application. That's the importance of repetition of words throughout the Scripture. Like words can be cross referenced.

The word *tempt*, or a form of it, is used 73 times in the King James Bible. MOST of these teach the reader the same consistent, picture—something evil is being depicted either by or to someone. The new versions remove most of these "pictorial" words: NKJV records tempt, or a form of it, only 45 times; the NASV 33 times, and the NIV 27 times. Study James 1:12-14.

> The internal Bible dictionary directly connects the character of Satan with that of the Pharisees.

The King James Bible, in Matthew 19:3, accurately transmits the wicked nature of the Pharisees with the word *tempting*. However, when the same underlying Greek root word is translated in Matthew 19:3 by the authors of the new versions, they not only chose less effective synonyms, *test* or *try*, but they use a totally different English root

69

word from what they used in Matthew 4:3. The Pharisees were not innocent "sheep" who were coming to get understanding from the LORD. They, instead, were <u>tempters</u> who wanted to destroy Him:

*I know that ye [Pharisees] are Abraham's seed; but ye seek to kill me [Jesus], because my word hath no place in you.* John 8:37

The King James Bible's *internal dictionary* (the words in the text) connects the character of Satan with that of the Pharisees because the translators selected the same English root word for the noun *tempter* in Matthew 4:3 as they did for the verb *tempting* in Matthew 19:3. That's because the underlying Greek text from which the English is translated has the same root word in both of Matthew's Scriptures, and they should contextually be translated into English using the same English root word. However, that's not what the new version translators have done.

**This is an example of the increasingly dangerous practice of subtly changing God's Word. This way of changing God's Word "quietly" changes who people are and what they do and say.** These kinds of subtle changes often go unnoticed by many Christians. They don't realize that in hundreds of places in their Bibles they are "hearing" the words of man rather than those of the LORD. This is as the LORD predicted would happen when He spoke through the Old Testament prophet Amos almost 3,000 years ago. There is a slowly creeping famine slithering unnoticed under the doors of many Christian homes—a famine of hearing God's Word:

> Satan works through subtle changes to God's Word which go unnoticed by many.

Chapter 7

*Behold, the days come, saith the Lord GOD, that I will send a famine in the land, not a famine of bread, nor a thirst for water, but of hearing the words of the LORD: And they shall wander from sea to sea, and from the north even to the east, they shall run to and fro to seek the word of the LORD, and shall not find it.* Amos 8:11-12

*...the words that I [Jesus] speak unto you, they are spirit, and they are life.* John 6:63

## Why did the Pharisees "tempt" Jesus?

It doesn't take much reading to figure out that the Pharisees, scribes, and Sadducees were in constant conflict with the LORD:

*Then went the Pharisees, and took counsel how they might entangle him* [Jesus] *in his talk.* Matthew 22:15

The Pharisees and other religious leaders tried to discredit Jesus. They were threatened by His growing popularity with the people because of His healings and miracles. They also hated Him because He claimed to be Who He was—the Messiah and the Son of God. Claiming to be the Son of God meant Jesus was God. For this, He was called a blasphemer. Even though the Pharisees knew what Moses had *suffered* (allowed) was for hardened hearts, they misapplied what he did in their ploy to try to manipulate the LORD into either discrediting Moses or contradicting His own "law of marriage."

There are several lessons to be learned from this confrontation with the Pharisees. Two of those are to not only learn the character of people through the <u>words</u> used to describe them but to take warning not to follow in the footsteps of those who wrongly interpret or quote God's Word. Study the table on the next page.

Jesus' Warning Is To Beware Of The Pharisees.

| **Jesus spoke some very explicit, graphic words directed to and about the Pharisees.** |
|---|
| ... *beware of the leaven of the Pharisees and of the Sadducees? Then understood they how that he bade them ... beware of the ... doctrine of the Pharisees and of the Sadducees.* Matthew 16:11-12 |
| *But woe unto you, scribes and Pharisees, hypocrites! for ye shut up the kingdom of heaven against men* [teach false doctrine]*: for ye neither go in yourselves ...* Matthew 23:13 |
| *Woe unto you, scribes and Pharisees, hypocrites! for ye devour widows' houses, and for a pretence make long prayer: therefore ye shall receive the greater damnation.* Matthew 23:14 |
| *Woe unto you, ye blind guides ...* Matthew 23:16 |
| *Ye fools and blind ...* Matthew 23:17 |
| *... for ye [Pharisees] are like unto whited sepulchres, which indeed appear beautiful outward, but are within full of dead men's bones, and of all uncleanness.* Matthew 23:27 |
| *Ye serpents, ye generation of vipers, how can ye escape the damnation of hell?* Matthew 23:33 |

What should studying the character of those to whom Jesus was speaking in these Scriptures tell readers about adopting Pharisaical doctrines, beliefs, or actions? As Christians, we should avoid having anything to do with such Pharisaical examples or doctrines. What was the sinful practice the Pharisees were tempting Jesus to accept in the encounter in Matthew 19?

> We should avoid having anything to do with wicked doctrines of the Pharisees.

*The Pharisees also came unto him, tempting him, and saying unto him, Is it lawful for a **man to put away his wife for every** [any] cause?* Matthew 19:3

## Our "Pharisaical" nation's legal system has exceeded the wickedness of the Pharisees.

America has gone one step further than even did the Pharisees in the way they dishonored God's "law of marriage." They have done this by instituting "No-Fault" divorce laws. These laws say no one is at fault for trying to dissolve God's marriage-covenant; yet, lawmakers are so blinded that they don't recognize they have underhandedly created a fault with their "No-Fault." They have specified a "cause" for their "no-cause." *Is it lawful for a **man to put away his wife for every*** [any] ***cause?*** This "cause," in today's courts, must be stated in the Petitioner's charge for divorcing his spouse, the Defendant. The "cause" is couched under the words: "This marriage is irretrievably broken." That's the "cause." The Court interprets this to mean that there are irreconcilable differences. However, no court or attorney has objectively, legally defined what the charge of "irretrievably broken" means; thus, there's no defense that the Defendant can offer to the Court as a reason not to bring the gavel down on his marriage.

Whenever the Plaintiff, the one who petitions the court for a divorce, states the above "cause," the judge automatically brings the gavel down against God's holy institution—marriage. Not only does the Court say the marriage is irretrievably broken, but it says it dissolves what God says is impossible for man to dissolve.

> This is the only claim in an American court where there's no defense allowed for the Defendant.

The Court refuses any counterclaim or defense the Defendant might present to try to prove what the Word of God says—that the marriage is *not* irretrievably broken. Thus, the Defendant (the person being sued for divorce) "… can never establish a lack of merit in the suit or a legal bar (any defense) to defeat the charge. This is the only claim in an American court where this happens; that is, where there's no defense allowed for the Defendant."* All divorce actions are an automatic "victory" for the one who seeks to do what God hates: to divorce.

*See *Judge, Please Don't Strike That Gavel ... On My Marriage*. Restoration Of The Family, PO Box 621342, Oviedo, FL 32762

"No-Fault" is the low estate to which America has bowed its corrupted knees. It's such a contrast to what our courts upheld in their earlier days. Our courts, like the new versions of the Bible, are changing the "face" of America and especially that of marriage.

| *Higher Courts historically recognized their *responsibility* to protect marriage versus the current focus to destroy marriage. |
|---|
| 1888: The Supreme Court of the United States characterized marriage as the most important relation in life ... |
| 1913: All of the duties and obligations that have existed at any time between husbands and wives **before** civil government was formed ... civil government has grown out of marriage ... from which government became necessary to ... protect ... |
| 1941: The government has an obligation to protect marriage ... |
| *See *Judge, Please Don't Strike That Gavel ... On My Marriage*, page 180. Restoration Of The Family, PO Box 621342, Oviedo, FL 32762 |

*Woe unto them that call evil good, and good evil; that put darkness for light, and light for darkness; that put bitter for sweet, and sweet for bitter! Woe unto them that are wise in their own eyes, and prudent in their own sight!*
Isaiah 5:20-21

All Christians today are to be keepers and teachers of God's law—to preserve it as it was recorded. None have been commissioned by the LORD to become changers of His law. No one is to *tempt* God, as the Pharisees did. All must beware of the teachings they adopt. Are they man's teachings or God's; the Pharisees' teachings or those of Jesus?

# 8

# Shall We Rend The Robe Of Jesus Though It Be Only A Jot Or Tittle?

Throughout most of the rest of this book, there will be many examples of word changes among the different Bible versions. Some, like those already covered, may seem insignificant to many. Yet, each of us must decide for ourselves if such changes matter to God when not only studying the Bible but also when we consider the accuracy of the Bible we are reading.

Even very small changes can lead to serious doctrinal errors, especially with marriage, divorce, and adulterous "marriages." Vital information may be missing, including important contextually related information between the Old and New Testaments.

## The Bible is one book, spiritually interlinked.

The Bible is interwoven as a one-piece tapestry, from Genesis through Revelation; and every Word has a significant part that helps to make up the whole. A case in point is the interlinking given in the previous chapter between Mathew 4:3 and Matthew 19:3. This is where the character of the Pharisees is linked with that of Satan, the Devil, with the words *tempter* and *tempting*.

Another more complex but related principle is explained in this chapter. It isn't complex in its reading level. The words to be studied are one and two syllables in length. The complexity is because these words are tied to the Bible's internal structure in a way that requires more study than that of the *tempter*. This is a teaching which Jesus gave as it is recorded in Matthew 5:18:

*For verily I say unto you, Till heaven and earth pass, one **jot** or one **tittle** shall in no wise pass from the law, till all be fulfilled.* Matthew 5:18

Can you explain what *jot* and *tittle* mean and how they are interlinked with the Old Testament? Perhaps from the context you can figure out the surface meaning. However, because *jot* and *tittle* are not words commonly used and understood, some may think it is acceptable with God to change them to words which may be more familiar. However, substituting what may *seem* to be acceptable synonyms for *jot* and *tittle* does three things:

1. It removes vital interlinking information between the Old and New Testaments.
2. It no longer reflects what is recorded in the underlying Greek text from which the English has been translated.
3. It violates God's command to not change His Word.

*Ye shall not add unto the word which I command you, neither shall ye diminish ought from it, that ye may keep the commandments of the LORD your God which I command you.* Deuteronomy 4:2

*And if any man shall take away from the words of the book of this prophecy, God shall take away his part out of the book of life, and out of the holy city, and from the things which are written in this book.* Revelation 22:19

## Why are *jot* and *tittle* little words with a big job?

These words, *jot* and *tittle*, preserved through the statement made by Jesus in Matthew 5:18, are words that link His timeless existence between the Old and New Testaments. These words tell readers that everything prophesied in the Old Testament will be fulfilled—every detail—which is indicated by the words *jot* and *tittle*. However, buried within this figure of speech are some facts that are overlooked by many readers—and in most new versions of the Bible.

These words, *jot* and *tittle*, spoken by Jesus, are recorded only in the gospel written by Matthew. They appear nowhere else in the entire Bible. Matthew is again recording another Jewish-related idiosyncrasy; but now in Matthew 5:18, he does it through a unique reference to the Hebrew language of the Old Testament. Recall that it was through the gospel of Matthew, who was of the Jewish heritage, that we learned important details about the Jewish engagement language: espousal and the two kinds of husbands and wives.

When Jesus spoke His succinct, many-pronged message, He was also giving an underlying *principle* for all of Scripture. Even though Jesus was specifically referring to the Old Testament (law), included was a truth which applies to both Testaments. The principle is that neither the law, nor any part of Scripture, changes with time or circumstances, and every word of Scripture will be fulfilled. Both Testaments are closed and are not subject to change or revision. They are canonized:

*... Till heaven and earth pass, one **jot** or one **tittle** shall in no wise pass from the law, till all be fulfilled.* Matthew 5:18

*Jot* and *tittle* are little words with a big job. Why would Jesus have chosen these words, *jot* and *tittle*, so uncommon to most today, to include in our Bible? A little background information may help to shed some light. First, the language in which the Old Testament was written was Hebrew even though there are some books which include other dialects, especially Aramaic in the books of Daniel and Ezra.

Second, writers often reflect their background and cultures in their writings. As noted above, both Matthew and Jesus were Jews, but the surrounding culture was predominantly Greek-speaking Gentiles. Matthew's teachings are recorded for all to read and study. However, they are written from his Jewish perspective and include words which are embedded with information unique to his Jewish and Hebrew heritage and background. The Jews had strong reverence not only for the Hebrew Old Testament words but for the Hebrew language itself—that in which the Old Testament was originally recorded.

> *Jot* and *tittle* retain Hebrew influence.

Third, and very important contextually, is that these two words, *jot* and *tittle*, <u>in combination, one with the other</u>, are relevant to no other language than that used to record the Hebrew Old Testament Scriptures. Here is another example which, in principle, is like that discussed with *an help meet* in Chapter 4. There is a unique combination of words seen in no other verses. However, as stated above, what is additionally important about **this <u>combination</u> (jot and tittle) is that it points to no other alphabet in any other language <u>except for</u> the Hebrew alphabet.**

In other words, the Hebrew language and its alphabet are directly related to the terms *jot* and *tittle* which Jesus spoke as recorded in Matthew 5:18. *Jot* is the English translation for the Hebrew letter y*od*. It's the 10th letter of the Hebrew alphabet and the smallest letter of that alphabet. It looks much like the English comma.

*Tittle*, however, isn't an actual letter of the Hebrew alphabet. It, instead, refers to the shaping and smallest extensions, strokes, or projections by which *Hebrew* letters are formed and which differentiate one letter from another.

Examine the image above. The Hebrew letter jod is at the left. On the right are two more Hebrew letters, *he* and *cheth*. Study closely the small fraction of an inch extension of the stroke on *cheth* which changes *he* to the letter *cheth*. That stroke is a tittle. Again, tittles are the tiny marks or strokes which distinguish Hebrew letters one from another. An English example of a tittle would be the small strokes that create the difference between our capital letters "L" and "I." The difference is in the small marks: the extension of the lower part of the "L" and the small horizontal extension at the top of the "I." We use phrases like "the dotting of the i" and the "crossing of the t" to transmit the idea that something is to be exact. That's the idea of *jot* and *tittle*.

## There are two "families" of Bibles with varying messages.

It's important to understand why we are talking about this. It ties into the reason the words *jot* and *tittle* must be retained in Matthew 5:18. How much more basic can one get than the simple letters of a language—the alphabet and the way the letters are differentiated one from another—to create the miracle of written communication?

It's also important to know that Jesus referred specifically to the Hebrew language. It wasn't an accident that His chosen words didn't refer to an Old Testament Greek, nor to Old Testament English, Spanish, or Latin; but it was to the Hebrew language. However, these unique Hebrew references, *jot* and *tittle*, are changed by most Bible version authors. Additionally, many readers gloss over them perhaps because they don't know what these specially chosen words mean and may feel their significance is not important.

You may or may not be aware that there are two different families of Bibles. Each differs in thousands of instances, including both the English translation and the underlying Hebrew and Greek texts from which the English Bible (and those of other languages) is translated. The one family or stream of Bibles for the New Testament is translated from a Greek collation of some 5,000$^+$ manuscripts (mss.) and collectively called the Textus Receptus (TR). The TR is that from which the King James Bible is translated. The other stream of manuscripts used for most new versions is translated from a Greek collation of basically only two major manuscripts (mss): Vaticanus and Sinaiticus. They are collectively called the Nestle-Aland/United Bible Societies Text (**NA**). These two texts reflect thousands of differences between them: 3,000 differences in just the gospels. Additional discrepancies are added in the English translation *from* these underlying texts.

> **TR**: collation of 5,000$^+$ mss. that underlie KJB; **NA**: collation of only 2$^+$ mss that underlie most new versions.

Don't be deceived by the *New* King James Bible. It's not an "updated" King James Bible. It is a different version of God's Word as are the NIV, NAS, ESV, et al. There are thousands of differences among each, and between each of the new versions and the King James Bible. The NKJV, for example, translates more than 100,000 words differently from those in the King James Bible.

It isn't just that there are thousands of differences in the words in the English translations between the two families of Bibles and their underlying texts, but these differences are bringing much confusion, division, and animosity among the body of believers.

## There is a purpose for the study of and reference to underlying languages.

This book is not meant to be a study on Hebrew and Greek languages. The author is in no way equipped to teach on these languages. However, it's impossible to fairly present the facts about changed doctrine in many Bibles without briefly showing the reader where some of the discrepancies initiate. They exist both (1) in the English translation and (2) in the Hebrew and Greek words from which the native tongue has been translated.

At times, there are discrepancies in the underlying Hebrew or Greek text; but in many of the examples, the differences lie in the fact that the translators do not accurately, *contextually* translate into English what is recorded in the text from which they are translating. For a more complete study of the Bible version issue, study two publications, *Bible Versions I* and *II* available through Restoration of the Family: www.RestorationOfTheFamily.org.

There are several Bible translation programs online and books available for those who are not schooled in Hebrew and Greek that can be used to assess the basics underlying most Bible translations. That's the approach used in this book. However, these programs, too, are not infallible. They are only guides and should not be used to discredit the accurately translated Word of God.

Chapter 8

## It's important to assess the accuracy of a translation with some textual facts.

Below is an illustration showing the underlying Greek text for *one jot or one tittle*. Over the top of the two circles are the *Greek letters* for the equivalent English letters *jot* and *tittle*. Directly below the Greek letters are the English equivalent for *jot* and *tittle*. The numbers under *jot* and *tittle*, 2503 and 2762 are from Strong's Concordance resource dictionary. (As mentioned previously, this is a book which provides references and information for the Hebrew and Greek Words used in the Bible.) At the bottom of the image are the equivalent English letters for the Greek alphabetic letters given over the top of each circle:

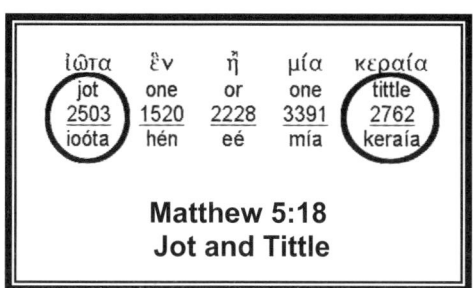

*For verily I say unto you, Till heaven and earth pass, one jot or one tittle shall in no wise pass from the law, till all be fulfilled.* Matthew 5:18

This is one of the formats used throughout this book to help the reader assess the accuracy or inaccuracy of the English translation—by looking at the text from which the English is translated. Equipped with

> There are contextual reasons to retain *jot* and *tittle*.

the above information, study the table on the next page to compare how several other Bibles record their substitutes for the specific Hebrew-related words, *jot* and *tittle*. *Jot* and *title* are words Jesus spoke. Using what has already been presented, determine what contextually is accurate and inaccurate with the following translations:

| **Matthew 5:18:** *Jot* and *tittle* are absent from all versions below, except for the King James Bible. ||
|---|---|
| *For verily I say unto you, Till heaven and earth pass, one jot or one tittle shall in no wise pass from the law, till all be fulfilled.* KJB | Greek Text NA and TR<br><br>ἰῶτα — ἓν — ἢ — μία — κεραία<br>(jot) — one — or — one — (tittle)<br>2503 — 1520 — 2228 — 3391 — 2762<br>ioóta — hén — eé — mía — keraía |
| *For truly I say to you, Until heaven and earth pass away, even a yoth[1] or a dash shall pass away ...* Lamsa (See next column for [1].)<br><br>*... not the smallest letter, not the least stroke of a pen ...* NIV<br><br>*For truly, I say to you, till heaven and earth pass away, not an \*\*iota, not a dot, will pass from the law until all is accomplished.* RSV<br><br>*For truly, I say to you, until heaven and earth pass away, not an \*\*iota, not a dot, will pass from the Law until all is accomplished.* ESV<br><br>*For truly I say to you, until heaven and earth pass away, not the smallest letter or stroke shall pass away from the Law, until all is accomplished.* NASV | [1]Lamsa footnote: "yoth is the smallest letter in the Aramaic and Hebrew." **[This is erroneous. *Yod* is the smallest letter in the Hebrew Alphabet,\* and Lamsa's dash could mean any language.]**<br><br>NIV: Smallest letter or stroke of a pen could refer to any language.<br><br>RSV and ESV: A dot could refer to any language. \*\*Iota is ninth letter of the Greek alphabet. It is not a Hebrew letter; *iota* is not an English translation of the underlying text.<br><br>NASV: Smallest letter could refer to any letter of any language; stroke could refer to many different things. |

\*Yod is the tenth letter of the Hebrew alphabet. The number ten plays an important part in the Bible. We have the Ten Commandments. There were ten plagues. BOTH *jot* and *tittle* are attached to the Hebrew language. \*\**Iota* (and Lamsa's *yoth*\*) is a transliteration, not a translation. *Transliteration* is changing letters from one alphabet into corresponding, similar-sounding characters of another alphabet, leaving the word untranslated from the underlying language. *Translation* is the transference of the *meaning* of words from one language to another. A transliteration in Matthew 5:18 removes important theological information and "threads" which interlink *jot* and *tittle*

## Chapter 8

and their Hebrew language "clues" as a bridge between the Old and New Testaments. Even more important is that *iota*, as recorded in the RSV and ESV, changes the internal language reference from Hebrew to Greek.

In the table above, it's only the King James Bible in which the underlying Greek text is properly *translated into* English. Other translators replace the Hebrew-derived words Jesus spoke. By doing so, they remove vital textual evidence. Additionally, by speaking these recorded words Jesus was "canonizing"—not English, not Spanish, not Greek, but Hebrew—the honored written Old Testament language of the Jews.

> It's important to recognize the difference between a translation and a transliteration.

There are many scholars who incorrectly teach that the preserved Old Testament underlying language was a <u>Greek</u> translation of the Old Testament rather than Hebrew. They support a corrupted Greek translation of the Old Testament called the LXX or Septuagint. The insertion of the Greek word *iota* into the English text in Matthew 5:18 by the RSV and ESV authors reinforces this faulty LXX teaching.

> It's not JUST a stroke of a pen; it's the Hebrew tittle; it's not JUST the smallest letter; it's a Hebrew alphabetic letter.

"The Palestinian Jewish community accepted only the Hebrew Scriptures. This was the community of Jesus and the Apostles ... the LXX is not the Bible of Jesus and the writers of Scripture ..."*

---

*A detailed, analytical and comparative study of selected Scriptures compared with the Septuagint is given in the publication: *Did Jesus and the Apostles Quote from the Septuagint (LXX)?* by Dr. Kirk D. DiVietro. B.F.T.#2707 (The Bible for Today, 900 Park Avenue, Collingswood, NJ 08108)

## Why should translators be so exacting?

The contextual study of *jot* and *tittle* should alert readers that even some Biblical scholars do not understand many of the nuances of Bible language. That's all the more reason for every person to equip himself to learn *how* to study so he can correctly interpret the Bible:

*Study to shew thyself approved unto God, a workman that needeth not to be ashamed, <u>rightly dividing</u> the word of truth.* 2 Timothy 2:15

Is God too particular? Does just a letter the size of a comma or a small change in the shape of a letter really matter? Yes, these changes are important. They are important for many reasons, but in this chapter it comes down to a principle expressed in John 10:35: ... *and <u>the scripture cannot be broken</u>*. Even though man changes God's Word, God's Word cannot be changed—broken.

> They could not *rend* His Word.

There is an interlocking, continuous thread that ties together all the words, and even letters, in the Bible. The question posed in the title of this chapter should be carefully considered: "Shall we **rend** the robe of Jesus though it be only a jot or tittle?"

The word *rend* highlighted above is a key word in the title for this chapter. It means to tear something into pieces. However, that's not the full meaning. It is to tear something into pieces <u>by force</u>. In the eyes of man, Jesus was taken into custody, beaten, and hung on the cross by force. Jesus, however <u>gave</u> his life and body to be beaten and hung on the cross. While he was dying a horrific physical death on the cross, do you recall what was happening at the foot of the cross?

## Chapter 8

*And they crucified him, and parted his garments, casting lots: that it might be fulfilled which was spoken by the prophet. They <u>parted my garments among them, and upon my vesture did they cast lots</u>.* Matthew 27:35

Luke records this same incident:
*... And they parted his raiment, and <u>cast lots</u>.* Luke 23:34

John gives other very important details:
*Then the soldiers, when they had crucified Jesus, took his garments, and made four parts, to every soldier a part; and also his coat: now **the coat was without seam, woven from the top throughout**.*

*They said therefore among themselves, **Let us not rend** it, but cast lots for it, whose it shall be: that the <u>scripture might be fulfilled</u>, which saith, They parted my raiment among them, and for my vesture they did cast lots. These things therefore the soldiers did.* John 19:23-24

Here, again, is that all important linking between the Old and New Testaments. This very incident was prophesized in the Old Testament:

*They part my garments among them, and cast lots upon my vesture.* Psalm 22:18

**The Word today is bartered as was the vesture of Jesus.**

The *vesture* of Jesus was not just any coat. It was a *coat without seam, woven from the top throughout*. His coat was "taken" into the hands of soldiers who hoped to profit from it. They even gambled for the clothing of Jesus. The value, to man, of what Jesus wore, came down to what today would be called "the throw of the dice." It won for the victor the very clothing that had covered the LORD's body. However, the coat of Jesus, like His Scriptures—and everything about Him—was (woven)

87

*without seam*: not broken, not torn, not rent. Even these wicked soldiers could not "rend" the garment of Jesus. What they did do was prophesied many years before the crucifixion took place. They would part His clothing and barter for it. However, these wicked men unknowingly fulfilled Old Testament prophecy exactly as it had been prophesied hundreds of years prior. This event, as well as many others, had been supernaturally recorded in the Old Testament through the hands of God's chosen holy men:

*For the prophecy came not in old time by the will of man: but holy men of God spake as they were moved by the Holy Ghost.* 2 Peter 1:21

They *parted* His items of clothing (divided them)

but they did not tear the "garment" of Jesus:

*They part my garments among them, and cast lots* [similar to throwing dice today] *upon*[for] *my vesture* [coat]. Psalm 22:18

*For these things were done, that the <u>scripture should be fulfilled</u>, A bone of him shall not be broken.* John 19:36 As prophesized, none of Jesus' bones were broken, even when the nails pierced through his hands and feet.

Is there any possible relationship between the rending of the garment of Jesus to the rending of the Word of God by man? Notice how the recorded words in the Bible reflect articles of clothing pictured as metaphors for the Word of God and what God does for us:

*I will greatly rejoice in the LORD, my soul shall be joyful in my God; for he hath <u>clothed</u> me with the <u>garments</u> of salvation, he hath <u>covered</u> me with the <u>robe</u> of righteousness ...* Isaiah 61:10

Every word of God has a significant part that makes up the entire Bible. So, another question might be considered: "Is it possible that those who are profiting from rending the Word of God, here and there—a word here, a verse there—that instead of throwing the "dice" to win a part of the vesture of Jesus, these men are unknowingly merely playing out the Old Testament prophecy given through the pen of Amos?"

*Behold, the days come, saith the Lord GOD, that I will send a famine in the land, not a famine of bread, nor a thirst for water, but of hearing the words of the LORD: And they shall wander from sea to sea, and from the north even to the east, they shall run to and fro to seek the word of the LORD, and shall not find it.* Amos 8:11-12

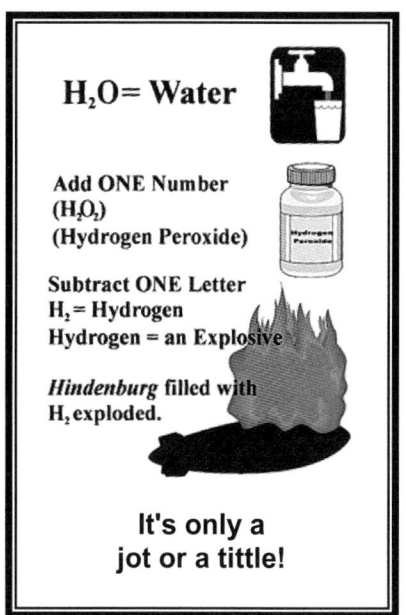

Many Christians when dealing with the above matters come to the sad conclusion that it's somehow okay to say: "Let's agree to disagree." Approaching these vital topics with such a flippant attitude is like saying God's Word is a matter of opinion. Oh, if only we had the same attitude or reverence about the Bible that we have for accuracy in other areas of life.

I leave you with additional food for thought with an analogy from the graphic given above. Adding only a small $sub_2$ to the chemical symbol for water $H_2O$ changes it to hydrogen peroxide $H_2O_2$. Which would you prefer to drink? Subtracting one letter from $H_2O$ changes it to an explosive gas $H_2$. It was this stroke of a letter that potentially made a difference in the lives of the 36 people who were killed in the explosion of the dirigible the *Hindenburg*.

We have also seen how the addition of the three letters "*n o t*" by the serpent to Adam and Eve ... *Ye shall not surely die* (Genesis 3:4) made a difference throughout the earth and in the lives of people who inhabit the earth. And so, does the elimination of a *jot* and *tittle* make a difference? Whether it's the Bible with its Ten Commandments and hundreds of other teachings and commandments or with science and its exacting formulas, God has a precise order and reason for everything He has done and written. Yet, the serpent, who is more *subtil than any beast of the field,* continues to say ... **yea, hath God said ...** (Genesis 3:1) through man's footnotes and versions of God's Words.

**Shall we rend the robe of Jesus though it be only one jot or one tittle?**

# 9

# The Jewish Engagement Is Not A Marriage.

In Chapter 5, you were introduced to the Jewish engagement language. This chapter will reinforce and build on that introduction. In the New Testament, the Jewish engagement is recorded as an espousal while in the Old Testament engagements are usually referred to as betrothals. Jewish engaged couples were called husband and wife, even though they had not been made one flesh (married) by God.

Conversely, most who become engaged today are called fiancé and fiancée. It isn't until after the marriage ceremony that the fiancé and fiancée are called husband and wife. As proof of the above-mentioned uniquely Biblical Jewish language, study the Scriptures below.

The Jewish Engagement Is Not A Marriage.

| **Betrothal and Espousal: Two Words for Engagement** ||
| **Old Testament Engagement** | **New Testament Engagement** |
| Deuteronomy 20:7<br>*And what man is there that hath **betrothed a wife**, and hath not taken her [not married her]?*<br><br>Deuteronomy 22:23<br>*If a damsel that is a virgin be **betrothed** unto an husband ...* | Matthew 1:18-19<br>*Now the birth of Jesus Christ was on this wise: When as his mother Mary was **espoused** to Joseph, before they came together [were married], she was found with child of the Holy Ghost. Then Joseph her husband, being a just man, and not willing to make her a publick example, was minded to put her away privily.* |

When a Jewish man wanted to marry, he often traveled to the house of the prospective bride where he negotiated a price for her. A **contract** of betrothal or espousal was established after which he returned to his father's house for a period of about twelve months. This was a man-made agreement drawn up by man and controlled by him. During the espousal/betrothal period, the betrothed bride and groom were called *husband* and *wife* even though there had not yet been a marriage ceremony.

> Engagements are man-made and man-controlled. Marriages are God-created and God-controlled.

The marriage ceremony occurred after a twelve-month period of separation. It was then that the two spoke their marriage vows before God and then that the LORD, through His marriage-covenant, made the two one flesh (a new creation), just as He does today. (Historical information varies widely on the specifics of the espousal contract. The important focus of this chapter is not based on what is found outside the Bible, but from what is recorded in the Word of God.)

God clearly and consistently gives one message about *what* it is that He joins together:

> ... she [is] *thy companion, and the wife of thy <u>covenant</u>.* Malachi 2:14

It's not what man has done. It's **What** *therefore God hath joined together* ... Mark 10:9 This supernatural joining is something impossible for man to create. Pastors, rabbis, priests, and justices of the peace do not "marry" people. They perform the ceremony. God does the joining, the creating of a marriage. After being made one flesh by God, the husband and wife remain two separate individuals, even though God "joins" them. There is an unseen creation of substance in the spiritual realm that we cannot see but can sense. It is something akin to faith. Faith is the substance of things <u>not seen</u>, but we know that faith exists; and thus, it is faith that becomes the "substance" of things not seen:

*Now faith is the substance of things hoped for, the evidence of things not seen.* Hebrews 11:1

> Man doesn't hold the creative power to join two people; he can only officiate over God's joining.

## Engagements and marriages are very different.

Engagements, both in Biblical times and today, are man-made. God is not a party to this *contractual* agreement in the sense that He doesn't join the two during the engagement. An engagement is a formalizing of an intended future life-time commitment. Conversely, a marriage is God-made and the terms thereof controlled by Him. A marriage is a supernatural, invisible, permanent **joining** BY God—not man. God calls it a covenant in Malachi and *one-flesh marriage* elsewhere. No one understands exactly *what* it is that God joins together or how.

The Jewish Engagement Is Not A Marriage.

The specifics we are given are the words spoken by Jesus, such as in Mark 10:8-9 and which are graphically described in Genesis 2:21-24. It's the two shall <u>be</u> one flesh; this is WHAT it is that God hath joined together. It's something that did not exist *before the LORD spoke it into existence* in Genesis, **much as he spoke the other "beginnings" into being.** *And God said ... and it was so.* Genesis 1:9, et al. How did He make something out of nothing? We don't understand. How does He make the two one flesh? We also don't understand. But if God says it happens, it is an immutable, unchangeable Truth:

> God speaks into existence a one-flesh creation called marriage. The "instrument" by which marriage is created is a covenant.

*And they twain shall be <u>one flesh</u>: so then they are no more twain, but one flesh. <u>What</u> therefore God hath joined together, let not man put asunder.* Mark 10:8-9

**Marriage and engagements are two different commitments from God's point of view.**

Study the illustration at the left. It depicts espousal and marriage. Those who are espoused are represented by the engagement ring. They haven't been made one flesh by God. Those who are married are represented by the image of woman being made from a rib taken from man. Distinguishing between a Jewish engagement and a

Chapter 9

marriage is vital to New Testament doctrine. This difference must be retained in the translated Scriptures. Study the Jewish language expressions below which are integral parts of Biblical language.

| It's important to understand that cultural practices influence word usages when studying and interpreting Scripture. | |
|---|---|
| Matthew 1:20, 24, 25 | |
| *20 But while he thought on these things, behold, the angel of the Lord appeared unto him in a dream, saying, Joseph, thou son of David, fear not to* **take** *unto thee* **Mary thy wife***: for that which is conceived in her is of the Holy Ghost.* This was during their espousal. The LORD was telling Joseph to "marry" his *espoused* wife, Mary. | *Take*, contextually means to marry.<br><br>Mary was an espoused wife. |
| *24 Then Joseph being raised from sleep did as the angel of the Lord had bidden him, and* **took** *unto him* **his wife***. Took* is the word for marriage in this context. It's not talking of sexual intimacy. Matthew 1:25 verifies they had no sex until AFTER the birth of Mary's firstborn son. | |
| *25 And* **knew her not** *till she had brought forth her firstborn son: and he called his name JESUS.* Matthew 1:25 *Knew* is the contextual word here for sexual intimacy. | *Knew*, contextually, is the word for sexual intimacy. |
| *And another said, I have* **married a wife** *…* Luke 14:20 Today, we say, "I got married." The Jewish espousal language serves as signposts to reflect important embedded teachings. | |
| Luke 14:20 teaches the reader there is an espoused wife who was subsequently married. This is similar to Matthew's recording to show Joseph "married a wife": ***Joseph … took unto him his wife.*** These language distinctions point out important unstated details. | He <u>married</u> his *espoused wife.* |

## The Jewish Engagement Is Not A Marriage.

Again, it's important to be keenly aware of not only every word in the Scriptures but <u>how</u> each is applied. It's not just the words that are written but *how* they are used in each specific verse which affects the correct application of each word. Study to see how the NIV authors err on two accounts as shown in the table below:

1. They do not translate using the Jewish cultural idioms.
2. They do not accurately translate from their underlying text:

| Translation from Greek Text by NIV Authors | Nestle Aland Greek text from which the NIV is translated |
|---|---|
| *... Joseph son of David, do not be afraid to take Mary \*home* **as** *your wife ...* Matthew 1:20 NIV  *When Joseph woke up, he did what the angel of the Lord had commanded him and took Mary \*home* **as** *his wife.* Matthew 1:24 NIV  \*Neither the NA (Nestle Aland) nor the TR (Textus Receptus) has the Greek word for *home* in verse 20 or 24. **What the Greek indicates is ...** ***fear not to take unto thee*** *Mary thy wife.* **KJB**  The NIV paraphrased translation, in verses 20 and 24, is misleading. It changes the emphasis from Joseph taking unto him [marrying] to taking Mary home **as** his wife. | **Matthew 1:20** Δαυίδ, μὴ φοβηθῇς παραλαβεῖν σοι, of David, not fear to take unto thee, 1138 3361 5399 3880 4671 Dauid meé fobeethees paralabein soi  Μαριὰμ τὴν γυναῖκά σου. τὸ γὰρ ἐν Mary wife: thy for in 3137 3588 1135 4675 3588 1063 1722 Mariám teén gunaiká sou tó gàr en  **Matthew 1:24** ὁ ἄγγελος κυρίου καὶ παρέλαβεν the angel of the Lord and took 3588 32 2962 2532 3880 ho ángelos Kuriou kai parélaben  τὴν γυναῖκα αὐτῷ αὐτοῦ· wife: unto him his 3588 1135 846 846 teén gunaiká autoó autoú  Nowhere in the entire first chapter of Matthew is there an underlying Greek word for home (oikos 3624).  The Greek text for both the TR (Textus Receptus) and NA (Nestle Aland) read the same in Matthew 1:24-25, but the NIV authors do not accurately translate their Greek text in English. |
| There's a difference between TAKING a wife—the Biblical word **to indicate marriage**—and taking someone home AS a wife. Many, today, "take another home" to live in sexual sin. ||

Study a similar pattern of the recording of the Jewish betrothal and marriage language in the Old Testament. What kind of *wife* and/or *husband* is represented in Deuteronomy 22:22-23? Is there a difference between someone who is betrothed and someone who is married? Notice the Jewish espousal language highlighted:

| Deuteronomy 22:22 | Deuteronomy 22:23 |
|---|---|
| *If man be found lying with a woman **married to an husband**, then they shall both of them die ...* | *If a damsel that is a virgin be **betrothed** unto an husband ...* |

Deuteronomy 22:22 describes a married woman. She has been made one flesh by God. We know that because of the Jewish cultural language: *married to an husband*. The damsel in verse 23 is betrothed or engaged. She is under a contractual agreement with her betrothed husband. Did you notice that both the Old and New Testament cultural language patterns are similar in the King James Bible translation? Thus, when a reader sees the expression, "married to a wife," whether it be in the Old Testament or the New, he should recognize it not as outdated language, but it is *Biblical language* that accurately reflects the underlying text from which it is translated.

It's also important to link the details of Joseph and Mary's espousal in Matthew 1:18-20 with the exception clause in Matthew 19:9. These are details only given by Matthew. It's crucial to understand that sexual sin during the espousal (contractual) period was fornication and grounds to end an engagement. This "permission" did not extend to a one-flesh marriage. Matthew lets us know that not only were Joseph and Mary espoused; but also, because Mary was pregnant, Joseph was going to exercise his right *to put her away*. *Putting away* is another Biblical term which means *to divorce*. "Taking her" to be his wife after she was pregnant could bring reproach to Joseph's character. Others would think (as did Joseph) that Mary was a fornicator and that he could have been a party to that sin. Joseph, however, was such a just man that he was hoping to divorce her secretly so as to not bring further shame upon Mary:

*Now the birth of Jesus Christ was on this wise: When as his mother Mary was <u>espoused</u> to Joseph, before they came together* [were made one flesh by God], *she was found with child of the Holy Ghost. Then Joseph her husband, being a just man, and not willing to make her a publick example, was minded to put her away privily.* Matthew 1:18-19

The Word of God distinguishes between engaged and married husbands and wives through the Jewish idioms for husbands and wives. This can be observed in both the Old and New Testaments. Furthermore, God gives man control over the terms of engagements but not over marriage. It's only the LORD who can create a marriage; a supernatural, invisible, permanent joining of a man and a woman, neither of whom has a living one-flesh spouse. If everyone understood the Biblically recorded cultural differences and basics between covenants and contracts, much of the confusion regarding Matthew 19:9 and "re-marriage" could be eradicated.

> There are major differences between contracts and covenants.

So what do we have? We have two very distinct acts and relationships. One is a covenant called *marriage* created and the terms thereof controlled by God. The other is a legal contract created and the terms controlled by man <u>which includes</u> *espousals* or *betrothals*. Carefully study some of the differences between God's covenant and man's contracts as noted below.

| **Marriage Covenant** | **Contract: Jewish engagements <u>and</u> other legal agreements** |
|---|---|
| **God made.** | **Man made.** |
| Spiritually created. | Legal contract/agreement. |
| God sets terms; He creates; He dissolves the covenant when a spouse dies. | Man sets terms; he creates; he dissolves per man-made stipulations. |
| Performance or nonperformance of terms or sin do not nullify. | Performance and nonperformance can nullify. |
| Only valid with one-flesh unions. | Valid among people of varying "marital" statuses. |
| Only valid between a male and a female neither of whom has another living one-flesh spouse. | Valid among those of the same or opposite sex. |

It's impossible to correctly comprehend Matthew 19:9 apart from: (1) understanding the primary purpose for which the exception clause *except it be for fornication* was included and (2) apart from proper understanding of the espousal language introduced by Matthew in Chapter 1 of his gospel. Likewise, it's difficult to correctly understand marriage without considering Genesis 2:21-24 and connecting it to the LORD's statements about the permanence of marriage in both Matthew 19:4-6 and Mark 10:6-9. Study the illustration on the next page. Notice there are differences between the language patterns for Jewish and Gentile engagements. There is, however, no difference Biblically between a Jewish and a Gentile covenant-marriage.

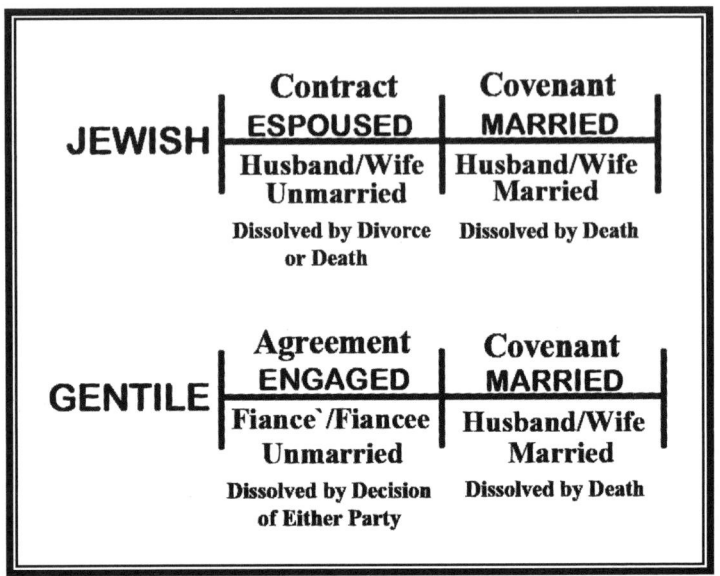

## You've heard it said, "But, Moses allowed for divorce."

The Bible also records the ungodly misuse of the Bill of Divorcement:

*When a man hath taken a wife, and married her, and it come to pass that she find no favour in his eyes, because he hath found some uncleanness in her: then let him write her a bill of divorcement, and give it in her hand, and send her out of his house.* Deuteronomy 24:1

The Pharisees asked Jesus, as recorded in Matthew 19:7, why Moses **commanded** this practice. However, they neglected to factor in one major point—the context. Jesus provides the context; that is, why it was **suffered** (allowed). It was allowed because those who were divorcing their wives had hardened hearts. This abusive practice had gotten so out of hand that husbands began signing Bills of Divorcement if their wives were guilty of some apparent frivolous "misdeed," called some uncleanness in Detuteronomy 24:1: ... *because he hath found some uncleanness in her* ...

Let's put this in perspective. Look at how this same thing is being practiced, but perhaps not recognized today. My experience in talking with people is that the number one sin associated with any reference to Deuteronomy 24:1 is that of adultery. These people incorrectly say, "According to Deuteronomy 24, divorce was allowed if someone committed adultery." Using Deuteronomy 24 as a loophole to allow a person to divorce a spouse is applying Scripture out of context.

First, it should be apparent from reading Deuteronomy 24:1 that the reason given there was not for adultery. The text says ... *he hath found some uncleanness in her* ... *Uncleanness* and *adultery* in the Old Testament are based on two different words. *Naap* is the Hebrew word translated *adultery* (or a form of it) and used 31 times in the Old Testament. Study three examples below:

- *Thou shalt not commit adultery.* Exodus 20:14
- *But whoso committeth adultery with a woman lacketh understanding: he that doeth it destroyeth his own soul.* Proverbs 6:32
- *And I will come near to you to judgment; and I will be a swift witness against the sorcerers, and against the adulterers* ... Malachi 3:5

The underlying Hebrew word used for uncleanness in Deuteronomy is *ervah*, Strong's 6172. Ervah is used 54 times in the Old Testament. It is most often translated *nakedness* but never translated *adultery*.

The context of Deuteronomy 24 is that they were putting away their spouses for trivial reasons: *some uncleanness*. In other words, they divorced for any reason they wanted to state. Conversely, those who committed adultery were to be stoned to death. The former is what is being done today by those with hardened hearts for what judicial family "courts of equity" call "irreconcilable differences"—a phrase which no court of law has been able to define.*

\*See *Judge, Please Don't Strike That Gavel ... On My Marriage:* Restoration of the Family, PO Box 621342, Oviedo, FL 32762-1342.

Secondly, God did not approve the ungodly Old Testament practice of putting away a spouse. It was that <u>ungodly conduct</u> which Jesus was <u>recognizing</u>. He, however, did not <u>approve</u> it. He allowed it, just as He *allows* it today. Both Matthew and Mark record the fact that (1) Moses allowed it, and (2) it was allowed because men had hardened hearts. This was a practice put in place BY MOSES to try to control the acts of hard-hearted husbands against their wives. Again, it was allowed or suffered, but not approved by God. He never approves sin:

> *They say unto him, Why did Moses then command to give a writing of divorcement, and to put her away? He saith unto them, Moses <u>because of the hardness of your hearts</u> suffered* [allowed] *you to put away your wives: but from the beginning it was not so. And I say unto you, Whosoever shall put away his wife, except it be for fornication, and shall marry another, committeth adultery: and whoso marrieth her which is put away doth commit adultery.* Matthew 19:7-9

Before leaving this teaching about why Moses suffered (allowed) divorce for the hard-hearted Israelites, think on this: How many murders and thefts are committed every day in the United States? How many man-made court divorces take place daily in the United

States? The answer is: thousands. As mentioned in Chapter 3, there are more than one million divorces every year. Does God approve of these sinful acts? Of course He doesn't. However, He permits man to have a free will to choose whether that free will is used for good or evil. This is one aspect of the love of God few understand.

## Two <u>kinds</u> of divorces are recorded: those approved and those not approved.

Those divorces which were Biblically allowed <u>and</u> approved include putting away an *engaged* wife because of the Jewish espousal practice. Espousals were contracts controlled by man, and the reason we are given for this putting away in the New Testament was for the sin of fornication. An example of that given in the same gospel would have been if Joseph had put away Mary during the time of their espousal contract, because ... *she was found with child of the Holy Ghost.* Matthew 1:18 However, the angel of the LORD appeared unto Joseph and helped him understand that the child Mary was carrying was conceived because of a supernatural miracle of Holy Ghost. It was not because of the sin of fornication.

> Jesus "allowed" for two different kinds of divorces, ... but ... beware.

The second **kind** of divorce, marital divorce, was also allowed but **NOT approved** by the LORD. It was **allowed** for ungodly acts by those who had hardened hearts. They were unsaved, unforgiving spouses acting outside the will of God. Jesus referred three times to their practice of putting away a married wife. It is recorded in

Matthew 5:31-32, Matthew 19:8-9, and Mark 10:5-12. He concluded each of these conversations with a warning—that another sin is often birthed out of putting away a covenant wife. Many who do the putting away subsequently marry another person as does the person who is put away. Jesus teaches us that those who do so put themselves into a continual state of adultery:

*And he saith unto them, Whosoever shall put away his wife, and marry another, committeth adultery against her. And if a woman shall put away her husband, and be married to another, she committeth adultery.* Mark 10:11-12

For some, this study on the Biblically recorded differences between the two kinds of wives may be a review; but for others, it has some new, very important information that may warrant reading the chapter again. It is vital for everyone to recognize the way in which the difference between a Jewish engagement and a God-created one-flesh marriage are carefully, but succinctly, worded. The idiosyncrasies in these Jewish language idioms, as they are tied to espousals, must be carefully observed, especially in the New Testament whenever marriage and divorce are discussed. Thus far, it has been shown:

- There are two kinds of husbands and wives.
- There are two kinds of divorces.
- There is a difference between a marriage and an espousal.
- There is an important contextual difference in the use of words such as *knew* and *took* as they relate to marriage.

The topic of divorce will be expanded in upcoming chapters, especially Chapter 17: *What Is A Divorce?* First, some additional groundwork must be laid.

# 10

# Are You Married Or Engaged To Jesus?

Now comes the test—to apply several principles already studied to another verse which has been the center of confusion because of a misunderstanding of the Jewish espousal language. Before looking at the main verse for this Chapter, let's review some of the principles taught in Chapter 6.

It was shown that the words *help* and *meet* are used many times in the Bible, but when they are combined as *(an) help meet*, in Genesis 2:18 and 2:20, there are unique applications of the underlying Hebrew words. The Hebrew word for the English word *help* (Strong's 5828) is usually translated as a name for God; but in two places, Genesis 2:18 and 2:20, it is uniquely tied to man's help meet. Additionally, the

Hebrew word underlying *meet* in Genesis 2:18 and 2:20 is usually translated as a preposition; but with *help meet*, there is a departure from that pattern. Thus, woman is given the "title," man's help meet—not helper or someone suitable for him, etc. These words, *helper* and someone *suitable for him*, do not accurately reflect the underlying Hebrew text, nor do they reflect what God is teaching.

There are many times when a study of how a word is used in one Scripture will help to determine the definition in another verse, and there are times when outside resources help. However, the final decision must line up with what has been <u>recorded in the English Biblical text</u>. That is, it must be a definition that will not violate the context. For example, studying the word *meet* in New Testament Scriptures such as Matthew 8:34 and Mark 14:13 would not properly define the <u>way</u> *meet* is contextually used in Genesis 2:18 and 2:20:

*And, behold, the whole city came out to **meet** Jesus: and when they saw him, they besought him that he would depart out of their coasts.* Matthew 8:34

*Go ye into the city, and there shall **meet** you a man bearing a pitcher of water: follow him.* Mark 14:13

The context of Genesis 2:18 and 2:20 should tell the reader that the above two verses in Matthew and Mark could not be properly used to define the word *meet* as it is used <u>in combination with</u> *help:*

*And the LORD God said, It is not good that the man should be alone; I will make him an help meet for him.* Genesis 2:18

The purpose for the study of *help meet* was not to get entwined with an analysis of Hebrew words. The purpose was to lay some principles

Chapter 10

for interpretation of God's Word, the most important of which comes down to context <u>and</u> believing what the LORD has preserved in English for us to study. That, of course, is possible only after determining that the text does not contain doctrinal errors.

The information in this chapter will reinforce and supplement the principles introduced with *help meet*, but an example from the New Testament will be used. Additionally, with this study, it will also be important to relate information learned about the Jewish engagement and marriage language idioms: *espoused* (engaged) and *married husbands and wives*.

Think about the title for this chapter. How would you answer the question posed; that is, do you think that you are married to Jesus, or do you think you are engaged to Him (or neither of these)? Write your answer on a piece of paper or below adding Scriptural evidence from the Word of God to support your belief.

Did you do that? Did you write your answer above?

Many believers say they are married to Jesus. Can that be proven or disproven in a study of the Scriptures? A study of 2 Corinthians 11:2 will shed Scriptural insight for the answer to this question. How would you interpret the word *espoused* as it is translated in this verse?

*For I am jealous over you with godly jealousy: for I have <u>espoused</u> you to one husband, that I may present you as a chaste virgin to Christ.*
2 Corinthians 11:2

Before getting to the heart of this question, think on some of the verses discussed thus far to show how the Scripture reflects many Jewish idioms, especially those which identify the two different kinds of husbands and wives: *espoused* and *married*. In Chapter 9, it was shown that espousals were tied to a formal, man-made <u>contract</u> which could be broken by an official Bill of Divorcement. On the other hand, marriages were and are created by God through a <u>covenant</u>. He controls the terms of His marriage-covenant. One of the foundational principles of a marriage-covenant is that no act of man can dissolve it. That's because God, in the beginning, set the duration of marriage as a life-long event—until one of the two spouses (a man or a woman) physically dies.

The focus in this chapter is to add more building blocks to reinforce ways to contextually interpret Scripture. This will be done, as mentioned above, through an expanded study of the Jewish espousal. Recall that betrothal or espousal means a mutual promise or contract for a <u>future</u> marriage, and the phrase *to put away* means *to divorce*. However, *putting away* has two very different applications:
- To put away an espoused husband or wife, and
- To put away a married husband or wife.

If a Jewish espousal contract were broken, those who were a party to that contract would be free to "contract" for another ("un-espoused") husband or wife. In so doing, neither party would commit adultery by giving their affections to their newly espoused husband or wife. That's because they had been engaged, not married. However, if a married

## Chapter 10

person (one joined by God) divorced and married someone else, he would become an adulterer (or adulteress if the person were a woman); that is, if one or both of the "re-married" spouses have a living one-flesh husband or wife. In other words, if while Doug and Judith are married (neither having another one-flesh living spouse), Doug divorces Judith and marries Sally, both Doug and Sally would put themselves into a continual state of adultery. This, however, is what most call, but incorrectly so, a "re-marriage." That is why, throughout this book, when a "re-marriage" is what the Bible calls adultery, it is always enclosed within quotes. If it isn't enclosed in quotes, *re-marriage* means a second marriage ceremony between the two original one-flesh spouses. That would be a valid re-marriage.

For example, if Doug would re-marry Judith after he divorced her, that would be a re-marriage. This, however, in the eyes of God, would not be necessary because they were still married even though Doug had chosen to "re-marry" and live with someone not his one-flesh wife. The act of re-marrying Judith could be to satisfy legal statutory requirements and perhaps to not give the appearance of evil.

The above scenario is not true with engagements. Jewish engagements were accompanied by a formal <u>contract</u>. A legal commitment was important for a Jewish engagement in one regard because the young man may have worked for years to gather the resources for the "purchase" of the betrothal or espousal contract:

*And Jacob loved Rachel; and said, I will serve thee seven years for Rachel thy younger daughter.* Genesis 29:18

Matthew, unlike any other New Testament writer, helps us to understand the espousal language through his writings about the espousal and marriage of Joseph and Mary. As shall be shown more conclusively later, Matthew Chapter 1:18-19 and 19:9 are interlinked:

*... When as his [Jesus'] mother Mary was <u>espoused</u> to Joseph, before they came together [were made one flesh by God], she was found with child of the Holy Ghost. Then Joseph <u>her husband</u>, ... was minded <u>to put her away</u> privily (except it be for fornication Matthew 19:9). But while he thought on these things, behold, the angel of the Lord appeared unto him in a dream, saying, Joseph, thou son of David, fear not to take unto thee Mary thy wife: for that which is conceived in her is of the Holy Ghost.* Matthew 1:18-20

*Then Joseph being raised from sleep did as the angel of the Lord had bidden him, and <u>took unto him his wife</u>.* Matthew 1:24 *Took* [or *take*] is the Bible sign that they were made one flesh by God. We use that term today: "I *take* thee Doug to be my wedded husband."

With the above review in mind, read the verse below again and interpret it in the context of the Jewish engagement language:

*For I am jealous over you with godly jealousy: for I have <u>espoused</u> you to one <u>husband</u>, that I may present you as a chaste virgin to Christ.* 2 Corinthians 11:2

Paul used the espousal language to portray our <u>engagement</u> to Christ. He was using Biblically consistent Jewish idioms to do so. He wasn't *espousing* an audience who had given their affections (married) to other gods. By analogy, those who are married are not to be engaged or "re-married" to another person. This is such a vital teaching. Paul is *espousing*—not marrying—his contemporaries to Christ. There will one day be, for faithful believers, a marriage—the *Marriage Supper of the Lamb*. Yet, as with believers today, Paul likewise knew ... *as the serpent beguiled Eve through his subtilty* ... believers of his day could be pulled astray by those who teach false doctrine: *But I fear ... your minds should be corrupted ...* 2 Corinthians 11:3

## They say …

Some teachers "say" the word *espoused* in 2 Corinthians refers to marriage because the underlying word used for *espoused* is a Greek word that <u>can</u> mean "to joint." (There's not an error here. It is the word *joint*.) It comes from the Greek word, *harmonzo*, but *harmonzo* also means *to woo*. *To woo* is one of the meanings man has given for this Greek word which contextually must be interpreted *espoused*.

## The Greek words for *joined* have several different meanings.

The Greek and English words for *joined* have several different meanings and applications. For example, Strong's 4801 *suzengnumi*, is used in two Scriptures where marriage is clearly defined as a joining between one man and one woman: Matthew 19:6 and Mark 10:9.

However, a different Greek word is used for *joined* (Strong's 2853, *kollao*) in Acts 8:29 when the Spirit told Philip to *… join thyself to this chariot.*

> Context in the native tongue clarifies correct interpretation.

*Kollao* is not the same word used for God's joining of a man and a woman in Matthew 19:6 and Mark 10:9. Likewise, and even *more important*, is the fact that <u>the context of the two events differ</u>.

Study the table on the next page. There are five different Strong's numbers representing different forms of Greek words that are each translated *join* or *joined*. What should be clear is that (1) there are several different Greek words which are each translated join(ed), *but (2) it's even more important to see that there are different contexts.* Context influences both the choice of Greek words originally penned, as well as the words chosen by those who translate the Greek words into another language:

| Scriptures using the word join or joined | Strong's # |
|---|---|
| *Wherefore they are no more twain, but one flesh. What therefore God hath joined together, let not man put asunder.* Matthew 19:6 | 4801 |
| *What therefore God hath joined together, let not man put asunder.* Mark 10:9 | 4801 |
| *Then the Spirit said unto Philip, Go near, and join thyself to this chariot.* Acts 8:29 | 2853 |
| *... whose house joined hard to the synagogue.* Acts 18:7 | 4927 |
| *For this cause shall a man leave his father and mother, and shall be joined unto his wife, and they two shall be one flesh.* Ephesians 5:31 | 4347 |
| *From whom the whole body fitly joined together and compacted by that which every joint supplieth, according to the effectual working in the measure of every part, maketh increase of the body unto the edifying of itself in love.* Ephesians 4:16 | 4883 |

In Acts 8:29, it's obvious the LORD wasn't telling Philip to marry the chariot. How do we know this? It's not that the underlying Greek word reveals this. **It's by the context in our native language that we understand the correct interpretation of *joined*.** Even, if for some reason, the underlying Greek word would have been the same in Acts 8:29 as that used in Matthew 19:6 and Mark 10:9, it's very clear from the context that Philip could not be made one flesh with a wooden chariot. Thus, context must prevail over Strong's Concordance and over what writers outside the Bible may teach—**if** those references make God's Word inconsistent.

In the last example given above, Ephesians 4:16, the word *joined* means being closely joined or knit together. However, <u>this</u> joining is in our beliefs and actions, as part of the church body, which will ultimately glorify God. We, within the body of Christ (the church), are not married to others within that body; that is, we have not been made one flesh with them such as when God joins a man and a woman through His covenant of marriage. Review 2 Corinthians 11:2 again:

*For I am jealous over you with godly jealousy: for I have <u>espoused</u> you to one <u>husband</u>, that I may present you as a chaste virgin to Christ.* 2 Corinthians 11:2

Even though the underlying Greek word for *espoused* in 2 Corinthians 11:2 is <u>derived</u> <u>from</u> a Greek word that <u>can</u> mean "to joint" (Strong's 719), Paul contextually isn't telling us that the joining in 2 Corinthians is to join as in a marriage. *Espoused* in 2 Corinthians is an engagement—as the word *espoused* means. Surely Paul was well aware of the difference between an espousal and a marriage. He understood the Jewish espousal and marriage language. He was a Jew and a well-educated Hebrew. He would not have made such a glaring error and neither would the translators. Paul was:

*Circumcised the eighth day, of the stock of Israel, of the tribe of Benjamin, an Hebrew of the Hebrews; as touching the law, a Pharisee.* Philippians 3:5

Study the illustration on the next page from 2 Corinthians 11:2. Words in all languages can have many different meanings. The correct choice of a word must be based on context—how it is used in like

Scriptures—so that conflict within the Word of God is not created. And that's what the translation committee did so well during the seven years they invested to translate the Hebrew and Greek texts into English to give us what is recorded in the King James Bible.

---

ἡρμοσάμην
I have espoused
718
heermosámeen

*harmozo* (har-mod'-zo); from NT:719; to joint, i.e. (figuratively) to woo (reflexively, to betroth):

*KJV* - espouse.

**Words must be translated so they do not violate context.**

---

As confirmed by the illustration above, the Greek word harmozo, according to Strong's Concordance, *can* mean "to joint" or "to woo" or "to betroth." Context, knowledge of the Jewish betrothal language, and Paul's leading by the Holy Spirit, along with his understanding of the language, confirm that the word *espoused* refers to an engagement, not to a marriage. These help to confirm what is written in the English translation. *Espoused* never means a one-flesh marriage—that supernatural, invisible, permanent joining made by God.

### The *Marriage Supper of the Lamb* is a future event.

Paul's teaching in 2 Corinthians 11:2 is showing, through the Jewish espousal language, that we are engaged to the LORD. This is consistent with other Scriptures, especially Matthew 1:18-25 and Revelation 19:7-9. Also recorded in Matthew's gospel is another event related to the *Marriage Supper of the Lamb*, the *Parable of the Ten Virgins* in Matthew 25:1-13. Five of the ten virgins had made themselves ready for the marriage to which they had been invited. The others had not made themselves ready:

*Afterward came also the other virgins, saying, Lord, Lord, open to us. But he answered and said, Verily I say unto you, I know you not.* Matthew 25:11-12 Symbolically, "the other virgins" were not ... *arrayed in fine linen, clean and white: for the fine linen is the righteousness of saints.* Revelation 19:8

John, who penned the book of Revelation, recorded a future event, the *Marriage Supper of the Lamb*. This is when those who are saved will be married to Jesus. It should be exciting to read 2 Corinthians 11:2 with a new insight—an understanding of the Jewish espousal language and how it definitively reflects the correct meaning when there are references to espoused and married husbands and wives.

Study the following verse in Revelation to help add some additional contextual information for the correct interpretation of 2 Corinthians 11:2 ... *for I have espoused you to one husband* ... and to reinforce the understanding that we are espoused or engaged to the LORD:

*Let us be glad and rejoice, and give honour to him: for the marriage of the Lamb is come, and <u>his</u> [engaged] <u>wife</u> hath made herself ready. And to her was granted that she should be arrayed in fine linen, clean and white: for the fine linen is the righteousness of saints. And he saith unto me, Write, Blessed are they which are called unto the marriage supper of the Lamb. And he saith unto me, These are the true sayings of God.* Revelation 19:7-9

A bride comes to her wedding as an engaged wife, not as a married wife. She is not married until after the vows have been given. This is the *espousal language* which is reflected in Revelation 19:7-9. The

Lamb, Jesus Christ, has paid the purchase price, His shed blood, for His <u>engaged</u> *wife*. The espoused of Jesus has *made herself ready*, through the purification/sanctification process. This righteousness (making oneself ready) is also spoken of in Ephesians 5:23-31, where the husband is to wash his wife with the water of the Word. Husbands symbolically do this by reading the Word to their wives:

*For the husband is the head of the wife, even as Christ is the head of the church: and he is the saviour of the body. Therefore as the church is subject unto Christ, so let the wives be to their own husbands in every thing. Husbands, love your wives, even as Christ also loved the church, and gave himself for it;* <u>*That he might sanctify and cleanse it with the washing of water by the word*</u>*, That he might present it to himself a glorious church, not having spot, or wrinkle, or any such thing; but that it should be holy and without blemish. So ought men to love their wives as their own bodies. He that loveth his wife loveth himself. For no man ever yet hated his own flesh; but nourisheth and cherisheth it, even as the Lord the church: For we are members of his body, of his flesh, and of his bones. For this cause shall a man leave his father and mother, and shall be joined unto his wife, and they two shall be one flesh. This is a great mystery:* <u>*but I speak concerning Christ and the church*</u>. Ephesians 5:23-31

## Context applies, whether it's the Hebrew, Greek, or English.

Now that some Biblical context and additional word study has been given for 2 Corinthians 11:2, those with discerning eyes can understand why Paul used the expression *espoused you to one husband* and why the Jewish espousal expressions must be maintained, recognized, and understood. Words are not generally used in isolation in the Bible. They are systematically interconnected:

*Which things also we speak, not in the words which man's wisdom teacheth, but which the Holy Ghost teacheth;* **comparing spiritual things with spiritual**. 1 Corinthians 2:13

# 11

# Was It Fornication Or Adultery?

In this chapter, we're going to examine more closely two words, *fornication* and *adultery* and relate this study to Matthew 19:9. Why will there be a focus on these two words, *fornication* and *adultery*? It's because they are two of the most discussed, misunderstood, and misapplied words when dealing with marriage and divorce. Thus, it's important to understand their Biblical applications.

*Adultery* is used twice in both Matthew 5:32 and 19:9, but is not in the exception clauses: *... saving for the cause of fornication ... except it be for fornication.* There are Scriptural reasons for this. The first and most important reason that adultery is not recorded in the exception clauses is because it isn't in the Greek text from which the English is translated.

The reader is reminded again that it's not necessary to learn the Greek language to understand and properly interpret the exception clauses recorded by Matthew (or any portion of Scripture). However, such studies can reveal additional nuances that can enrich understanding of the Scriptures. The Greek is shown below and in several other places in this chapter for a different reason. That reason is to point out that the Greek texts from which both the King James Bible and other versions are derived all have the same Greek word *porneia* to support the English translation *fornication* in the exception clauses. (Unless otherwise stated, the Bible referenced is the King James Bible.) Most other Bibles do not accurately and contextually translate *porneia* as *fornication*. When they inaccurately translate *porneia*, they:

- Are changing God's Word.
- Are teaching false doctrine.
- Are removing the cultural interlinking information.
- Are incorrectly recording the purpose for the exception clause.

Changing God's Word can introduce serious doctrinal error. This is true whether it be printed in a version of the Bible or taught from the pulpit.

Study the illustration on the next page which shows the underlying Greek text for *except it be for fornication.* At the top of the <u>outlined boxed</u> text are the Greek letters for the equivalent English letters for *porneia* which are given at the bottom of the outlined box. Directly below the Greek letters is the English equivalent word translated for the Greek word *porneia*, which is *fornication*. The number 4202 is from Strong's Concordance.

> | εἰ μὴ | | ἐπὶ | πορνείᾳ |
> |---|---|---|---|
> | except | it be | for | fornication |
> | 3361 | 9999 | 1909 | 4202 |
> | eí meé | | epí | porneía |
>
> **TR (KJB) and NA (new versions) Greek texts are the same for the Matthew 19:9 exception clause.**

- The Greek text underlying the King James Bible is the TR (Textus Receptus).
- The Greek text underlying the new versions is the NA (Nestle Aland, short for Nestle-Aland/United Bible Society text NA/UBS).

As mentioned previously, there are two main underlying Greek texts. One is used for most new versions; the other, for the King James Bible. Both Greek texts record the Greek word in the Matthew 19:9 exception clause as *porneia*. That Greek word should be translated *fornication* in English. (This is the same pattern that is found in the Matthew 5:32 exception clause. The focus of this chapter is Matthew 19:9. Matthew 5:32 will be discussed in Chapter 16.)

Another illustration is given on the next page which shows the exception clause and the phrase that follows the exception clause, *and shall marry another, committeth adultery*. The Greek text is the same for all Bible versions for the underlying Greek word for *adultery*, *except it be for fornication, and shall marry another, committeth <u>adultery</u>*.

Was It Fornication Or Adultery?

| εἰ μὴ | | ἐπὶ | πορνείᾳ | καὶ | γαμήσῃ | ἄλλην | μοιχᾶται. |
|---|---|---|---|---|---|---|---|
| except | it be | for | fornication, | and | shall marry | another, | committeth adultery: |
| 3361 | 9999 | 1909 | 4202 | 2532 | 1060 | 243 | 3429 |
| eímeé | | epí | porneía | kaí | gameésee | álleen | moichátai |

**Both Greek texts record the same Greek words for fornication and adultery in Matthew 19:9.**

As illustrated above, there are two distinctively different Greek words for *fornication* and *adultery*. These differences should be reflected in the English translation. Without any Greek language background, a reader can, through the illustration above, see the contrast between the underlying Greek word for *fornication* and that for *adultery*.

Now it's time to examine how several Bible versions mistranslate what the underlying Greek text indicates should be *fornication* in the exception clause (*except it be for **fornication***). *Adultery,* in the phrase following (*and shall marry another, committeth **adultery***), shows a contrast. Study the table on the next page. Refer to the illustration above which shows the Greek from which these English translations have been taken. A common practice in new Bible versions is the insertion of hundreds of *critical footnotes* which often include spurious information. For example, see the NGSB footnote below. These authors, in one of their footnotes, add unscriptural information explaining their exception clause worded: "except for sexual immorality":

> "The Greek word for 'sexual immorality' is fairly broad, including a number of sexual sins besides adultery. In this clause (present also in 5:32 but omitted in Mark 10:11), Jesus recognizes that marital infidelity potentially destroys the marital tie between spouses and is,

therefore, ground for legal divorce ..." The section of the critical footnote underlined is **unbiblical. There is no Scripture in which Jesus says any sin destroys the "marital tie" and is grounds for legal divorce.** These authors inserted statements about Jesus that He did not support, but were sins against which He specifically taught.

| Bible* | Study the English text from Matthew 19:9 with the exception clause in a *different font* for emphasis. |
|---|---|
| KJB | *And I say unto you, Whosoever shall put away his wife,* ***except it be for fornication****, and shall marry another, committeth adultery:* **\*\****and whoso marrieth her which is put away doth commit adultery.* |
| NKJV | *And I say to you, whoever divorces his wife,* ***except for sexual immorality****, and marries another, commits adultery;* **\*\****and whoever marries her who is divorced commits adultery.* |
| NGSB | *And I say to you, whoever divorces his wife,* ***except for sexual immorality****, and marries another, commits adultery;* **\*\****and whoever marries her who is divorced commits adultery.* |
| NIV | *I tell you that anyone who divorces his wife,* ***except for marital unfaithfulness****, and marries another woman commits adultery.* |
| NASV | *And I say to you, whoever divorces his wife,* ***except for immorality****, and marries another commits adultery.* |
| ESV | *And I say to you: whoever divorces his wife,* ***except for sexual immorality****, and marries another, commits adultery.* |
| HCSB | *And I tell you, whoever divorces his wife****, except for sexual immorality****, and marries another, commits adultery.* |

*Key for above Bibles: KJB: King James Bible; NKJV: New King James Version; NGSB: New Geneva Study Bible; NIV: New International Version; NASV: New American Standard Version; ESV: English Standard Version; HCSB: Holman Christian Standard Bible

**The double asterisk (\*\*) shown in the KJB, NKJV, and NGSB, indicates the Bibles which include the additional warning for anyone who marries the person who has been put away: *and whoso marrieth her*

*which is put away doth commit **adultery**.* In other words, all parties involved in a "re-marriage" (an adulterous "marriage") place themselves in an on-going sin, adultery. This final clause is important because without it some people think that it's permissible to marry a person they call the "innocent party" (the one who didn't want the divorce). The NASV has a footnote which reads: "Some early mss. add: and he who marries a divorced woman commits adultery."

God's words clearly indicate that it is only death, not sin, which destroys or dissolves the marital tie (bond or joining). Most new version Bibles record a conflicting message from what Jesus spoke in the exception clauses. Jesus would never preserve Scripture that would make His own words inconsistent. The Holy Ghost didn't commission holy men to record words preserved in the Bible which create untruths and inconsistent doctrines:

*For the woman which hath an husband is bound by the law to her husband so long as he liveth; but if the husband be dead, she is loosed from the law of her husband.* Romans 7:2

> The words of Jesus and all of Scripture cannot conflict.

*... God, that cannot lie ...* Titus 1:2 *God is not a man, that he should lie; neither the son of man, that he should repent: hath he said, and shall he not do it? or hath he spoken, and shall he not make it good?* Numbers 23:19
*For the prophecy* [word of God] *came not in old time by the will of man: but <u>holy men of God spake as they were moved by the Holy Ghost</u>.* 2 Peter 1:21

*And I say unto you, Whosoever shall put away his wife, except it be for fornication, and shall marry another, committeth adultery: and whoso marrieth her which is put away doth commit adultery.* Matthew 19:9

*And he* [Jesus] *saith unto them, Whosoever shall put away his wife, and marry another, committeth adultery against her. And if a woman shall put away her husband, and be married to another, she committeth adultery.* Mark 10:11-12

Chapter 11

## *Adultery* and f*ornication* in Matthew 19:9 and Matthew 5:32 are different sins used in contrast.

Confusion has been created in the new versions over the two words *adultery* and *fornication* because most of these authors have not correctly and contextually translated what is in their underlying Greek text. Also, as show above, critical footnotes in new versions add more confusion and often spurious information.

By a visual comparison of the Bibles listed in the table on page 121, only one of the Bibles translates the underlying Greek word *porneia* as *fornication* in the exception clause. That Bible is the King James. Many say, "These other words mean the same thing." That's not true as will be seen in further studies. Additionally, none of the underlying Greek texts record the Greek words *sexual immorality*, *martial unfaithfulness*, or *adultery* in the exception clauses.

> Paraphrasing in the new versions bring error and confusion into their Bibles.

A study of the paraphrased words used in the exception clauses in the new versions reveal some common doctrinal errors. Carefully assess their paraphrased words: *sexual immorality, immorality,* and *marital unfaithfulness.* What comes to your mind when you read these words?

1. Do these words accurately translate, word-for-word, the underlying text? No.
2. Do these words accurately reflect what Jesus is contextually teaching? No.
3. Are these words consistent with other parallel Scriptures and cross-references? No.
4. Are these words doctrinally correct in this context? No.

## Definitions of words used in the exception clauses

Even though many Christians know that man should not tamper with God's Word, they read from Bibles which do exactly that. Perhaps they, like a rebellious child, do not understand that driving the wrong direction on a one-way busy highway can end in death. God's Words are designed ... *for doctrine, for reproof, for correction, for instruction in righteousness.* 2 Timothy 3:16. Study the definitions on the next two pages. There are two sets of them. The first set includes those for *fornication* and *adultery* based upon Scriptures from the King James Bible. The second set is taken from societal sources. Outside resources are used because these are not words reflected by the underlying Greek. They are, however, definitions for words normally used in the new versions of the Bible in Matthew 5:32 and 19:9: *immorality, sexual immorality,* and *martial unfaithfulness.*

The first set of definitions (adultery and fornication) is based on God's Word from the King James Bible, which, unlike man's words and standards, doesn't change doctrinally with time or circumstances. Both Jesus and His Word agree, and they do not change: ... *the same yesterday, and to day, and for ever.* Hebrews 13:8

Even though *adultery* is not named in either of the exception clauses in the King James Bible, or in most of the new versions, the definition of *adultery* is included to show there is a Biblical contrast between *fornication* and *adultery* and that is reflected in Matthew 19:9. What many people wrongfully include, represent, or describe as a part of the exception clauses would be the sin of adultery.

## Contextual definitions of *adultery* and *fornication* based on the KJ Bible for Matthew 5:32 and 19:9:

**Adultery**: Wrongful sexual thoughts and acts by a spouse in a covenant-marriage toward someone other than his spouse; such as when a one-flesh spouse divorces and marries another while his one-flesh spouse is living.

**Fornication**: A sinful act or thought, usually sexually driven, among persons not part of a covenant-marriage.

**Definitions based on societal standards of words used in new versions' exception clauses in Matthew 5:32 and Matthew 19:9:**
(Emphasis is added to draw attention to the focus on opinions.)

<u>Sexual immorality and immorality</u>: Shown below are some of the varying definitions of ***immorality*** taken from <u>**opinions**</u> posted online:

- A wide variety of **socially** unacceptable behavior patterns.
- Evil ascribed to sexual acts that violate **social** conventions.
- Morals which **vary** from person to person.
- Sexual immorality must be looked at from a **social** perspective.
- Sexual immorality includes dishonesty and taking advantage of another.
- Morals are something you get from your parents, your schools, and the things around you.
- **Moral and immoral are all subjective between people.** What's good for one isn't necessarily good for another. You can pass along your morals to another or you can force your morals on another. You can force your immorality on another.
- It's all **subjective** to what you were taught; What I would consider immoral may not be what you would consider immoral and vice versa, but there are some rules that <u>we can all agree on</u>. Now we all just have to agree on those.
- The Bible is not a valid source of information unless we put it side by side with every other piece of religious text in the world dealing with sex.

The bullet points listed above are quoted from non-biblical sources to show what the authors of the new versions are reflecting by their wrongful practice of inserting *immorality* into God's Word.

Marital Unfaithfulness: Below are some statements **found online** in which people gave their definitions of *marital unfaithfulness*, also referred to as infidelity, cheating, adultery, or having an affair:

- It is the **subjective feeling** that one's partner has violated a set of rules or relationship norms, and this violation results in feelings of sexual jealousy and rivalry.
- A violation, sexual in nature with another individual outside of the relationship or **emotional in nature**; for example, sharing intimate thoughts, expending great amounts of trust or other emotional resources with an individual outside of the relationship.
- What constitutes an act of infidelity is **dependent** upon the exclusivity **expectations** within the relationship.

The above bullet points are quoted from **non-biblical** sources to show what the authors of the new versions are reflecting by their **wrongful insertion** of *marital unfaithfulness* into God's Word.

## What's the danger of secularizing God's Word?

Can you see a common thread in the way people define *immorality* and *marital unfaithfulness*? The way the average person defines sexual immorality and marital unfaithfulness varies and is based upon subjective opinions. This is the DANGEROUS THREAD COMMON IN OUR SOCIETY. These definitions are subjective; the terms are defined according to socially acceptable and constantly changing values rather than THE UNCHANGING WORD OF GOD.

*Fornication* is the word in English that accurately and contextually translates the Greek underlying word *porneia*. The Greek word *moichao* (adultery) is not found <u>in the exception clause</u> in either of the two families of Greek texts. Neither are there Greek words in the underlying text for the words *sexual immorality* or *marital unfaithfulness* used by authors of the new versions. Again, it's important to note that the foundation for the new versions appears to be based upon man's beliefs rather than God's unchanging standards.

## Dynamic equivalency has been coined by the authors of the new versions.

The societal "norms" expressed in the new versions' exception clauses are largely subject to evolving social beliefs and practices. They are reflective of the popular translation technique, *dynamic equivalency*, used by authors of the new Bible versions. That is, they use the term *dynamic equivalency* to describe their method of translating the underlying languages into English. This method is based on man's opinion rather than a strict word-for-word translation. Dynamic equivalency relies a great deal on paraphrasing—adding to and subtracting from the text—when there's no reason to do so, even for translation equivalence. The sentence structure is often changed as well as parts of speech. Nouns are changed to verbs and pronouns and vice-versa. The term *dynamic equivalency* may sound impressive, but even this coined term is flawed. *Dynamic* is a word characterized by constant change; equivalency indicates stability or equality. These are opposites. They are oxymoronic. Dynamic equivalency, a form of paraphrasing, is <u>the practice of replacing God's words with man's, rather than translating God's words</u>.

What is happening is that the authors of the new versions give the impression that the exception clause is an escape clause from a one-flesh marriage for adultery rather than reflecting the exception for a "divorce" for <u>fornication</u>. This is because they insert incorrect words into statements made by Jesus. It's not an insignificant matter to wrongly suggest that Jesus would support what He hates and what He consistently teaches against and to substitute words that do not reflect the underlying Greek words from which they are translating.

The effect of what authors of new versions of the Bible are doing is even more clearly evident in children's Bibles. In the table below are two examples taken from the International Children's Bible. This illustration shows some of the contextual errors that are being programmed even into minds of little innocent ones.

| Unscriptural teachings from International Children's Bible* ||
|---|---|
| *But I tell you that anyone who divorces his wife is causing his wife to be guilty of adultery. The only reason for a man to divorce his wife is if she has sexual relations with another man. And anyone who marries that divorced woman is guilty of adultery.* Matthew 5:32 | *I tell you that anyone who divorces his wife and marries another woman is guilty of adultery. The only reason for a man to divorce and marry again is if his first wife has sexual relations with another man.* Matthew 19:9 |
| *The tag line for this Bible is: "The Version Children Can Read and Understand."* ||

Children's Bibles can be very deceptive. They are often purchased because of attractive, colorful graphics. What is written in the text can be very deceptive and surely is not what children should be reading. Those who are leading not only children but adults astray with false doctrine might carefully assess the following Scripture:

*Whosoever therefore shall humble himself as this little child, the same is greatest in the kingdom of heaven. And whoso shall receive one such little child in my name receiveth me. But whoso shall offend one of these little ones which believe in me, it were better for him that a millstone were hanged about his neck, and that he were drowned in the depth of the sea.* Matthew 18:4-6

The Scripture passage above is another of the many metaphoric teachings of Jesus. It is staged around children but the spirit of the message is universal in that it applies to all those who come to the LORD while alluding to those who are "young" or new to the faith. They, by implication, could be easily pulled aside by false teachings.

## Interconnectivity means there is a connection.

The King James Bible is written with an underlying, invisible thread in which the words are interconnected and systematically placed. When man changes these words, then important connectives which tie everything together and give contextual continuity to the Bible are removed. This connective thread regretfully is missing in the new versions. Much important cross referencing is removed because of their paraphrasing.

An example of this lack of interconnectivity, as found in the new Bible versions, is in their often overlooked omission of the interconnectivity between Matthew 19:9 and two related verses: 1 Corinthians 6:9-10 and Galatians 5:19-21. The latter two passages tell believers and nonbelievers the punishment awaiting those who do not repent of <u>fornication</u> and <u>adultery</u> (as well as other sins). Those who live in these lifestyles will not inherit the Kingdom of God—if they do not turn from these sins and to the LORD. Yet, the link between these sins and the judgment for them has been removed in new versions

## … except it be for fornication …

*Marital unfaithfulness* and *sexual immorality* are the names of sins incorrectly inserted in the new versions' exception clauses; that is, in both Matthew 5:32 and Matthew 19:9 (as well as in other verses). This is done even though their underlying text does not support those words. However, even beyond that, few readers notice that <u>marital unfaithfulness</u> and <u>sexual immorality</u> are not among the sins listed in 1 Corinthians 6:9-10 and Galatians 5:19-21 as sins that keep a person from inheriting the Kingdom of God. Again, that is because they are not sins listed in the underlying Greek text or anywhere in a text which has been accurately translated. See below:

*Know ye not that the unrighteous shall not inherit the kingdom of God? Be not deceived: neither **fornicators**, nor idolaters, nor **adulterers**, nor effeminate, nor abusers of themselves with mankind, Nor thieves, nor covetous, nor drunkards, nor revilers, nor extortioners, shall inherit the kingdom of God.* 1 Corinthians 6:9-10

*Now the works of the flesh are manifest, which are these; **Adultery**, **fornication** ... and such like: of the which I tell you before, as I have also told you in time past, that they which do such things shall not inherit the kingdom of God.* Galatians 5:19-21

Even though *unfaithfulness* and *sexual immorality* are sins, they are not named sins the LORD inspired His holy men to include in the exception clauses. These sins, as they are recorded in most new versions, are not contextually reflective of the sins named in their underlying Greek text; nor do they reflect, in English, the correct <u>meaning</u> in the exception clauses. As shown above, the words they insert, instead, reflect changing societal norms: changing opinions, subjective feelings, rules with which the majority of people agree, human expectations, and socially defined norms. See below:

| Most new versions (1) do not correctly translate the exception clauses, and they (2) don't include the named sins they substitute, for *fornication,* in Matthew 19:9, in 1 Corinthians 6:9. ||
|---|---|
| πόρνοι / fornicators, / 4205 / pórnoi    οὔτε / nor / 3777 / oúte    εἰδωλολάτραι / idolaters, / 1496 / eidoololátrai    οὔτε / nor / 3777 / oúte    μοιχοὶ / adulterers, / 3432 / moichoí | The Greek text for both the KJB and that used for the new versions have the Greek word for *fornication* in the underlying text in 1 Corinthians 6:9. |
| Exception Clause | 1 Corinthians 6:9 |
| except it be for <u>fornication</u> KJB | ... Neither <u>fornicators</u>, nor idolaters, nor adulterers ... KJB |
| except for sexual **immorality** NGSB | ... Neither fornicators, nor idolaters, nor adulterers ... NGSB |
| except for sexual **immorality** NKJV | ... Neither fornicators, nor idolaters, nor adulterers ... NKJV |
| except for **marital unfaithfulness** NIV | ... Neither the sexually immoral nor idolaters nor adulterers ... NIV |
| except for **immorality** NASV | ... neither fornicators, nor idolaters, nor adulterers ... NASV |
| *Key for above Bibles: KJB: King James Bible; NGSB: New Geneva Study Bible; NKJV: New King James Version; NIV: New International Version; NASV: New American Standard Version ||

The table above illustrates these two related major issues with new versions: (1) not correctly translating *porneia* as *fornication* in the exception clauses because of their use of dynamic equivalency and (2) not interlinking their paraphrased choice of words to 1 Corinthians 6:9-10 and Galatians 5:19. From the table above, it's obvious that only the King James Bible is correctly interlinked. The others are not.

There's a real danger for those who study from Bibles or listen to teachings from Bibles which include doctrinal error. By doing so, some may believe, or rationalize, that they can commit these sins (marital unfaithfulness, sexual immorality, and immorality) and think God's Word doesn't hold them accountable if they don't repent.

They could have these false assurances in part because their Bibles do not list these sins in 1 Corinthians 6:9-10 and in Galatians 5:19-21. Those who commit these sexual sins which their Bibles call sexual immorality, marital unfaithfulness, or immorality could come to the conclusion that they will inherit the kingdom of God, instead of **will not inherit the kingdom of God**.

> Everyone will be accountable for living according to God's Word correctly interpreted.

However, regardless of what the text says in the new versions, fornicators and adulterers (those who commit fornication and adultery and do not turn from these sins) will not inherit the Kingdom of God. Even though new versions of the Bible are not being doctrinally true to their readers, they have not really changed God's Word and His judgments for sin. How could they have <u>changed God's Word</u> and, at the same time, <u>not changed God's Word</u>? That question and the answer to it are important to consider.

The reason is that even though men change God's Word with their dynamic equivalency, God's Word is not changed. It's still in effect. So even if the Bible a person reads has doctrinal error, he will still be held accountable for Truth on judgment day. It should be alarming to those who are studying from a Bible containing mistranslations to find that it has major doctrinal errors, but ... is it alarming enough? Each person should examine himself and his Bible knowing these facts.

### "I study all the versions ... to get an understanding of what the Scripture means."

I want to preface my opinions regarding the heading of this section. As mentioned previously, my purpose is not to offend any reader and especially pastors who study the many different versions of the Bible to gain understanding for a particular passage. We can all learn from one another and gain nuances about word usage from studies outside the Bible. However, I offer a word of caution that comes from a concept I used to teach as a college professor of economics. The topic of counterfeit money was a part of my teaching about the Federal Reserve and their employees' duties of overseeing our currency. Those who work for the Federal Reserve in the capacity of discovering counterfeit money are trained to detect counterfeit coins and bills. Even though this training includes some inspection of counterfeit currency, the counterfeit is not the focus. The focus is on the genuine currency. When a person is thoroughly knowledgeable about the genuine, he will recognize most fraudulent imitations.

> We learn from what we read, whether what we read is true or false.

Because there is a continual stream of new ways to counterfeit money, it would be almost impossible to become and remain an expert on all counterfeits. However, when a person KNOWS the feel, look, and key characteristics of the real thing, he has a treasure house of expertise to detect counterfeits. Thus, the time and focus is on the genuine.

That principle (focusing on the genuine), in my opinion, is one that Christians might benefit from considering. If I read the exception clause from six different versions that are all flawed, will that teach me what the genuine is, or will such repetition reinforce error in my thinking processes?

*Whom shall he teach knowledge? and whom shall he make to understand doctrine? them that are weaned from the milk, and drawn from the breasts. For precept must be upon precept, precept upon precept; line upon line, line upon line; here a little, and there a little.* Isaiah 28:9-10

*Which things also we speak, not in the words which man's wisdom teacheth, but which the Holy Ghost teacheth; comparing spiritual things with spiritual.* 1 Corinthians 2:13

What we must focus on is:
*... whatsoever things are true, whatsoever things are honest, whatsoever things are just, whatsoever things are pure, whatsoever things are lovely, whatsoever things are of good report; if there be any virtue, and if there be any praise,* **think** *on these things.* Philippians 4:8

*But let him ask in faith, nothing wavering. For he that wavereth is like a wave of the sea driven with the wind and tossed.* James 1:6

## Review the purpose for which a Bible passage is written.

Another guideline to help correctly interpret the Bible is to consider, if possible, the purpose for which a Bible verse or passage has been included. That information can reveal important contextual information. Matthew 19:9, for example, is a rebuttal to the wicked Pharisees who came "tempting" Jesus by trying to get Him to approve sin. They were looking for an acceptable reason to divorce a wife. Jesus, however, quickly and succinctly turned the tables on their ploy. He gave no permission for divorce, and He gave no permission for "remarriage." This is one of the things that many miss in this important teaching. He warned that if anyone in a covenant-marriage "married" another spouse, he would be committing adultery.

Jesus wasn't teaching in Matthew 5:32 and 19:9 that divorce and "remarriage" are permissible if "sexual unfaithfulness" occurred. It's impossible for Jesus to say something which goes against Who He is as recorded in Scripture; that is, it's impossible for Him to give permission to divorce a covenant-spouse and marry another spouse because that would go against what the Scripture says in other places. One thing that Jesus can be affirming in the exception clauses is that the Jewish <u>engagement</u> or espousal can be dissolved for the cause of fornication *during* the espousal contractual period. This kind of putting away a wife (espoused) and later marrying someone else would not be adultery because the *putting away* was from an engagement. The two had not been made one flesh by God. Other types of "put-aways" will be discussed in Chapter 19.

The key word in the exception clause is, and must be, *fornication*. Sadly, most Bible version authors have replaced the word *fornication* with erroneous substitutes: marital unfaithfulness, sexual immortality, etc. By doing this, they change the meaning of the text so that it could include those who are in a covenant-marriage rather than those to whom it was addressed: sin committed among those who <u>aren't married in God's eyes</u>. Textual confusion, which man has created, enters right into the midst of the holy and pure words of our LORD. It's where Satan first attacked in the garden of Eden by suggesting to Adam and Eve that God did not really mean what He so clearly told them: *... for in the day that thou eatest thereof thou shalt surely die.* Genesis 2:17

## … but my Bible says …

I would sadly venture to say that most regular church attendees can identify with the graphic on the next page. It seems to speak very loudly to the sad demise of what has happened within the very walls where God's pure Word is to reign supreme; yet, most Christians have become so anesthetized to this horrific tragedy—changing the Word of God—that they do not recognize it for what it is, and they freely partake in it:

*Will ye steal, murder, and commit adultery, and swear falsely, and burn incense unto Baal, and walk after other gods whom ye know not; And come and stand before me **in this house**, which is called by my name, and say, We are delivered to do all these abominations?* Jeremiah 7:9-10

> The key word in the exception clause, contextually and culturally, is *fornication*; yet, that is the very word which most authors of new versions remove.

*Behold, the days come, saith the Lord GOD, that I will send a famine in the land, not a famine of bread, nor a thirst for water, but of **hearing the words of the LORD**: And they shall wander from sea to sea, and from the north even to the east, they shall run to and fro to seek the word of the LORD, and shall not find it.* Amos 8:11-12

Chapter 11

The low estate of confusion and division to which God's Word has been brought.

## Joseph and Mary knew the difference between fornication and adultery.

The Biblical language in Matthew 1:18-25 introduces the reader to the important distinction between a sexual sin committed before marriage, which is fornication, and that after marriage, which is adultery. Even though those two sins are not named in the first chapter of Matthew, they are very closely related to the account of the espousal and marriage of Joseph and Mary.

> We must discern the difference in the Scripture between sins committed before marriage and those committed after marriage.

Fornication (Greek: *porneia*) was the sin that gave grounds to end an *engagement* for those who took part in the Jewish espousal custom. So when Joseph discovered that Mary, his espoused wife, was pregnant, Joseph thought he had reason to divorce Mary—to end the engagement (espousal). Thus, he was planning to divorce her.

However, once they were married, indicated by the words *take* and *took*, Joseph could no longer divorce Mary for any reason, including adultery ... *Joseph ... fear not to take ... Then Joseph ... took unto him his wife.* Matthew 1:20, 24 It is only through Matthew's gospel that we learn about the Jewish espousal custom of divorcing an engaged wife. The other gospels do not mention this. Neither do they mention the exception clause. Each of the gospels has a different focus and purpose. That is a major interrelated reason **why** the exception for fornication is recorded in Matthew 19:9—to dissolve an engagement contract. Many readers do not recognize the <u>link</u> between Matthew 1:18-25 and Matthew 19:9, just as they don't <u>link</u> fornication together with those sins listed in 1 Corinthians 6:9 and Galatians 5:19. They, instead, refer to Matthew 19:9 as a man-made exception to God's perspective on marriage as a lifetime joining by removing the word *fornication*. They restructure the exception clause so it appears to give a reason to divorce a one-flesh spouse and marry another.

The **interlinking** between the words *except it be for fornication* in Matthew 19:9 and Joseph's initial response to divorce his espoused wife (... *was minded to put her away privily* Matthew 1:19) is also very important. The Pharisees would have known about the Jewish espousal practices so it was needful for Jesus to include what He said about an espousal divorce to reflect this practice. He succinctly gave a contrast for putting away for fornication and a putting away for adultery. After all, the Pharisees were coming to Jesus to tempt Him— to look for a weakness in His teachings or in how He responded.

Let's summarize some of the information related just in the book of Matthew that could serve to link the Matthew 19:9 exception clause to the espousal and marriage of Joseph and Mary:

1. Only Matthew records the details about the espousal and marriage of Joseph and Mary.
2. Matthew introduces the Jewish espousal language, *Joseph her husband* [espoused] and *Mary thy wife* [espoused], important terms to interlink a major reason for the Jews' practice of putting away for fornication in both Matthew 1:19 and 19:9.
3. Only in Matthew do we learn that Joseph was minded to put away (divorce) his espoused wife. Joseph was a just man who would have had "cause" (*except it be for fornication*) to break the espousal **contract**—to put away his espoused wife.
4. Only in Matthew do we learn that the reason Joseph was planning to put Mary away is because he thought she had gotten pregnant out of wedlock. This could only be identified as the sin of fornication because Mary had not married a man (not been made one flesh by God). Married spouses who commit sexual sin with others are adulterers. They commit the sin of adultery. Those who are not married and commit sexual sin are called fornicators. They commit the sin of fornication.
5. If Joseph had divorced his espoused wife for fornication, he could have contracted for another (espoused) wife. Having a different, second (**espoused**) wife would not put him into a state of adultery. This, however, is not the case if a married husband puts away a married one-flesh wife and "marries" another. That "married" husband puts himself into a state of adultery. This is all verified in Matthew 19:9.
6. In Matthew 19:4-6, Matthew records the reinforcement of the indissolubility of the only God-ordained marriage. It is that which was established in the beginning—Genesis 2:21-24.
7. The espousal history, especially Joseph's original intent of putting away his engaged wife, is given only in Matthew 1:18-25 and is reflected in Matthew 19:9:

*And I say unto you, Whosoever shall put away his **wife, except it be for fornication,** and shall marry another, committeth adultery: and whoso marrieth her which is put away doth commit adultery.* Matthew 19:9

## Scripture confirms and defines Scripture.

When the Bible was being recorded, and for many years before and after that, becoming pregnant outside the bonds of a one-flesh marriage was a sin that was very seriously frowned upon. Mary and Joseph surely faced much persecution and ridicule because Mary had been chosen by the Holy Ghost to bear the **seed** of our LORD and Saviour. Those who knew Mary and her pregnant-while-engaged condition but did not **interlink** her divine prophesied mission as given "in the beginning," would have thought that she had committed the sin of fornication. Joseph, initially, surely had those thoughts:

*And I will put enmity between thee and the woman, and between thy seed and her **seed**; it shall bruise thy head, and thou shalt bruise his heel.* Genesis 3:15

*And the angel answered and said unto her* [Mary], *The Holy Ghost shall come upon thee, and the power of the Highest shall overshadow thee: therefore also that holy thing which shall be born of thee shall be called the Son of God.* Luke 1:35

Mary's conception was by the Holy Ghost. God created the woman's **seed**. The angel's explanation to Mary as recorded in Luke 1:35 fulfilled the prophecy of Genesis 3:15.

## We be not born of fornication.

There is a Scripture that could "quietly" support not only the possibility that Mary and Joseph faced persecution because of her first pregnancy, but one that also can confirm the primary contextual definition of fornication as it applies to Matthew 19:9. Study John 8:41. Focus on the Pharisees' words, *We be not born of fornication.* How might these words spoken by the wicked Pharisees relate to the misunderstood circumstance by and for which Jesus was conceived and its <u>interrelationship</u> to the exception clauses?

> *Then said they* [Pharisees] *to him* [Jesus], ***We be not born of fornication****; we have one Father, even God.* John 8:41

Many, even today, do not have the faith to believe the supernatural circumstances by which Mary could conceive, yet be a virgin. The important passage in Luke 1:34-35 confirms that Mary was a virgin when Jesus was conceived and relates the circumstances under which she was told of the miraculous conception. Review this again:

> *Then said Mary unto the angel, How shall this be, seeing I know not a man? And the angel answered and said unto her, The Holy Ghost shall come upon thee, and the power of the Highest shall overshadow thee: therefore also that holy thing which shall be born of thee shall be called the Son of God.* Luke 1:34-35

Recall this birth was foretold hundreds of years before it happened: ... *Behold, a virgin shall conceive, and bear a son, and shall call his name Immanuel.* Isaiah 7:14

We are also told by Matthew that Mary's other children were not conceived by the Holy Ghost. **She did not remain a virgin.** She and Joseph had sexual intimacy after the birth of Jesus Christ, and Scripture confirms that Jesus had several siblings. There are recorded interactions between Jesus, His mother, and His siblings. It's important to notice that **there is additional information recorded in Matthew 1:25 from what was prophesied in Isaiah 7:14.** Matthew's gospel lets us know that Mary did not remain a virgin and that she had other children. The King James Bible records the fact that this was not just a Son but Mary's firstborn Son. That's because the underlying

Textus Receptus Greek text has the word *prototokos* for *firstborn:*

*And* [Joseph] *knew her not till she had brought forth her firstborn son: and he called his name JESUS.* Matthew 1:25 Scripture states Jesus was her **"firstborn"** son. It doesn't say He was a son but her firstborn son.

<u>Other Scriptures recorded by Matthew</u> verify important textual facts. Mary gave birth to other children:
*Is not this the carpenter's son? is not his mother called Mary? and his brethren, James, and Joses, and Simon, and Judas? And his sisters, are they not all with us? Whence then hath this man all these things?* Matthew 13:55-56

*While he yet talked to the people, behold, his mother and his brethren stood without, desiring to speak with him. Then one said unto him, Behold, thy mother and thy brethren stand without, desiring to speak with thee.* Matthew 12:46-47 (See also: Luke 8:19 Mark 3:31, John 7:1-10, Acts 1:14, and Galatians 1:19.)

The Pharisees were known for trying to find ways to discredit Jesus. The confrontation by them in John 8 is another example of the many times Jesus and the Pharisees had intense debates. In this passage, Jesus is addressing the Pharisees who were pridefully boasting that they were Abraham's children. Jesus responded by telling them ... *If God were your Father, ye would love me* ... John 8:42

Jesus had just told the Pharisees in verse 41: *Ye do the deeds of your father* ... He was telling them something that cut very deeply into their false religious facade—that God was not the One whom they served. It was, instead, Satan. So the retort from the Pharisees was not one of friendliness. Consider also the circumstances and the way Jesus describes, through other Scriptures, the character of the Pharisees, such as in Matthew 23:13-33. He called them hypocrites, blind guides, and serpents. With those facts in mind, and a review of the Scriptures given above, consider the statement given by the wicked Pharisees to the charge given by Jesus (*Ye do the deeds of your father.*):

> Then said they [Pharisees] to him [Jesus], **We be not born of fornication**; we have one Father, even God. John 8:41

The response of the Pharisees could be an answer with a dual meaning. Knowing their character and their constant attacks against Jesus, this could have been a double-edged sword of these *tempters* to imply that Jesus was born out of wedlock and that they were asserting that this out-of-wedlock sin was fornication—something worth pondering. Sadly, some of the new version authors change the noun *fornication* in John 8:41 to their paraphrased inaccurate terms, removing the contextually interrelated Scriptural impact of this statement. They do this, again, unsupported by their underlying Greek text that includes the Greek noun *porneias*. With *fornication* removed in their English translation, vital cross-referencing and **interlinking** becomes impossible.

| ʻΗμεῖς | ἐκ | πορνείας | οὐ | γεγεννήμεθα· |
|---|---|---|---|---|
| We | of | fornication; | not | be born |
| 2249 | 1537 | 4202 | 3756 | 1080 |
| Heemeís | ek | porneías | ou | gegenneémetha |

TR and NA Underlying Greek Text for John 8:41

... *We are not illegitimate children, they protested* ... NIV John 8:41
... *We were not born of sexual immorality* ... ESV John 8:41

The King James Bible correctly and contextually translates from the Greek text: ... *We be not born of fornication* ... John 8:41

## Quick Guide Test to Check Bibles for Translation Errors

This guide is to help evaluate if you have a Bible which contains doctrinal translation errors in the main text and/or in critical footnotes which question the text. The partial list of Scriptures listed below are ones commonly changed in new Bible versions, especially the bolded words. This list is adapted from: *Bible Versions II* www.RestorationOfTheFamily.org. There are hundreds of additional examples, but those listed are more than enough to give a guide to evaluate the Bible you are reading. Write us if you do not understand why changes to the following Scriptures are serious doctrinal errors.

## Are the following verses/words changed, missing, or footnoted as not being in "some mss." (manuscripts)?

Genesis 2:18: And the LORD God said, It is not good that the man should be alone; I will make him **an help meet** for him.

Genesis 2:24: Therefore shall a man leave his father and his mother, and shall cleave unto his wife: and they **shall be** one flesh.

Deuteronomy 20:7: And what man is there that hath **betrothed a wife**, and **hath not taken her?** let him go and return …

Jeremiah 3:1: **They say**, If a man put away his wife, and she go from him, and become another man's, shall he return unto her again? shall not that land be greatly polluted? but thou hast played the harlot with many lovers; **yet return again to me, saith the LORD.**

Matthew 19:9: And I say unto you, Whosoever shall put away his wife, **except it be for fornication**, and shall many another, committeth adultery: **and whoso marrieth her which is put away doth commit adultery.**

Matthew 5:32: But I say unto you, That whosoever shall put away his wife, saving for the **cause** of **fornication**, causeth her to commit adultery: and **whosoever shall marry her that is divorced committeth adultery.**

Matthew 22:25: Now there were with us seven brethren: and the first, when he had **married a wife**, deceased, and, having no issue, left his wife unto his brother.

John 8:9: ... they which heard it, being convicted by their own conscience ...

Romans 1:31: Without understanding, **covenantbreakers, without natural affection**, implacable, unmerciful.

1 Corinthians 7:2: Nevertheless, to avoid **fornication**, let every man have his own wife, and let every woman have her own husband.

1 Corinthians 7:15: But if the unbelieving depart, let him depart. A brother or a sister is not under **bondage** in such cases: but God hath called us to peace.

Galatians 5:19: Now the works of the flesh are manifest, which are these; Adultery, **fornication**, uncleanness, lasciviousness.

Revelation 19:7: Let us be glad and rejoice, and give honour to him: for the marriage of the Lamb is come, and his **wife** hath made herself ready.

*Extra Points of Interest*

# 12

# Let's Go Fishing: Specifically, Generically, And Proximately.

In Chapter 10, it was shown how the word *joined* was used in several different contexts. The proper determination of meaning was derived from the context. The same principle held true with the teaching on the words *adultery* and *fornication* in Chapter 11. If you skipped over Chapter 11, it would be best to go back and read it.

There are, however, some additional internal signposts which can aid in correctly interpreting Scriptures, especially Scriptures which include *fornication* and *adultery*. The focus of this chapter is to create an awareness of how words are used in contrast to one another as well as their ability to be exclusive or inclusive.

As stated previously, it's common knowledge that words have different meanings depending on the context. There are, however, two additional guidelines that may be helpful to further correctly interpret Scripture. These are guidelines that require no knowledge of a foreign language and are helpful for the correct interpretation of fornication and adultery, especially as they are used in the New Testament. These guidelines have been overlooked by many because they are intertwined with the English text in patterns of word usage. **They are part of Biblical language patterns that may or may not be true in secular writings.** They include:

> You can know when fornication does not include adultery.

- Whether the words are located in the same verse or in close proximity to one another; i.e., in the same or adjoining verses.
- Whether the words take on specific or generic (inclusive) meanings.

## Proximity is a sign to help differentiate between fornication and adultery.

In this chapter, it will be shown that both fornication and adultery have a variety of applications and that there are even times when fornication can include adultery. However, there are many times when it does not. Context should alert the reader to discern which is correct; however, there's a usage principle, an internal key, which helps to show when fornication cannot include the sin of adultery. That also becomes very important to further prove the fact that fornication, as it is used in Matthew 19:9, cannot refer to marital unfaithfulness; that is, adultery. This internal sign is what is called, in this book, *proximity*.

When two different words are located near or in close proximity to each other, that is, in the same verse or in a verse before or after, **the two words, especially *fornication* and *adultery*, do not mean the same thing.** As with most rules, there can be exceptions, but this rule holds true with New Testament uses of fornication and adultery.

Thus, when fornication and adultery are located in close proximity, they take on their specific meanings. Adultery identifies the specific sin of marital adultery (which usually means "re-marriage"), and fornication represents illicit relationships outside the bonds of a one-flesh marriage; that is, sexual sin among those who are not in a covenant-marriage. Study Matthew 5:32 and Matthew 19:9 again. Notice how the rule of proximity can act as a signpost to tell the reader that the two words, *fornication* and *adultery* do not refer to the same sin. They are represented by two different nouns because the underlying Greek text is written that way and because the context tells the readers these are two distinctively different kinds of sexual sins:

| **Both exception clauses follow the rule of proximity.** |
|---|
| *But I say unto you, That whosoever shall put away his wife, saving for the cause of fornication, causeth her to commit adultery: and whosoever shall marry her that is divorced committeth adultery.* Matthew 5:32 |
| *And I say unto you, Whosoever shall put away his wife, except it be for fornication, and shall marry another, committeth adultery: and whoso marrieth her which is put away doth commit adultery.* Matthew 19:9 |

Consider another example, 1 Corinthians 6:9: *Know ye not that the unrighteous shall not inherit the kingdom of God? Be not deceived: neither fornicators, nor idolaters, nor adulterers, nor effeminate ...* The words *fornicators* and *adulterers* are both used in this verse. That being the case, the two do not mean the same thing. Biblically, when this happens with fornication and adultery, the two words are meant for contrast, not to redefine the same sin. *Fornication* does not include adultery, and *adultery* does not include fornication else there would be no need to list both. It would be like saying, "neither adulterers, nor idolaters, nor adulterers, nor effeminate …"

Again, the most important things to notice for purposes of the teaching in this chapter is that when *fornication* and *adultery* are used in the same passage, they take on their specific meanings, and they are not interchangeable—in that verse; that is, one does not encompass the other. Thus, it would be an incorrect interpretation to say that *fornication* and *adultery* have the same meaning in Matthew 19:9 or that *fornication* includes *adultery*: *...Whosoever shall put away his wife, except it be for fornication, and shall marry another, committeth adultery: and whoso marrieth her which is put away doth commit adultery.* Matthew 19:9

> It's important to recognize the specific and generic use of words.

There are reasons other than proximity which explain why these two nouns take on contrasting meanings as they are used in Matthew 19:9. They are distinctive words to differentiate between two different sins, just as fornication and adultery are delineated as two different sins in 1 Corinthians 6:9 and several other verses. In Matthew 19:9, they are pointing out a difference between:
- Sexual sin among those outside God's "law of marriage," and
- Sexual sin by those joined in a covenant-marriage.

In Matthew 19:9, the words *fornication* and *adultery* are used <u>in contrast</u> to each other. This consistently fits with the rule or principle of proximity. This is in addition to the hypothetical signpost indicated by the words *except it be for* used with fornication. This signpost also serves to tell the reader there is something different or in contrast to the remainder of the verse.

The table below shows other examples to illustrate the principle of proximity and how this principle applies **where the two words *fornication* and *adultery* are writte**n in the same Scripture or in Scriptures that are closely located. In each example, both words take on their specific meanings.

| **If *fornication* and *adultery* are used in the same Scripture or in a verse before or after, they typically are not interchangeable; they do not mean the same thing.** |
|---|
| *But I say unto you, That whosoever shall put away his wife, saving for the cause of <u>fornication</u>, causeth her to commit <u>adultery</u>: and whosoever shall marry her that is divorced committeth <u>adultery</u>.* Matthew 5:32 |
| *For out of the heart proceed evil thoughts, murders, <u>adulteries</u>, <u>fornications</u>, thefts, false witness, blasphemies.* Matthew 15:19 |
| *And I say unto you, Whosoever shall put away his wife, except it be for <u>fornication</u>, and shall marry another, committeth <u>adultery</u>: and whoso marrieth her which is put away doth commit <u>adultery</u>.* Matthew 19:9 |
| *Now the works of the flesh are manifest, which are these; <u>Adultery</u>, <u>fornication</u>, uncleanness, lasciviousness.* Galatians 5:19 |
| *And I gave her space to repent of her <u>fornication</u>; and she repented not. Behold, I will cast her into a bed, and them that commit <u>adultery</u> with her into great tribulation, except they repent of their deeds.* Revelation 2:21-22 |

## Specific and generic uses are also signposts.

Many words can have specific uses as well as generic ones. Specific means it applies to one specific use; it is exclusive; it excludes others.

Generic applications mean that words can refer to more than one alternative. This <u>principle</u> includes both pronouns and nouns. *He* and *she*, *man* and *woman*, *male* and *female* are examples of words, which, depending on the context, can refer to one specific person or thing (specific reference), or they can take on their generic characteristics to include different genders or circumstances. *Whosoever* is another pronoun that can include one specific person or any number of persons or genders.

Some examples are given below. They include words that can be specific or generic depending on how they are used. Noticing these differences is important because many people apply Scriptures on marriage and divorce out of context. They don't understand that there are generic and specific applications of words. What happens is that if a verse doesn't specifically say male <u>and</u> female, or man <u>and</u> woman, or him <u>and</u> her, they incorrectly feel it doesn't apply to both genders:

> There are patterns of word usage in the Bible that may or may not be true in secular writings.

*But if the unbelieving depart, let <u>him</u> depart. A brother or a sister is not under bondage in such cases: but God hath called us to peace.* 1 Corinthians 7:15

Even though the pronoun *him* is male in gender, this verse equally applies to women. Thus, the Scripture also means "But if the unbelieving depart, let *her* depart ..." There is contextual information following the first sentence that confirms the fact that this directive applies to both genders: ... *A brother <u>or</u> sister is not under bondage ...* The same gender application principle applies to Romans 7:2-3:

*For the <u>woman</u> which hath an husband is bound by the law to her husband so long as he liveth; but if the husband be dead, <u>she</u> is loosed from the law of her husband. So then if, while <u>her</u> husband liveth, <u>she</u> be married to another man, <u>she</u> shall be called an adulteress: but if <u>her</u> husband be dead, <u>she</u> is free from that law; so that <u>she</u> is no adulteress, though <u>she</u> be married to another man.* Romans 7:2-3

Some people wrongly believe that because Romans 7:2-3 addresses *the woman which hath a husband*, it doesn't equally apply to a "man which hath a wife"; but, that is not true. God's "law of marriage" applies equally to both genders, male and female as do the pronouns in Romans 7:2-3. However, this must not be applied out of context to violate God's "law of marriage" to include same sex marriages.

Study two additional examples below which do not have anything to do with marriage; yet, the principle of generic interpretation applies. Context and hearing from the Holy Sprit should guide a student of the Word to correct interpretation when there are exceptions:

*Behold, what manner of love the Father hath bestowed upon us, that we should be called the <u>sons</u> of God: therefore the world knoweth us not, because it knew him not.* 1 John 3:1 *Sons* is normally a noun referring to men; however, in 1 John 3:1, it refers equally both to men and women.

*For I testify unto every <u>man</u> that heareth the words of the prophecy of this book, If any <u>man</u> shall add unto these things, God shall add unto <u>him</u> the plagues that are written in this book: And if any <u>man</u> shall take away from the words of the book of this prophecy, God shall take away <u>his</u> part out of the book of life, and out of the holy city, and from the things which are written in this book.* Revelation 22:18-19

Each of the underlined words above is male in gender; however, they are all generic or inclusive; that is, they also apply equally to both genders and thus include women as well as men.

## God doesn't approve of sin for one gender while requiring holiness of the other.
## He's no respecter of persons.

Luke 16:18 is another of many examples of this generic application. *Whosoever putteth away his wife, and marrieth another, committeth adultery: and whosoever marrieth her that is put away from her husband committeth adultery.* The warning also means "whosoever putteth away [divorces] her husband and marrieth another also committeth adultery."

Thus, the pronoun w*hosoever* in Luke 16:18 is generic because it applies to everyone, in the context of this verse: Everyone includes anyone (male or female) who divorces a covenant spouse.

> Covenant love is like charity. It's something you give with nothing expected in exchange.

*Whosoever* is translated from the same underlying Greek word *pas* that is used in John 3:16: *For God so loved the world, that he gave his only begotten Son, that whosoever believeth in him should not perish, but have everlasting life.* Some Christians debate whether *whosoever* in Luke 16:18 applies to both genders; yet, those same persons don't debate whether *whosoever* in John 3:16 applies to both genders. The same principle is also true for the word *whosoever* in Mark 10:11: ... *Whosoever shall put away his wife, and marry another, committeth adultery against her.* No one is excluded if this marriage is a one-flesh joining:

*And the woman which hath an husband that believeth not, and if he be pleased to dwell with her, let her not leave him.* 1 Corinthians 7:13

First Corinthians also applies to a married man: "Ánd the *man* which hath a *wife*..." No one is given an excuse to leave an unsaved or saved spouse. Living with an unsaved spouse can be extremely challenging, but that's when the saved spouse can experience growth and learn the kind of unconditional love explained in 1 Corinthians 13:1-7 called *charity*—a love you give away but expect nothing in return. It's dying to self—a kind of love few are willing to extend.

However, if a separation becomes necessary for perhaps a safety issue, the guidelines are for a spouse to <u>remain</u> in an unmarried state or <u>be reconciled</u> "to her husband." Likewise, the man is to remain in an unmarried state or return to his wife. (Study 1 Corinthians 7:11.) **This, "departing," however, is not a dissolution. It's a separation. Only physical death dissolves a covenant-marriage. Separation leaves no open door for dating, inordinate affections, or "re-marriage."**

## Adultery is used in a specific sense throughout the New Testament.

In the New Testament adultery is usually specific. That is, it most often refers to the sin committed after someone divorces his one-flesh spouse and marries another person such as in Matthew 5:32, 19:9, Mark 10:11-12, Luke 16:18, Romans 7:2-3, et al. However, there are a few examples where adultery is used to define a type of lust that is specifically identified with the eyes. It is fitting that this kind of lust is called adultery as it often leads to martial adultery.

This kind of adultery is often not taken as seriously as it should, especially when the offenders' eyes focus on sexually stimulating body parts. This *could* include all forms of pornography: *But I say unto you, That whosoever <u>looketh</u> on a woman to lust after her hath <u>committed</u>*

*adultery with her already in his heart.* Matthew 5:28 Both the noun *woman* and the pronoun *his* are also used in their generic sense in that this verse also applies to a woman who looks at a man with lust or views pornographic images.

## Beware: The eyes can commit a heinous crime.

The eyes are used in a comprehensive way to encompass the entire body. This includes a person's heart, ways, and footsteps. Job succinctly summarized this principle; that is, how a person should consider where he permits his eyes to look: *I made a covenant with mine eyes; why then should I think upon a maid?* Job 31:1 Job also lets us know not only that God sees everything but how abhorrent the LORD considers the wrongful use of one's gift of sight—it is a heinous crime:

*Doth not he* [the LORD] *see my ways, and count all my steps? If I have walked with vanity, or if my foot hath hasted to deceit ... If mine heart have been deceived by a woman, or if I have laid wait at my neighbour's door ... For this is an <u>heinous crime</u>; yea, it is an iniquity to be punished by the judges. For <u>it is a fire that consumeth</u> to destruction, and would root out all mine increase.* Job 31:4-12

Job, whom God described as a man that ... *was perfect and upright, and one that feared God, and eschewed* [hated] *evil* Job 1:1, would not have violated the directives given in Psalm 101:2-3 and neither should we: *I will behave myself wisely in a perfect way. O when wilt thou come unto me? I will walk within my house with a perfect heart. <u>I will set no wicked thing before mine eyes</u>: I hate the work of them that turn aside; it shall not cleave to me.* Yet, many Christians walk unashamedly into theaters and use the LORD's resources to watch wrongful images and hear offensive words or music. They bring such sins into their homes through TV and also download them onto their cell phones, iPads, and computers.

## Many have grown anesthetized to the feeding of visual sin in their homes.

The proliferation of sin which drives Hollywood and most TV programming and ads has anesthetized the world to what the LORD is saying in Psalm 101:2-3. We should *set no wicked thing before mine eyes*, and we should ***hate*** *the work of them that* produce these ungodly things. We should have nothing to do with these works. For example, what if a typical TV bedroom scene were physically played out in your home? Would you allow two people to have sexual intimacy in front of you and your children by setting up a bed in your TV room and watching a man and woman remove their clothes and continue their sinful acts by getting into that bed for sexual intimacy, or even for the pretense of doing the same?

> Many should be horrified with what they do under the guise of entertainment.

Some would be horrified; yet, many of these same people so horrified at that thought are anesthetized to sexually driven advertisements and sinful sexual scenes playing through their TVs, computers, iPads, and smart phones. The LORD is very jealous over what we permit our eyes to gaze upon or our ears to hear. How many movies or TV programs can be watched without hearing someone take the LORD's name in vain? *Thou shalt not take the name of the LORD thy God in vain* ...

Exodus 20:7 Neither should we consider it entertainment to listen to someone who speaks the same. It would seem like a premeditated sin of adultery to walk into a movie theater or watch any type of entertainment when the rating is PG, R, or X-rated (now NC-17). What is it that generally gives "entertainment" such ratings? Is it not the profanity, violence, or sex which is included that is not appropriate for general audiences? Walking into the theater is followed by setting wicked things before the eyes—the sin of visual adultery. No one should use entertainment as a platform to watch or participate in what God says are sinful acts:

> Many Christians have committed premeditated adultery.

*The light of the body is the <u>eye</u>: therefore when thine eye is single, thy whole body also is full of light; but when thine eye is evil, thy body also is full of darkness. Take heed therefore that the light which is in thee be not darkness.* Luke 11:34-35

*Having **<u>eyes full of adultery</u>**, and that cannot cease from sin ...* 2 Peter 2:14

*But I say unto you, That whosoever <u>looketh</u> on a woman to lust after her hath <u>committed adultery</u> with her already in his heart.* Matthew 5:28 (This also includes women looking at men with lust.)

> There's no adulterer who didn't first entertain a wrongful thought about the opposite sex.

The above may seem like an unnecessary rabbit trail, but it is not. These images, no matter what their source, are a feed-bed for thoughts which enter through the eyes, are incubated in the heart, and emerge through the flesh where they are played out in fornication, adultery, divorce and "re-marriage." There's no drunkard who didn't start with one drink of wine or bottle of beer. There's no fornicator or adulterer who did not first entertain a wrongful thought about someone of the opposite sex. Man commits adultery with his eyes before he does so with his body. See James 1:14, keeping in mind that the noun *man* is generic. It also means "every woman is tempted":

*But every man is tempted, when he is drawn away of his own lust, and enticed. Then when lust hath conceived, it bringeth forth sin: and sin, when it is finished, bringeth forth death. Do not err, my beloved brethren.* James 1:14-16

## Adultery is specific as defined by its context.

There are several other examples below which illustrate the specific nature of adultery in the New Testament. "Re-marriage" is adultery when that "marriage" is one which includes those who have a one-flesh spouse who is living. The context of these verses tells the reader that the sin being addressed is an adulterous one. All except for the last one (John 8:3-4) teach how God looks at "re-marriage." John, in the gospel he penned, records an adulterous act by someone who had sexual intimacy with a man who wasn't her one-flesh husband. Jesus forgave her BUT He also gave her warning as recorded in John 8:11 not to commit adultery again: ... *go, and sin no more.* John 8:11 Study the examples below:

*Whosoever putteth away his wife, and marrieth another, committeth adultery: and whosoever marrieth her that is put away from her husband committeth adultery.* Luke 16:18

*And I say unto you, Whosoever shall put away his wife, except it be for fornication, and shall marry another, committeth adultery: and whoso marrieth her which is put away doth commit adultery.* Matthew 19:9

*So then if, while her husband liveth, she be married to another man, she shall be called an adulteress: but if her husband be dead, she is free from that law; so that she is no adulteress, though she be married to another man.* Romans 7:3

*But I say unto you, That whosoever shall put away his wife, saving for the cause of fornication, causeth her to commit adultery: and whosoever shall marry her that is divorced committeth adultery.* Matthew 5:32

*And if a woman shall put away her husband, and be married to another, she committeth adultery.* Mark 10:12

*And the scribes and Pharisees brought unto him a woman taken in adultery; and when they had set her in the midst, They say unto him, Master, this woman was taken in adultery, in the very act.* John 8:3-4

## Fornication includes a broad range of sins, sometimes specific; other times, generic, depending on the context.

Fornication includes a much broader range of sins than does adultery. It is used in both a specific and generic sense. Below are examples of some of the varied ways fornication is used in the New Testament to represent specific sins:

- To represent the sin of incest—wrongful illicit relationships between those who are closely related as with the example in 1 Corinthians 5:1.
- To identify those who sin against the marriage bed, described in Hebrews 13:4 as a whoremonger—a male fornicator.
- As a metaphor or simile (comparison) signifying idolatry or spiritual unfaithfulness as in Revelation 19:2.
- To indicate a lack of holiness or a disdain for the gifts of God as with Esau in Hebrews 12:16.
- To indicate miscellaneous sinful illicit sexual relationships such as sodomy and premarital sex as in Jude 1:7; 1 Corinthians 7:2.

In 1 Corinthians 5:1 *incest* is called *fornication*: *It is reported commonly that there is fornication among you, and such fornication as is not so much as named among the Gentiles, that one should have his father's wife.* This is an example of a specific use of fornication. The word *incest* itself is not used in the Bible. Its many "faces," however, are listed in Leviticus. Study these as shown in Leviticus 18:6-18. This list of varying kinds of incest is introduced in verse six: *None of you shall approach to any that is near of kin to him, to uncover their nakedness ...* It is context that must, in most verses, be used to tell the reader the correct meaning of words such as *fornication*. In 1 Corinthians 5:1, *fornication* would not include other sins such as idolatry, sodomy, covetousness, etc. as the context tells the reader what specific sin fornication is representing—incest. He "had" his father's wife.

> Incest is called *fornication* in 1 Corinthians 5:1

Sexual sin outside the bonds of a one-flesh marriage by those who are not married is called *fornication* or whoredom. Readers can determine what kind of sexual sin is being pictured through word usage:

*Nevertheless, to avoid fornication, let every man have his own wife, and let every woman have her own husband.* 1 Corinthians 7:2

*For true and righteous are his judgments: for he hath judged the great whore* [Babylon], *which did corrupt the earth with her fornication, and hath avenged the blood of his servants at her hand.* Revelation 19:2

Revelation 19:2 is an example of spiritual idolatry, called *fornication*. *Whore* is a female fornicator. Nations are identified by the female gender. *Whore usually* represents a person, but as above, it represents the nation Babylon, and *fornication* represents the sin itself.

In Jude 1:1:7 *fornication* refers to the specific sin of sodomy: *Even as Sodom and Gomorrha, and the cities about them in like manner, giving themselves over to fornication, and going after strange flesh are set forth for an example, suffering the vengeance of eternal fire.*

Esau is called a profane person in the same verse that warns readers not to be fornicators. (Profane means irreverence for God or sacred things; unholy, heathen, pagan.) The context contrasts *fornication* with *holiness*. *Fornication* can be steeped in the root of bitterness. This is what happened to Esau who offered to sell his birthright to his brother Cain and then was bitter against his brother when he bought it. Read this tragic incident in Genesis 25:29-34. See Hebrews 12:15-17 below:

*Looking diligently lest any man fail of the grace of God; lest any root of bitterness springing up trouble you, and thereby many be defiled; Lest there be any <u>fornicator</u>, or profane person, as Esau, who for one morsel of meat sold his birthright ... for he found no place of repentance, though he sought it carefully with tears.* Hebrews 12:15-17

Fornication can also refer to sexual sin among those who are not in a covenant-marriage as is shown in the two exception clauses in Matthew's gospel. What should be evident is that fornication has several other uses in addition to those studied in previous chapters. Those teachings focused more on divorce and its relationship to the espousal contract, *except it be for fornication*. However, *depending on the context,* fornication can become quite broad—much more so than adultery. The above quoted diverse uses of fornication show the need for readers to be acutely aware of context and signposts. Context, however, isn't always in the immediate verse or even in the immediate chapter. It may be in other chapters or other books of the Bible. Spiritual discernment must be exercised so that other seemingly related Scriptures are not misapplied to create unbiblical doctrine. An example of such misuse was introduced in Chapter 2 with the wrongful combination of Matthew 27:5 and Luke 6:31.

*And he* [Judas] *cast down the pieces of silver in the temple, and departed, and went and hanged himself. And… do ye also …* Matthew 27:5; Luke 6:31

## Fornication, harlotry, and whoremonger are used interchangeably.

To complicate things even more with the study of fornication is the fact that there are other words that are also used for *fornication* and *fornicator* in the Bible. *Fornication* represents the sin, and *fornicator* is the one who commits that sin. Other words used for *fornication* and *fornicator* are *harlotry* and *harlot* and *whoremonger* and *whore*.

These words usually refer to those who are not married but caught up in sexual sin. Yet, these words, in other Scriptures, refer to the spiritual idolatry of a nation, especially God's spiritual wife *Israel*. He called the nation of Israel a *whorish wife* because she made allegiances with pagan nations and worshipped their idols, statues, and gods, and she, Israel, coveted their military power instead of relying on God.

*Whoredom* is a very important word that should be studied to get a fuller picture of the way the LORD looks at all sexual sins. Studying the many Scriptures in which *whoredom(s)* is used in the Old Testament gives an eye-opening awareness of how God views sinful thoughts and acts—all sexual sins. Absent a study of *whoredoms*, much rich background understanding is missed that would tell the reader the perverted depth to which God generically says all sexual sin reaches. *Whoredom*, or a form of it, is used 30 times in the book of Ezekiel and 15 times in the book of Hosea. Both books use a form of *adultery* six times. One of those uses in Hosea specifically refers to the adultery of Gomer, his one-flesh wife. She had divorced him and "re-married" one of her lovers. *Yet*, God told Hosea to buy back his adulteress wife and love her with the kind of unconditional love the LORD extends—according to the love of the LORD:

> *Then said the LORD unto me, Go yet, love a woman beloved of her friend, yet* [still is] *an adulteress, according to the love of the LORD toward the children of Israel, who look to other gods, and love flagons of wine.* Hosea 3:1

Fornication is also used in a general sense to refer to a number of specifically unidentified sins, and it *can* also include adultery **if**:

- Adultery is not used in the same verse.
- The context does not suggest a specific meaning for adultery.

An analogy of a basket of fruit may help in the study of the **generic or inclusive uses of fornication** (and other words in the Bible). The fruit

at the left contains a number of fruits. Generically, the word *fruit* encompasses all the fruit in the basket, even though each fruit is very distinctive in color, shape, and taste and each can be eaten alone or in combination with the others. Likewise, fornication is a basket or container that can hold many different sins including sodomy, idolatry, harlotry, incest, inordinate affections, covetousness, etc. It, at times can even include adultery which is shown on the outside of the basket.

162

Because fornication *can* include a variety of sins when it is used in a verse with other sins, a careful inspection of those other sins must be assessed. That's when the rule of proximity can be a helpful guide. If other sins are listed in the same verse, fornication does not include those sins. For example, sometimes fornication *could* include all types of sexual sins including spiritual idolatry and adultery; but, if any of these sins are specifically listed in the same verse, or content deems otherwise, then fornication does not encompass those other sins listed in that same verse. Even though fornication could encompass adultery, it is never used in the New Testament to specifically represent marital adultery. Adultery, not fornication, is always used to represent those sins identified with marital unfaithfulness; that is, those who are in a covenant-marriage who are unfaithful. Study some examples below:

*Being filled with all unrighteousness, fornication, wickedness, covetousness, maliciousness; full of envy, murder, debate, deceit, malignity; whisperers.* Romans 1:29 Fornication could include adultery and sodomy in Romans 1:29; however, because these sins are listed in verse 31, fornication becomes more specific than generic: *Without understanding, covenant-breakers, without natural affection, implacable, unmerciful.* Romans 1:31 *Covenant-breakers* are one-flesh spouses who divorce, and one-flesh spouses who divorce and "re-marry." If spouses break their covenant, they become covenant-breakers. Breaking a covenant, however, does not dissolve a marriage-covenant. This will be discussed in Chapter 17.

*But fornication, and all uncleanness, or covetousness, let it not be once named among you, as becometh saints.* Ephesians 5:3 Fornication could include all sexually illicit sins because none of those types of sexual sins are specifically listed here. This is another example of the generic use of *fornication*. Context, however, limits its scope.

*Neither repented they of their murders, nor of their sorceries, nor of their fornication, nor of their thefts.* Revelation 9:21

In Revelation 9:21, fornication could represent all sexually illicit sins. This is a generic use example.

*But that we write unto them, that they abstain from pollutions of idols, and from fornication, and from things strangled, and from blood.* Acts 15:20

*Fornication* above is applicable to all illicit sexual sin; thus, it is a generic application. It could include incest, adultery, sodomy, etc.

*Mortify therefore your members which are upon the earth; <u>fornication</u>, uncleanness, <u>inordinate affection</u>, evil concupiscence, and <u>covetousness, which is idolatry</u>.* Colossians 3:5

*Fornication*, in Colossians 3:5, could include many forms of sexual or spiritual sins; but, in this verse, it would not include uncleanness, inordinate affection, or idolatry, because these other sins are specifically listed. In other contexts, *fornication* could include idolatry, but it doesn't here because this verse includes another word for idolatry: *covetousness*, which is called *idolatry*.

> Two terms, such as *fornication* and *inordinate affection*, used in contrast and/or "in proximity" do not mean the same thing.

This illustrates the rule of proximity. Proximity tells the reader that words used in the same verse take on meanings which exclude other sins in that verse. This is especially important when the exception clauses are studied. This simple rule should alert a reader that the <u>exception clause</u> could not include marital unfaithfulness or adultery because both fornication and adultery are used in that verse. They are listed as two different sins—two different names. Thus, they aren't a substitute one for the other, nor do they include the other in that verse.

> Read not just the words but how they are used with other words.

## God is very serious about the need to be faithful to one's <u>own</u> spouse.

There are many specific warnings to not become involved with a wife belonging to someone else. *Wife* in the examples below is generic:

*Thou shalt not covet thy neighbour's house, thou shalt not covet thy neighbour's wife, nor his manservant, nor his maidservant, nor his ox, nor his ass, nor any thing that is thy neighbour's.* Exodus 20:17

*So he that goeth in to his neighbour's wife; whosoever toucheth her shall not be innocent.* Proverbs 6:29

*Whosoever putteth away his wife, and marrieth another, committeth adultery: and whosoever marrieth her that is put away from her husband committeth adultery.* Luke 16:18

*For the woman which hath an husband is bound by the law to her husband so long as he liveth; but if the husband be dead, she is loosed from the law of her husband. So then if, while her husband liveth, she be married to another man, she shall be called an adulteress: but if her husband be dead, she is free from that law; so that she is no adulteress, though she be married to another man.* Romans 7:2-3

God doesn't sugar-coat the abhorrent sin of marital unfaithfulness as we do today by calling it an affair or a "re-marriage." He, instead, expresses such aberrant behavior as He views it: *They were as fed horses in the morning: every one neighed after his neighbour's wife.* Jeremiah 5:8 I've never heard anyone express an affair or "re-marriage" in the way that Jeremiah recorded how God sees it.

> They were as fed horses, neighing after their neighbour's wife.

In addition to *whoredom* being a word for spiritual fornication, the word *whoremonger* in the New Testament is also used to describe someone who defiles (sins against)

> Defiling the marriage bed is a very serious sin.

the marriage bed. *Marriage is honourable in all, and the bed undefiled: but <u>whoremongers</u> and adulterers God will judge.* Hebrews 13:4 Both *fornicators* and *whoremongers* are translated from the same Greek word in the New Testament.

However, w*horemonger* and *adulterer*, like *fornicator* and *adulterer*, are two different words. They are properly interpreted from their distinctively different underlying Greek words. Thus, Hebrews 13:4 is an example of the rule of proximity where the writer is indicating two different sins, but here both sins are against the marriage bed. *Marriage bed* means a covenant-marriage.

## Sexual sin does not affect
## the validity of God's covenants.

God's marriage-covenant is both unilateral and bilateral. It's <u>unilateral</u> in that the LORD totally has charge of the terms which He sets. Nothing man can do changes God's terms. The LORD unilaterally creates a marriage-covenant, and He alone joins the two. The <u>bilateral</u> aspect of a marriage-covenant is the relationship between each of the spouses, <u>a male and a female</u>, neither having a living one-flesh spouse when they take their vows. They do this bilaterally between the two of them and unilaterally between them and God. The standards that God sets for marriage are binding <u>between</u> the two spouses, <u>and</u> the standards are binding individually <u>between</u> each of the spouses and God. It's this latter two-way relationship between the husband and wife that is misunderstood in that even if one of the spouses does not fulfill his commitment to the other spouse the commitment to honor those vows is still in place **because it is also being held by the unilateral bonding or joining power of God**.

If either or both spouses decide to rebel and violate the terms of a God-made covenant, judgment will come down—and harshly so—if they do not repent. Their ability to alter the time frame of God's joining is impossible because it is done and held by God. Regardless of the circumstances or what either spouse does or doesn't do, each spouse is unilaterally, individually, bound to the covenant between each of them and God, and the husband and wife are bilaterally "bound" until one of them physically dies.

God's covenants are unilateral and bilateral.

In the graphic at the left, the Godhead (God the Father, Son, and Holy Ghost) is represented by the crown, thorns, and dove. God unilaterally creates the covenant of marriage. The covenant is represented by the Ark of the Covenant within the scroll. The two spouses below the scroll are accountable (1) unilaterally, to God, to uphold His covenant-marriage terms and (2) both bilaterally, to one another, to uphold their vows until death parts them. That's why a dissolution has no effect on a covenant-marriage.

The time frame of God's act of joining two people into one flesh is part of the *WHAT therefore God hath joined together* and is why the warning*: let not man put asunder.* Matthew 19:6 *Time* <u>cannot be separated from the covenant</u>. God tells us it's a serious offence to commit adultery against His covenant. Those who do so and do not repent will <u>not</u> inherit the Kingdom of God. Totally forsaking the sin of unbiblical marriage relationships means to honor what the Word says, even if, through those relationships, children have been birthed. Neither will hiding the sins of fornication and adultery behind the cloak of salvation or grace appease the wrath of God for violating His sacred one-flesh joining:

> Hiding behind the cloak of salvation or grace will not appease the wrath of God. He will judge all whoremongers and adulterers.

*What shall we say then? Shall we continue in sin, that grace may abound? God forbid. How shall we, that are dead to sin, live any longer therein? ... Let not sin therefore reign in your mortal body, that ye should obey it in the lusts thereof.* Romans 6:1-2; 12

Sin committed by those who are in a marriage-covenant has absolutely no effect **on the validity of the terms of that marriage.** It's death, not sin, whatever sin it might be, that dissolves a God-created marriage-covenant. Those who sin against the marriage bed (a covenant-marriage), absent repentance, will be under God's judgment. God's rules and judgment apply whether the sin is:

- Because of sexual intimacy by those not married (fornicators) with someone who is.
- By someone who is married and becomes sexually intimate with another person.
- Because someone who is married has divorced and "re-married" another person.

## It comes down to context, context, context.

It should be clear that the way *fornication* is used in Matthew 19:9 is not the same as the way *fornication* is used in Revelation 19:2. Matthew 19:9 is a physical non-covenant wife (or husband) who is a fornicator; Revelation 19:2 refers to spiritual apostasy:

| The context is different between Matthew 19:9 and Revelation 19:2 and so are the contextual definitions for *fornication* in each verse. ||
|---|---|
| *And I say unto you, Whosoever shall put away his wife, except it be for fornication, and shall marry another, committeth adultery: and whoso marrieth her which is put away doth commit adultery.* Matthew 19:9 | *For true and righteous are his judgments: for he hath judged the great whore, which did corrupt the earth with her fornication, and hath avenged the blood of his servants at her hand.* Revelation 19:2 |

Likewise, the way the word *adultery* is used in Matthew 19:9 is not what is intended for its meaning in Matthew 5:28:

| The context is different between Matthew 19:9 and Matthew 5:28 and so are the contextual definitions for adultery in each verse. ||
|---|---|
| *And I say unto you, Whosoever shall put away his wife, except it be for fornication, and shall marry another, committeth adultery: and whoso marrieth her which is put away doth commit adultery.* Matthew 19:9 | *But I say unto you, That whosoever looketh on a woman to lust after her hath committed adultery with her already in his heart.* Matthew 5:28 |

## I discovered a new kind of "family feud."

The statement has been made several times in this book that it is not necessary to study or know Hebrew or Greek to understand the Word of God if you have a translation that is true to the underlying text; yet, there are examples in most chapters thus far of the Hebrew and Greek words underlying the English translation. Again, the reason for including these is not to teach these languages, but to help the reader discern with some concrete proofs that many of the Bibles which publishers claim to be accurate are not accurate. The authors of these Bibles have, in many places, incorrectly translated the underlying text and have paraphrased the English text creating many doctrinally inaccurate words and phrases. Many of these inaccuracies deal directly with salvation issues. Yet, many readers continue to study from them. It's like having the wrong ingredients in a prescription. Wouldn't that be of concern to people who take that prescription drug?

## The focus has changed.

In the past forty years, teachings from the pulpit and through many ministries have greatly changed. They have changed <u>from</u> an emphasis on studying directly from the English text in the Bible <u>to</u> teachings which include and focus on many references to the Hebrew and Greek texts as well as how words are defined in Strong's Concordance.

Because there is now so much focus on the Hebrew and Greek, many are reading their Bibles thinking that some person must explain to them what God "really" said in Hebrew or Greek, or they must learn to read Scripture in these other languages. Thus, the focus has changed. It has become man's wisdom in Hebrew, Greek, and sometimes Aramaic, rather than the words written upon the pages of the Bible in English. Yet, the LORD magnifies HIS Word even above

> Forty years ago the pastor in our church didn't make references to the Hebrew and Greek.

His Name (See Psalm 138:2.), and God says He will preserve His Word pure unto a thousand generations. Has God not done that? Of course He has. The English text, if correctly translated, is directly related to the preserved underlying Hebrew and Greek texts:

*He hath remembered his covenant for ever, the word which he commanded to a thousand generations.* Psalm 105:8 *The words of the LORD are pure words: as silver tried in a furnace of earth, purified seven times. Thou shalt keep them, O LORD, thou shalt preserve them from this generation for ever.* Psalm 12:6-7

Which option should we believe: man's wisdom or God's Word? Thousands of martyrs gave their lives up to torment and death to bring the Bible to the common man in a language <u>he could read for himself</u>, in his own language without an interpreter. (Review page six.) They did this for naught if we must (as many church leaders are implying) have a teaching on the Hebrew or Greek words to properly interpret the Word of God. Again, I urge those who have expertise in Hebrew and Greek not to take these statements out of context.

Let me put this on a personal level. When my husband left our marital home after he became ensnared in the sinful lifestyle of adultery, I fell on my knees and prayed as I was destroyed emotionally. I started combing the Scriptures day and night from Genesis through Revelation. I fasted and prayed for many days, sometimes for weeks at a time. I reached out to several pastors and ministries nationwide.

I was shocked to hear pastors and ministries consistently telling me that my Bible was not written correctly—that it didn't correctly reflect the underlying Hebrew and Greek. Tragically, they tried to console me by also telling me that since my husband committed adultery, I was free from our marriage, and God would bring me another husband. That was so offensive to me as the LORD had shown me, in my Bible, that my husband and I were married until one of us physically died. Furthermore, my love for my husband never waned. I hated **what** he was doing, but I **loved him**. Circumstances could not change those vows we took or my unconditional love for him.

I had for months immersed myself in the study of the Word. I asked the LORD for answers to what was going on in our family and for an understanding regarding the conflicting, supposedly Biblical counsel I was receiving. I was in an additional state of shock to find that ministers and ministries were telling me that my Bible (the King James) wasn't accurate. They didn't believe what the words said which were written in English in my Bible because, according to them, there were more accurate texts in a language <u>that I couldn't read</u> and about which I knew nothing. It was then, and only then, that I became aware of a Biblical "family feud"—a feud among the different versions of the Bible. There are, I learned, two different and conflicting families of Bibles.

I didn't have a clue what all this Hebrew and Greek talk was about, as the pastor of the church my husband and I had attended didn't make references to the Hebrew and Greek from the pulpit. This was 40 years ago, a time when there wasn't the infiltration of so many versions of the Bible or the infusion into sermons of explanations as to what the Bible supposedly "really means"—in Hebrew and Greek. Being wrongly told that my marriage was dead in God's eyes and that my Bible was inaccurate could have put me onto a paved road that could have led to my spiritual destruction.

Fortunately, I felt led to search for myself. I went to the library at a local seminary to investigate what this Hebrew and Greek "thing" was that threatened to put my whole spiritual belief system in jeopardy:

- How could these theologically trained men be wrong?
- Could it be that my Bible was flawed?
- Could it be that my marriage was no longer valid?
- Would I need to learn two new languages to properly understand the Bible?
- Was it possible that what they told me was true: "You are emotionally upset and therefore cannot understand what your Bible is really saying"?

I found myself on totally foreign territory with totally foreign books and languages. This was quite apparent to the librarian who seemed shocked that I didn't know which Hebrew and Greek texts I wanted to check out. I, however, didn't let my apparent stupidity deter me and told the librarian I needed all of them—not having the slightest idea what that meant. I returned day after day to study and search.

After months of research, I began to see that what I had been told about the inaccuracy of my Bible was not true. It was not any truer than the untruth that my marriage was invalid because my husband had committed adultery and even "re-married."

What I discovered was that my Bible consistently and contextually reflected the words from which it was translated. The other Bibles were flawed as were the doctrines and theories so many theologians told me about my covenant husband. The Holy Spirit had rescued me.

## Put together the fishing tackle box.

This small window into my life is shared to hopefully help you to see the **necessity** to search the Scriptures <u>for yourself</u>. Through the study presented in this book, it has been shown that there is no need to feel required to understand Hebrew or Greek to know what God clearly says about marriage *from a correctly translated text*. **Yet, my search of the underlying languages is still ongoing because some people were and are misusing their skills in these languages to discredit God's Word.** Again, such abuses could have been a catalyst that would have sent me in a direction that could have put me on a road to eternal destruction.

More importantly, why this chapter? In this chapter the "rule of proximity" was introduced as well as the importance of differentiating between the specific and generic use of words. Also included were

> There is a danger when the Hebrew and Greek **become** the message **rather than** the gift that we have through a Bible accurately translated into words that we can study in a language we can read for ourselves.

discussions on the many different ways fornication, whoredom, and adultery can be contextually applied. These precepts have been taught because a thorough grounding of *how* words are *used in the Bible* can be, for many, a matter of correct or incorrect doctrinal beliefs. The latter is something we don't want to put in the hands of another person. <u>Each person</u> must be able to determine, in English, the correct interpretation of important doctrinal truths. This was the goal of Tyndale. These additional tools for study are meant to serve as aids to help in discerning between correct and incorrect doctrine.

DISCLAIMER: Again, PLEASE, don't take this out of context. I also believe there is a time and place for the study of the original languages. After all, without those linguistic experts in these languages, we wouldn't have our Bible in English today.

Many theologians study the Hebrew and Greek words underlying the English translation to enrich their messages for their congregations and to help them grow in understanding the Bible. Several theologians have helped to guide me to grow in my still limited understanding of the Hebrew and Greek manuscripts. The LORD has given us apostles, prophets, evangelist, pastors and teachers *for the perfecting of the saints, for the work of the ministry* ... Ephesians 4:12

Where the dividing line exists for me is when the original languages become the focus <u>instead</u> of what is contextually correctly translated in English. If I cannot read my Bible with understanding and correctly interpret basic doctrines without a Strong's Concordance or a Hebrew and Greek Interlinear Bible, then there is something amiss. What may be amiss with some is a wrong belief that the Holy Spirit Who has promised that He will teach us cannot do so. Perhaps what may be the even bigger issue is that many Christians do not spend quality time alone reading and <u>studying</u> the Bible. They invest more time listening to man (including TV preachers) **rather** than "hearing" directly from the Author of the Bible by <u>studying from the Bible itself</u>. There is a difference between (1) reading, (2) listening, and (3) studying. The first two are important aids; however, the key is for each person to study from the Bible itself. The Word never tells us that our source for understanding is the wisdom of man; it is the Word of God. *It is the spirit that quickeneth; the flesh profiteth nothing: <u>the words that I</u>* [Jesus] <u>*speak unto you,*</u> ***they*** <u>*are spirit, and*</u> ***they*** <u>*are life*</u>. John 6:63

> The bigger issue may be that many Christians are not **studying** the Bible by themselves.

Do not lightly dismiss the fact that thousands of martyrs died for the purpose of bringing the Word of God to the common man in his native tongue. This was so important that these men and women gave up their lives and endured horrific torture and self-denial. They were hunted down like animals. For a glimpse of the kinds of hardships they bore, review Hebrews 11:35-38. Are we slowly and tragically returning to a dependence upon languages we do not understand and where we think we must have someone interpret the Scriptures for us? Let's hope not!

**Study** *to shew thyself approved unto God, a workman that needeth not to be ashamed, rightly dividing the word of truth.* 2 Timothy 2:15

*Then opened <u>he</u>* [Jesus] *their understanding, that they might understand the scriptures.* Luke 24:45

*Which things also we speak, not in the words which man's wisdom teacheth, but which the <u>Holy Ghost teacheth</u>;* **comparing spiritual things with**

***spiritual**. But the natural man receiveth not the things of the Spirit of God: for they are foolishness unto him: neither can he know them, because they are spiritually discerned.* 1 Corinthians 2:13-14

*Only the LORD give thee wisdom and understanding ... that thou mayest keep the law of the LORD thy God.* 1 Chronicles 22:12

*Whom shall <u>he teach</u> knowledge? and whom shall <u>he make to understand doctrine</u>? them that are weaned from the milk, and drawn from the breasts. For precept must be upon precept, precept upon precept; line upon line, line upon line; here a little, and there a little.* Isaiah 28:9-10

Every person must decide for himself what to believe. However, I pray that God will provide you with the skills to be able to determine whether your Bible has doctrinal errors and:

- You will have the tools to equip yourself to be able to assess whether specific doctrines are true or false.
- If you are studying from a Bible that has doctrinal errors (such as those pointed out in this book) that you will set it aside and pick up one that doesn't have such errors.
- You will know without a doubt, from a consistent, contextual analysis of the Scriptures, in English, that there is one man for one woman until the physical death of one of the two spouses.
- Finally, you will come to the above conclusions because you can prove them consistently **through Scriptures from a correctly translated Bible in English (your native tongue)**, especially when you see doctrinal errors about marriage.

Then you will have learned how to fish. You've heard it said, "Give a man a fish and he will eat for a day. Teach a man to fish and he will eat for a lifetime." So pick up that fishing pole and your tackle box and move on to the next chapter!

---

Note: The teaching on the generic application of words is in no way suggesting a gender-neutral Bible. That is taking out of context the purpose of these teachings. Translation of God's words must be retained to reflect the underlying text.

## God's Word is not bound—copyrighted.

What does it mean if something is copyrighted? Copyright is a law which grants to the <u>creator</u> of an **original work** exclusive right to its use and distribution for a given number of years. New versions of the Bible, however, come under the <u>derivative</u> copyright law. Derivative works (Bibles) are based on preexisting works, but they must be **changed significantly** from those existing works to qualify under the U. S. Derivative Copyright Law. That is, "new" versions must contain thousands of words that differ from the original or other existing works. This includes differing significantly from a *public domain* publication (one which can be reproduced freely) such as the King James Bible.

Unlike the new version Bibles, **the <u>words</u> in the King James Bible cannot be copyrighted**. The King James translation, as we know it today, was completed in 1769. This was a few years prior to the passage of the first copyright law in the United States in 1790 which gave copyright protection to authors of original works from that day forward. It is the notes, footnotes, formatting, etc. added by an author and made a part of a King James Bible that <u>can</u> be copyrighted because these are created by the author; however, the Scriptures may not. Anyone can freely quote, copy, and publish every word of Scripture from the King James Bible, but no one can obtain a copyright—exclusive right to the words in this Bible: ... *the Word of God is not bound.* 2 Timothy 2:9

That, however, is not true with the new versions. Their works are "bound" by copyright because these are considered works created by the authors of these Bibles. They have avowed that their Bibles are significantly changed from any preexisting Bible, enough so they are considered an original work. Permission must be granted from these authors to quote beyond a certain number of words. (Copyright laws allow for quotes from others' works when they are made for comparative purposes.) **Thus, to qualify under the derivative copyright law for Bibles, those authors must violate God's law** which instructs man <u>not</u> to change His Word for any reason and gives eternal damnation warnings for doing so.

God has preserved His Word, copyright free unto all generations. *The words of the LORD are pure words: as silver tried in a furnace of earth, purified seven times. Thou shalt keep them, O LORD, thou shalt preserve them from this generation for ever.* Psalm 12:6-7

# 13

# *A Grammatical Idiosyncrasy Is Embedded In Matthew 19:9.*

A grammatical idiosyncrasy in Matthew 5:32 and Matthew 19:9 is seldom recognized, but it is an important silent internal signpost—an aid in properly interpreting these Scriptures. It is related, in principle, to something students of past years were required to learn—how to analyze a sentence for correct structure by diagramming it. One of the many purposes of diagramming is to help readers to be able to visualize parts of a sentence. For example, if a sentence has a single subject but two verbs, it would be diagrammed much like the illustration above. Jesus, the subject, both wept and taught.

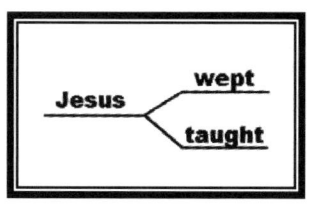

## A Grammatical Idiosyncrasy Is Embedded In Matthew 19:9.

The above simplified, illustrated sentence structure can lend additional understanding to the total message presented in Matthew's two recorded exception clauses: Matthew 5:32 and 19:9. The key is in Matthew's unusual, unique sentence structure which is misunderstood. First, recall that in the Jewish culture there were two different kinds of husbands and wives: betrothed (Old Testament language) or espoused (New Testament language) husbands and wives, and married husbands and wives.

Those who are betrothed or espoused and become involved in sexual sin are *fornicators*. They commit the sin of fornication. Those who are married and become involved in sexual sin and/or a "re-marriage" (adulterous "marriage") are called adulterers or adulteresses. The later (those in a one-flesh marriage) commit the sin of adultery in two ways: (1) through an affair (a sexual encounter or mental fantasy with someone other than their one-flesh spouse), or (2) by committing the sin of (marital) adultery if they marry another person while their one-flesh spouse is alive.

Those who "re-marry" put themselves into an ongoing state of adultery which is usually indicated in the Bible by the *eth* ending on the verb commit:

> The *eth* ending on a verb tells the reader that this is an ongoing sin.

committ**eth**. It's this latter type of adultery—an ongoing state of adultery—that is the focus of most of the New Testament teachings on divorce. However, most new version Bibles do not record this important aspect of adultery.

## The Dual Application of *wife* must be applied.

The word *wife* in the clause, *Whosoever shall put away his wife*, in both Matthew 5:32 and 19:9, reflects a dual application of the word *wife*. That is, the noun *wife* encompasses two kinds of wives, espoused (or non-covenant) and married.

In addition to the dual nature of a Jewish wife (and husband), there is also a grammatical sentence structure expressing this idiosyncrasy in Matthew 19:9. The sentence structure reflects both an "engagement or a non-covenant putting away" (divorce) and a "marriage putting away." However, these two "putting aways" are introduced by <u>one</u> introductory clause given for both types of divorces: *Whosoever shall put away his wife.* **Wife is the key word which ties everything together; that is, the word *wife* encompasses both kinds of wives.**

Matthew's sentence structure is shown below. The word *wife* <u>acts</u> in its dual nature (espoused and married) for two different sins. However, instead of verbs following the subject (wife), as shown on page 179, what follows are two different kinds of sins: fornication listed on the first line and the sin of adultery listed on the second line.

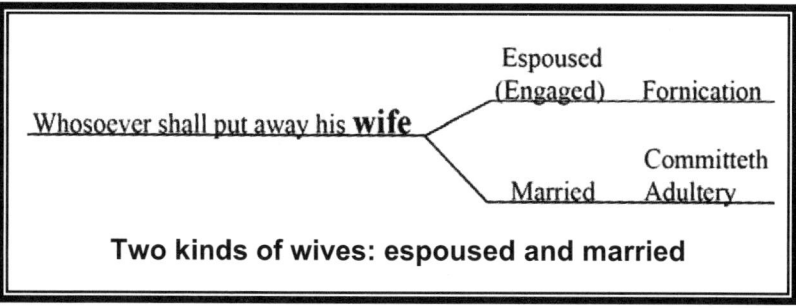

**Two kinds of wives: espoused and married**

A Grammatical Idiosyncrasy Is Embedded In Matthew 19:9.

The diagram above is designed to help the reader visualize what is being taught in the exception clauses as they relate to the Jewish cultural practices:

1. Two kinds of wives: espoused and married.
2. The sexual sin committed by an espoused wife: fornication.
3. The sexual sin committed by a covenant wife: adultery.

As recorded in Matthew 1:19, Joseph was planning to put away (divorce) his wife, Mary. What kind of a wife was he planning to put away, an espoused or a married wife? Why was he thinking of divorcing Mary? Was it for fornication or adultery? The context gives the answers. Joseph was planning to put away an espoused wife because he thought she had committed fornication.

What would have been different about the "divorce" if Joseph had been planning to put Mary away after they had been made one flesh by God? What if Joseph, after divorcing Mary, married another wife while Mary was still living? The answers are all in Matthew's gospel, and specifically in 19:9.

If, while they were engaged, Joseph would have put Mary away, it would have been for fornication, and he could have contracted for another espoused wife. In so doing, he would not have committed adultery because he was engaged, not married; assuming, of course, that the second espoused wife did not have a living one-flesh husband:

... *Whosoever shall put away his wife, except it be for fornication* ... Matthew 19:9

However, if after Joseph was made one flesh with Mary, he put her away (divorced his married wife) and married another, he would then have become an adulterer.¹ Similarly, if Mary had married someone else after being divorced from a one-flesh marriage, she³ and the man² who married her would both become adulterers:

*¹... Whosoever shall put away his wife ... and shall marry another, committeth adultery: ²and whoso marrieth her which is put away doth commit adultery.* Matthew 19:9

*³So then if, while her husband liveth, she be married to another man, she shall be called an adulteress: but if her husband be dead, she is free from that law; so that she is no adulteress, though she be married to another man.* Romans 7:3

## The exception clause is a subjunctive: a hypothetical exception.

Read again the question posed by the wicked Pharisees:
*The Pharisees also came unto him, tempting him, and saying unto him, Is it lawful for a man to put away his wife for every cause?* Matthew 19:3

Consider the immediate audience—the Pharisees. Who were they? They were devoted Jews who knew very well the Jewish espousal practices; yet, Jesus called them *vipers, hypocrites, whited sepulchres,* and *blind guides.* That's because their doctrines were wicked. Jesus knew they were looking for loopholes. That might explain why He succinctly included both kinds of wives in His answer. It could have been so neither the Pharisees—nor anyone else—would have room to doctrinally manipulate His reply. He, additionally, however, gave no "cause" for putting away a *married* wife. He only gave the judgment *if* a covenant spouse *were* to divorce and marry another. Jesus told them that those who do so become adulterers. Many today, instead of accepting the answer Jesus gave, look to Him for a way to not only divorce but to "re-marry."

A Grammatical Idiosyncrasy Is Embedded In Matthew 19:9.

## The exception clause is uniquely structured.

The exception clause is structured as a subjunctive. Technically, it is called the *subjunctive mood*. *Subjunctive* is not a commonly used word, but it describes a very important grammatical Biblical structure that needs to be recognized. Subjunctives are used hundreds of times throughout the Bible. There are different kinds of subjunctives; but the focus of this study is to show how their conditional characteristic serves as a signpost to help readers identify Matthew's sentence structure. The focus, however, shouldn't be the structure itself but WHY it is used. The subjunctive structure in Matthew 19:9 *except it be for* serves as a tool to set apart these five words *except it be for fornication* from the remaining message in the verse.

> A subjunctive sets apart important contrasting information.

A subjunctive is an exception or addition to the main part or thought of the verse. It includes information that is not the same as what was stated before or directly thereafter. It can be a hypothetical statement; that is, it often is an exception or a clause stating a condition. Even though the sentence or verse is complete without the subjunctive, the subjunctive includes important information.

That's the unrecognized important structural aspect of the exception clauses in Matthew 5:32 and 19:9. The information included in the exception clauses is that **the husband who puts away a wife for fornication is not subject to the remainder of the verse**. One example of that would be an espoused wife as Matthew teaches in the first chapter of his gospel. Other examples will be studied later.

Words which most often signal the subjunctive mood in the New Testament are *if* and *except* combined with *be; whether* combined with *be;* and *saving for*. These words are signposts that the clause is a subjunctive and that the words which follow these words include an exception to, a possibility, or something contrary to what has been stated before, or which is to follow. In other words, subjunctives point to or include something that is different in some way. They can be used in many different ways:

> Words are more than containers for meanings. They also can serve as signposts.

- As a warning.
- As a possibility.
- As a universally accepted principle or rule (axiom).
- As something that may or might be.
- As something that is conditional.
- As something contrary to the speaker's main viewpoint.
- As something that is in addition.

It's only Matthew who includes the subjunctive *except it be for fornication* in his gospel, and it's only in the book of Matthew where the specific Jewish example of the espousal, espousal divorce, and marriage of Joseph and Mary are clearly given. It's only in Matthew that these two, the example and the exception clause, can be interlinked from within the information given in that book.

What was the exception? The exception, for those in the Jewish culture, could have been someone whose espoused wife committed the sin of fornication. These are facts specifically included within Chapter 1 of the book of Matthew:

A Grammatical Idiosyncrasy Is Embedded In Matthew 19:9.

*Now the birth of Jesus Christ was on this wise: When as his mother Mary was espoused to Joseph, before they came together, she was found with child of the Holy Ghost. Then Joseph her husband, being a just man, and not willing to make her a publick example, was minded to put her away privily.* Matthew 1:18-19

The engaged husband could put away (divorce) his engaged wife, and then he would be free to contract for another engaged wife and not commit adultery. This is an example which fits the parameters of the exception in Matthew 19:9.

## All but (except) the subjunctive refers to those who are in a covenant-marriage.

The <u>remainder</u> of the verse, that which follows the exception clause, is <u>no longer an exception that applies to a non-covenant wife</u>. The words which follow the exception clause apply totally to a wife and husband joined by God; that is, they are married in His sight. This is the second application for the word *wife* and the reason for the bottom line in the diagram in the graphic repeated below: Married Committeth Adultery.

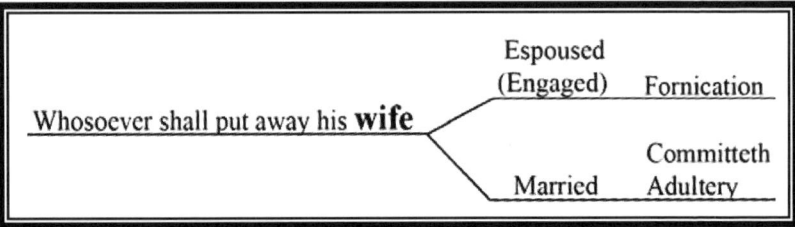

Jesus, unlike most today, refused to be involved in vain conversations about *reasons* to put away a one-flesh wife because there are none. Even though the Pharisees specifically asked: *Is it lawful for a man to*

*put away his wife for every cause?* (Matthew 19:3), Jesus did not focus on *for every cause*. Instead, His conversation with the scribes and Pharisees states, very clearly that if anyone (whosoever) puts away a married wife AND marries someone else, or if she that is put away marries someone else, everyone so involved committ**eth** adultery. There's no innocent party; there's no desertion clause; there are no grounds for divorce given by Jesus for those in a covenant-marriage.

## Subjunctives are important signposts used throughout the Bible.

Subjunctives (clauses beginning with *if, except, whether* and including the word *be*) are important signposts. They, when recognized, should call the reader's attention to something that not only breaks the flow of thought but adds some important, relevant information. Study the Scripture below.

*For by one Spirit are we all baptized into one body ... and have been all made to drink into one Spirit.* 1 Corinthians 12:13

The Scripture above is complete in thought; however, you may or may not have noticed that there is something missing. What is missing are two subjunctive clauses: **whether** we **be** *Jews or Gentiles,* **whether** we **be** *bond or free.* What words or signposts indicate these clauses are subjunctives? Hopefully you recognized the words *whether* and *be*. Important information is added through these subjunctives. It is information that God has decided is necessary:

*For by one Spirit are we all baptized into one body,* **whether we be Jews or Gentiles, whether we be bond or free***; and have been all made to drink into one Spirit.* 1 Corinthians 12:13

A Grammatical Idiosyncrasy Is Embedded In Matthew 19:9.

## Subject and verb idiosyncrasies

The following may be too much "grammar" for some but "catch" what you can. It has a very important purpose. There's another signpost pointing to hypothetical subjunctives, in addition to the signpost words (*except it be; whether it be; if it be*). It's what normally would be considered a subject/verb conflict. When the normal pattern of single subject-single verb and plural subject-plural verb are broken, accompanied by the above-mentioned words, the reader should look closer at the information and think on the reason for the added words. When that happens, there is an embedded reversal in meaning. Subject/verb disagreement isn't inserted in the Bible because the writer didn't understand rules of grammar, but because he did. Study the difference between normal sentence structure and abnormal structure because of a hypothetical example being given:

> Subject/verb disagreement is a grammatical structure which serves as a signpost for conditional subjunctives.

- Normal grammatical pattern: She was going to study her Bible. (*She* is a singular subject. *Was* is a singular verb.)
- Abnormal grammatical pattern: <u>If</u> she <u>were</u> going to study her Bible … She is a singular subject, but now there is a plural verb, and **the meaning has been changed from a statement of fact to a hypothetical thought**: *IF she were to study*. The singular verb *was* is properly changed to the plural *were* because this is now a hypothetical example. Subject-verb disagreement is a signpost for something that is hypothetical. It's recording what **might** happen.

This plural verb signpost above is an example of a sentence which was changed from the indicative mood (making a statement of fact) to the subjunctive mood (a hypothetical example).

## Other examples of the subjunctive mood are used in the Bible.

Listed below are a few of the many times the subjunctive mood is used in the Bible. Within each verse, there is a consistent grammatical structure for these subjunctives. Notice the signposts *if ... be, except ... be*, or a combination of these words, and subject-verb disagreement. Many hypothetical statements begin with the conditional *if* and include *be* which give the clause its hypothetical

> It's the difference between a stop sign and a stop sign with a flashing light.

characteristic. It helps some readers to have the hypothetical "flashing light" to alert them that **this is not an ordinary pause**—that there is something different to be noted. However, what is even more fundamental is that the underlying Hebrew and Greek texts must be accurately translated which is the case with each of these examples below. They are correctly translated as subjunctives because the text from which they are translated records them as subjunctives:

| Signposts identify hypothetical subjunctive mood: something contrary to an immediate situation. |
|---|
| *... if the thief be found let him pay double.* Exodus 22:7 |
| *If a damsel that is a virgin be betrothed unto an husband ...* Deuteronomy 22:23 |
| *... If thou be a great people ...* Joshua 17:15 |
| *If the foundations be destroyed, what can the righteous do?* Psalm 11:3 |
| *And when the tempter came to him, he said, If thou be the Son of God ...* Matthew 4:3 |
| *And if a house be divided against itself, that house cannot stand.* Mark 3:25 |
| *... If God be for us, who can be against us?* Romans 8:31 |
| *... except it be for fornication ...* Matthew 19:9 |
| *... My kingdom is not of this world: if my kingdom were of this world, then would my servants fight ...* John 18:36 |

## A Grammatical Idiosyncrasy Is Embedded In Matthew 19:9.

It isn't just the <u>conditional</u> word *if* that helps the reader know that what follows is something hypothetical or not certain to happen. It's also when *if* is combined with **subject-verb disagreement.** For example: "**If** she **were** to study ... **If** I **were** a rich man ..."

<u>However</u>, when there is a clause beginning with the conditional word *if* <u>followed</u> by subject/verb **agreement** then *if* **takes on the meaning of "since"** making the statement declarative—a statement of fact.

> A declarative sentence is not a hypothetical sentence.

It may be difficult to discern the *slight* difference between a true hypothetical statement and one that isn't. Study the following examples on the left with the hypothetical signs, *if ... be*. Compare the ones on the right that have been changed to declarative statements in the new versions:

| New versions remove the hypothetical "if" "be" and insert subject/verb agreement reflecting a declarative statement. ||
|---|---|
| *... if the thief **be** found, let him pay double.* Exodus 22:7 KJB | **\*\****... if he **is** caught, must pay back double ...* Exodus 22:7 NIV |
| *If a damsel that is a virgin **be** betrothed unto an husband ...* Deuteronomy 22:23 KJB | **\*\****If there **is** a girl who is a virgin engaged to a man ...* Deuteronomy 22:23 NASV |
| *... If thou **be** a great people ...* Joshua 17:15 KJB | **\*\****... If you **are** a numerous people ...* Joshua 17:15 ESV |
| *If the foundations **be** destroyed, what can the righteous do?* Psalm 11:3 KJB | **\*\****if the foundations **are** destroyed, what can the righteous do?* Psalm 11:3 ESV |
| *And when the tempter came to him, he said, If thou **be** the Son of God ...* Matthew 4:3 KJB | **\*\****Now when the tempter came to Him, he said, "If You **are** the Son of God ...* Matthew 4:3 NKJV |
| *And if a house **be** divided against itself, that house cannot stand.* Mark 3:25 KJB | **\*\****And if a house **is** divided against itself, that house cannot stand.* Mark 3:25 NKJV |
| *Key for above Bibles: KJB: King James Bible; NASV: New American Standard Version; ESV: English Standard Version; NKJV: New King James Version; NIV: New International Version    \*\***Each of these should have used *be* or the plural verb *were*.** ||

Chapter 13

## *If it be* and *except it be* ...
## are important "jots" and "tittles."

The new versions remove the hypothetical statements by changing *if thou be* to *if you are*, etc. God, unlike us, sees the whole intent of the Bible and has a purpose for each word and how each may have special significance in the way it is used or is used in combination with other words. When we refer to accurately translating word-for-word from one language to another, there are some words that do not translate word-for-word for which words may need to be added to complete a thought. However, accurate translation avoids indiscriminately changing parts of speech and tenses of verbs, adding to and taking from the underlying text, and changing subjunctives to declarative statements.

Review Chapter 8 to examine the highlighted words in the Scripture below as they might apply to the study of hypothetical Scriptures:

*For verily I say unto you, Till heaven and earth pass, one **jot** or one **tittle** shall in no wise pass from the law, till all be fulfilled.* Matthew 5:18

The principle behind jot and tittle applies to all of God's Word, including the signposts *except it **be**; if ... **be**; whether ... **be***. Recall the examples already given of the *Hindenburg* explosion and the "quiet explosion" recorded in Scripture when the serpent added only three letters—*N O T*—to what God had spoken.

Bible translation is not the same as translating secular materials. It's not just a matter of having the correct underlying text. It's also being faithful with contextual interpretation, including applying consistent rules of grammar as they relate to the context in the immediate text and to other related Scriptures. Those who translate from the underlying languages must also be holy men directed by the Holy Ghost. Absent this, many important doctrinal teachings will not be properly translated, even though the translators know Hebrew and Greek. It is holy men of God that we're told the LORD chose to record His Word.

*Knowing this first, that no prophecy of the scripture is of any private interpretation. For the prophecy came not in old time by the will of man: but holy men of God spake as they were moved by the Holy Ghost.* 2 Peter 1:20-21

## STOP does not require a degree in language exploration!

Consider a similar secular example, the familiar stop sign. It is a signpost which those who drive a car observe. Because drivers understand nuances of our language, such as when there is an imperative sentence or short command, such as STOP, or even the shape of the sign, they know what it means.

There is an understood subject and that subject is *you*—whosoever is driving on our highways. Drivers who approach this octagonal sign  know they are to stop. The sign means YOU stop, even though the subject is not given. We don't have to examine the etymology of the word, or research who made the sign, or take a college class on stop signs. Drivers know to stop because there is a standard in place throughout the land that stop signs are red and white in color and octagonal in shape; and those who drive on our highways are held responsible to observe legal road signs. They observe the law of the land. However, if everyone designed his own stop sign in his favorite color and shape and with his own words to express *stop*, total confusion would break out on our roadways. Yet, that's what is happening with Bibles today, especially with the exception clauses. Man is making his own "Biblical road signs" and people are having devastating crashes.

The removal of just the two letters "b" and "e" (the word "be") in the exception clause by the NIV and other versions seems so small. This subtle omission goes unnoticed by many. However, in so doing they change not only the words of the Creator God, but they change the signpost and the reason for the exception clause when they replace *fornication* with their unscriptural insertion of *marital unfaithfulness*. They further also fail to see the need for 51 additional letters, 11 words: *and whoso marrieth her which is put away doth commit adultery:*

| How many "jots" and "tittles" are too many to remove? ||
|---|---|
| And I say unto you, Whosoever shall put away his wife, **except it be for fornication**, and shall marry another, committeth adultery: **and whoso marrieth her which is put away doth commit adultery**. Matthew 19:9 KJB | I tell you that anyone who divorces his wife, **except for marital unfaithfulness**, and marries another woman commits adultery. Matthew 19:9 NIV |

## Why did Jesus insert the exception clause?

From my more than 40 year's experience of defending God's perspective on marriage, I have found Matthew 19:9 and Matthew 5:32 have been two of the most often misapplied verses by those who are looking for Biblical loopholes to justify divorcing a one-flesh spouse and marrying someone else. Typical remarks are "Jesus allowed divorce for marital unfaithfulness, (or adultery, or sexual immorality)." They quote from versions of the Bible in which the authors have used these incorrect terms, creating mass confusion and division among even strong Christians. Do we really think that Jesus meant these clauses to be so troublesome for us today? Absolutely not. It's man, not God, who has made the simplicity of the gospel into a multiple choice "fiasco" with man-created doctrines and hundreds of critical footnotes that are often convoluted, misapplied, and troublesome. These practices have prospered to a large extent because most do not understand or accept one or more of the following:

(1) God's picture of marriage in Genesis 2:21-24 has never, and will never, change.
(2) The contextual definition of fornication.
(3) The fact that "**except it be**" is a signpost for a hypothetical statement—not a loophole to put away a spouse and marry another.
(4) The subjunctive clause is multifaceted.
(5) The exception clause is purposely given only in the gospel of Matthew.
(6) The exception clause addresses a cultural practice introduced specifically only by Matthew through the recording of the espousal and marriage of Joseph and Mary.
    a. This practice included two kinds of husbands and two kinds of wives: espoused (engaged) and married.
    b. Espousals were man-made and man-controlled. The Jews instituted a legal divorce for fornication during the espousal (engagement period).
(7) Marriage was and is God-created and controlled. Man cannot put away a married wife in a way that such an

action dissolves WHAT it is that God has joined. Only death dissolves WHAT it is that God has joined together.

In Matthew, the subjunctive clauses, especially that of Matthew 19:9, help to reinforce the espousal practice of the Jews of Jesus' day. As stated before, the espousal is succinctly introduced in the first chapter of Matthew's gospel through the example of Joseph who could have put Mary away from their espousal contract if she had committed fornication. However, that same clause no longer applied once Mary became a married wife instead of an espoused one.

Why did Jesus include teachings that the Pharisees, who professed to be devout religious Jews, already knew about divorce and "re-marriage"? Read the entire passage in Matthew 19 from the beginning of the chapter up to and including verse nine. In this short passage, the Pharisees tried, not once but twice to maneuver Jesus into agreeing to a loophole for putting away a wife. The Pharisees weren't really interested in being reminded about the immutable "law of marriage." They, like many today, refused to accept the teaching given so clearly in Genesis 2:21-24 to which Jesus referred. <u>Hearing the Word and accepting It are two very different things</u>. Many people hear the Word, but they do not act upon It. They have a dead faith as James explains:

*Thou believest that there is one God; thou doest well: the devils also believe, and tremble. But wilt thou know, O vain man, that faith without works is dead?* James 2:19-20

As mentioned previously, verse 3 of Matthew 19 shows the character of the Jews. They came, *tempting* Jesus. They were not asking what marriage was but were trying to *tempt* Jesus into agreeing with putting away a wife. **Finding a loophole was their agenda**. Many today, likewise, come to Jesus looking in the Bible with the same wrong motive. The Pharisees tried, not once but twice, to achieve their purpose. Thus, we have two different answers by Jesus. Study carefully the wording in each of the responses of Jesus, including His words: *And I say unto you.*

> First attempt:
> **Pharisees**: *The Pharisees also came unto him, tempting him, and saying unto him, Is it lawful for a man **to put away** his wife for every cause?* Matthew 19:3
> **Jesus' response**: *And he answered and said unto them, Have ye not read, that he which made them at the beginning made them male and female, And said, For this cause shall a man leave father and mother, and shall cleave to his wife: and they twain shall be one flesh? Wherefore they are no more twain, but one flesh. What therefore God hath joined together, **let not man put asunder**.* Matthew 19:4-6 Jesus totally avoided any reference to any cause for divorce even though that WAS their question. He clearly said to not divorce—not to put asunder.
> Second attempt:
> **Pharisees**: *They say unto him, Why did Moses then command to give a writing of divorcement, and **to put her away**?* Matthew 19:7
> **Jesus' response**: *He saith unto them, Moses because of the hardness of your hearts suffered you to put away your wives: but from the beginning it was not so. **And I say unto you**, Whosoever shall put away his wife, except it be for fornication, and shall marry another, committeth adultery: and whoso marrieth her which is put away doth commit adultery.* Matthew 19:8-9

What did the Pharisees do to try to *tempt* Jesus into giving a loophole to put away a wife? When they didn't get the answer they wanted from Jesus in their first question, they asked a second time, but they slyly couched the **same issue** in different circumstances. In the second question, they tried to incriminate Jesus through what Moses allowed. They implied "the man YOU chose" commanded: *Why did Moses command to give a writing of divorcement, and to put her away?* Jesus replied that Moses did not command but suffered [allowed] this to happen. In His answer, Jesus included the reason for Moses' allowing what he did: *because of the hardness of **your** hearts.* Matthew 19:7-8

Notice how Jesus prefaced Matthew 19:9: *And I say unto you*. He had already clearly told them what the "law of marriage" is, but that didn't satisfy their sinful flesh. He replied through what is recorded in verse nine to perhaps ironically give them a "cause" for a divorce, but this "cause" was for a <u>non-covenant dissolution</u>: *except it be for fornication*. If Jesus had answered just for a covenant-marriage, they could have said, "but we were talking about an espousal writing of divorcement—that's the kind of *wife* about which we were asking." Conversely, if Jesus would have only spoken about an espousal, then they could have gone away saying that He allowed the putting away of a covenant-marriage. Jesus followed the subjunctive exception clause (*except it be for fornication*) with what would apply to those who put away a married (covenant) spouse and subsequently "re-marry" someone else.

It's typical for sinful man to keep looking for the answer he wants instead of accepting what should be obvious: Truth. Review these two questions again.

*The Pharisees also came unto him, tempting him, and saying unto him, Is it lawful for a **man to put away his wife** for every cause?* Matthew 19:3

## A Grammatical Idiosyncrasy Is Embedded In Matthew 19:9.

*They say unto him, Why did Moses then command to give a writing of divorcement, and **to put her away**?* Matthew 19:7

Jesus totally answered their first question by referring these wicked men to Genesis 2:21-24. If two people are made one flesh and can never be two again then it should be obvious that there's no way to put the two apart. There was no more Jesus could say about the indissolubility of a one-flesh marriage. Because the Pharisees were intent on finding a way to divorce a wife, Jesus, in response to their second *tempting*, continued by contrasting two kinds of divorce: that from a non-covenant "wife" and that from a covenant "wife." They *could* put apart both kinds of wives (as allowed by Moses) because of their hardened hearts, BUT if they did so with a one-flesh wife—**and** married someone else, they would put themselves into a continual state of adultery: committ**eth** adultery. Once anyone "takes" a wife; that is, once he is made one flesh by God, there is no exception.

Furthermore, whatever the LORD's reason for the exception clauses, man "tempts" Jesus by quoting his altered version, and he then uses this counterfeit version as an excuse to put away what it is that God has joined together. Rarely does anyone quote the entire verse of Matthew 19:9. It does not have just five words, 24 letters *(except it be for fornication)*. It has 33 words consisting of 155 letters. I challenge you to ask anyone who brings to you a question about the exception clause to ask them to quote the entire verse. Most cannot. What about you? Can you quote all of Matthew 19:9, or do you only know what the exception clause says?

# 14

# When...
# Is A Marriage Consummated?

You may be ready for a break from the heavy "work" session from Chapter 13. However, the LORD does tell us to study as <u>work</u>men. And there are many other important doctrinal issues to consider:

*Study to shew thyself approved unto God, a workman that needeth not to be ashamed, rightly dividing the word of truth.* 2 Timothy 2:15

How would you answer the question as it is titled for this chapter: *When is a marriage consummated?* What Scriptures would you quote to prove or disprove what you feel you have learned regarding your answer? Please write your answer on the next page or on another sheet of paper so you can refer to it when you complete the study of this chapter.

## When ... Is A Marriage Consummated?

> When is a marriage consummated? Please write your answer here:

You've probably heard someone say their marriage wasn't consummated, or they consummated their marriage. The attachment of *consummation* to *marriage* comes with many faces. For example, many years ago I met a nun whose position in a large Catholic Church was to be in charge of annulments. (I'm not of the Catholic faith and wasn't then but was pulled into this arena because of a personal issue with which I was dealing.) The nun shared with me that they "offer" hundreds of annulments every year. That was a shock to this naive neophyte in the arena of fighting for one-flesh marriages—as I sat there mentally multiplying by hundreds the untold numbers of churches who offer this "service."

As best I can recall, what I was told was that the "church" determined whether a marriage was valid based on whether the marriage had truly been consummated. Consummated, in this context, meant that there had been sexual intimacy. Yet, I also learned that people who had been married for many years, and even those with several children, were also granted annulments. I, of course, had difficulty trying to figure out how the latter was possible; that is, how one bears children without having sexual intimacy. I'm sure there must be more to all this, but that's about the depth of my remembrance of this encounter.

I have also heard this term, *consummate*, used by many Protestant believers and even those who are highly educated theologically and who have written extensively on marriage and divorce. One such paper which was forwarded to me included some of the following statements: "…until there is actual intercourse, the two have not become one flesh, therefore there cannot be adultery following such a 'divorce.'" The

> A little leaven permeates the entire loaf.

author of this quote is very strong on teaching against the sin of adultery; however he also alludes to legitimate marriages and illegitimate marriages as including marriages that have been and have not been "consummated sexually."

The unseen full effect of what happens with these statements about the

consummation of a marriage is that the "Spaceship Consummate" fires from the launch pad a few degrees off course. The entire flight subsequently becomes out of control and major corrections have to be made to <u>try</u> to redirect it so that it will reach the correct destination.

Let's follow through what happens because of a couple of degrees differential in the trajectory of the spacecraft and how it can "… skip off the atmosphere and out into space forever." The first major shortcoming is starting off not understanding or totally accepting Who it is that creates marriage.

There have been expressions repeated many times throughout this book about the creation of marriage: "What therefore <u>God</u> hath joined together," "made one flesh by <u>God</u>," "joined by <u>God</u>." What do these expressions clearly say about the joining of a man and a woman?

It's God and God alone Who does the *joining* of the two—not man, not clergy, not the justice of the peace, not the church. There is no Scripture that says man has anything to do with the joining—other than of course agreeing to become a part of the covenant of marriage. Being a part of and creating are two very different functions. Pastors, priests, rabbis, justices of the peace, etc. do not join the two; they officiate at the ceremony where God does the joining. God is the Potter; we are the clay.

> Being a part of and creating are two very different functions.

The LORD doesn't force anyone to be joined to another person through His covenant of marriage. However, when a man and a woman (neither of whom has a living one-flesh spouse) agree to be married, God joins the two supernaturally, usually in a formal ceremony, officiated by a member of the clergy. That joining is until one of the spouses leaves this earth through physical death.

Let's review what should be, in essence, the understanding of the joining of a man and woman by reviewing vows taken in a typical marriage ceremony. Below are the vows for the woman. This is to be understood in a <u>generic</u> sense; that is, the vows apply equally to the husband who repeats the same words with the appropriate changes.

> I, Judith, take thee, Doug, to be my wedded husband, to have and to hold, from this day forward, for better, for worse, for richer, for poorer, in sickness and in health, to love and cherish, **till death us do part**, <u>according to God's holy ordinance</u>.

The underlined words of these vows need to be reviewed: *according to God's holy ordinance.* They may or may not be spoken, but that is what takes place. How do we know these vows are according to God's holy ordinance? It's because the Word of God teaches the following about marriage:

1. Marriage is until death with no exceptions: Romans 7:2-3; 1 Corinthians 7:39.
2. It is between a man and a woman: Genesis 2:21-24.
3. It is God who creates the covenant and sets the terms for it: Malachi 2:14; Mark 10:6-9.

God does not join, through His covenant of marriage, those relationships He condemns, including:

- Incestuous—those of kin (1 Corinthians 5:1).
- Same sex (Romans 1:27).
- Adulterous (Luke 16:18).
- Other miscellaneous aberrations (Leviticus 18).

Some clergy read the following at the end of a ceremony:

> O Eternal God, Creator and Preserver of all mankind, Giver of all spiritual grace, the Author of everlasting life; send Thy blessing upon this man and this woman, whom we bless in Thy Name; that they may surely perform and keep the covenant and vows now <u>made between them and Thee</u> ... (and then admonishes the newly-married couple) ... that you may so live together in this life that in the world to come you may have life everlasting. Amen.*

## When ... Is A Marriage Consummated?

*WITH THIS RING I THEE WED: The Marriage-Covenant and Vows; What do they mean? (Restoration of the Family, PO Box 621342, Oviedo, FL 32762; www.RestorationOfTheFamily.org)

When are the two made one flesh? Is it after they have given their vows and before they leave the marriage altar, or is it that evening after they have had sexual intimacy? They are made one flesh

> The two are one flesh before they leave the wedding altar.

before they leave the altar—after their vows were made. Their being made one flesh has nothing to do with the marital privilege of sexual intimacy. It has to do with WHAT God spiritually does <u>during</u> a marriage ceremony. If the man and woman had an accident on the way to their home and one of them were incapacitated and could not enjoy the pleasures of sex, they would still be married.

Sexual intimacy does absolutely nothing to make two people one flesh. That physical "act" is in no way permanent—it is a short momentary pleasure. If sex made the two people one flesh, then there would be no need for a wedding ceremony in which God joins the two making them one flesh. Millions of people who are fornicators, adulterers, sodomites, etc. would be made one flesh repeatedly by their sinful acts. No—marriage, just as with man's *help meet*, must not be lowered to mankind's molding of the clay. It is God who makes woman *an help meet* for man (Review Chapter 6.), and it is God who joins a man and a woman into one flesh.

When man starts believing that he does the supernatural (creates a one-flesh marriage) through a sexual act or "re-marriage," he has gotten his spaceship trajectory askew. He has tried to take control of a creation property of which only God has control. And what happens? Man takes "by violence" what he has no Scriptural right to touch:

*For the LORD, the God of Israel, saith that he hateth putting away: for one covereth violence with his garment, saith the LORD of hosts: therefore take heed to your spirit, that ye deal not treacherously.* Malachi 2:16 ... *but they shall not touch any holy thing, lest they die* ... Numbers 4:15 Man was instructed to not even touch the ark which held the covenant agreement terms: *And when they came to Nachon's threshingfloor, Uzzah put forth his hand to the ark of God, and took hold of it; for the oxen shook it. And the anger of the LORD was kindled against Uzzah; and God smote him there for his error; and there he died by the ark of God.* 2 Samuel 6:7

This kind of violence—disobedience—is played out in millions of lives and in countless churches. Because man, including many clergy, wrongly thinks that he has control of the covenant of marriage, he thinks he can join what God says cannot be joined (adulterous and sodomite "marriages").

Man further takes God's marriage-covenant "by force." He does this when he thinks he can dissolve or annul, through a man-made piece of paper (dissolution of marriage or church annulment), what God says cannot be dissolved—marriage—except through physical death.

What deceived man has done is to build something that is an anomaly—something that God does not recognize other than as being what it is—adulterated. Recall the definitions of *adulterated* from Chapter 4: to corrupt, debase, make impure by adding a foreign or inferior substance, often by replacing valuable ingredients with inferior ones; to contaminate or depreciate; to make impure or inferior by adding alien or less desirable materials; altered; adulterer, adulteress. God's covenants need no additional act by man to make them complete.

If man were following God, he would obey and not rebel. God looks at rebellion as a type of wickedness so evil that He compares it to witchcraft. *For rebellion is as the sin of witchcraft, and stubbornness is as iniquity and idolatry. Because thou hast rejected the word of the LORD, he hath also rejected thee ...* 1 Samuel 15:23 Even though the LORD was judging Saul for his rebellion, the reason for quoting this Scripture is to emphasize just how important God considers it for man to be obedient to His Word.

## One flesh is a supernatural, permanent, invisible joining <u>by God</u>. Sexual intimacy is not.

Sexual intimacy is not a permanent joining between a husband and a wife. It is a privilege sanctioned by God for those who are in a one-flesh marriage. Sexual intimacy is a <u>temporary</u> pleasure between a husband and wife. It has nothing to do with joining the two any more than does holding hands or kissing. Yet, it's not uncommon to read such remarks as:

- We became soul mates.
- The two become one-flesh in the sexual union.

## Neither God nor man joins our souls to another person.

We don't have soul mates. No one should want his soul to be joined to another person's soul. If that happened and one of the persons so joined was spiritually lost in sin and died in that state, then would not the saved person's soul also go into eternal damnation with the lost person? Whether a person is saved or lost, he will exist eternally—either in heaven or hell—not as a soul mate joined to another but as an individual. All souls belong to God, not to man: *Behold, all souls are mine; as the soul of the father, so also the soul of the son is mine: the soul that sinneth, it shall die.* Ezekiel 18:4 Keep in mind the important teaching on the generic application of words. *Son* and *soul* are used generically in Ezekiel 18:4. Each of these nouns includes both male and female. If you haven't done so lately, please read all of Ezekiel 18. It includes vital information for basic understandings about soul mates as well as other foundational Truths.

> It's vital to stop now and read Chapter 18 of Ezekiel.

Sadly, there are many who teach and many who wrongly believe that their soul can be joined to another person here on this earth. The term *soul mate*, however, cannot be found in God's Word. It can be found in secular writings and in many of man's teachings. It is man, not God, who teaches that we have soul mates. The term *soul mate* has been coined to wrongly express what many consider to be an intimate relationship between two people. God, however, has no such reference. He categorizes relationships between mankind as righteous or unrighteous. He permits us to develop and refine intimacy through His covenant of marriage. However, even within marriage the Word never teaches that our souls are joined. Every person is made up of three parts: body, soul, and spirit. Study the illustration on the next page.

When ... Is A Marriage Consummated?

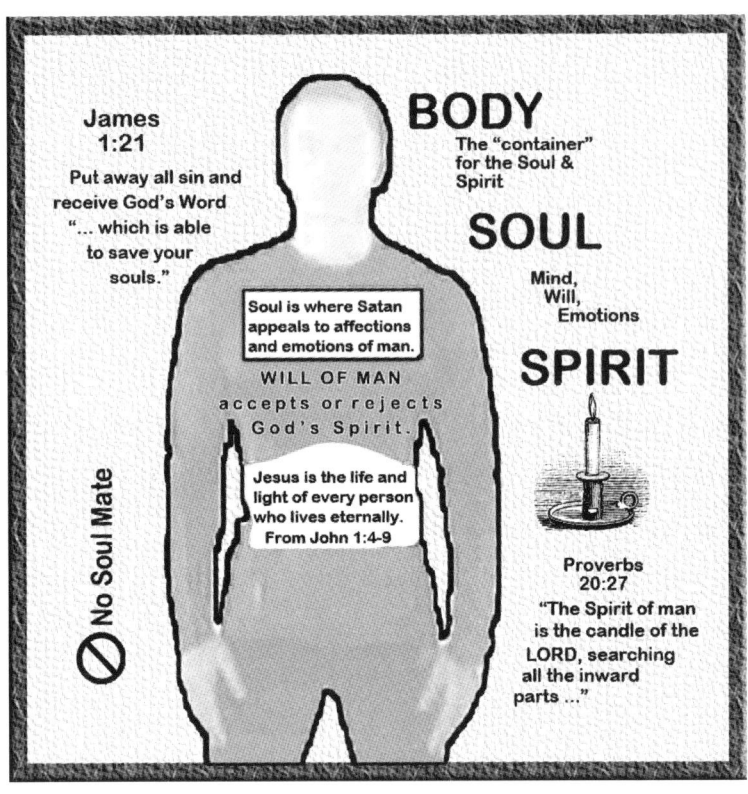

Wrong beliefs about soul mates could be partially fueled by misunderstandings from 1 Corinthians 6:15-17. These verses teach so much in a few words with <u>rhetorical questions</u>. These words, without some of the teachings shared thus far, could be taken out of context resulting in doctrine created that opposes other Biblical precepts The rhetorical questions are noted with numerical superscripts[1,2,3,4]:

*15 Know ye not that your bodies are the members of Christ?[1] shall I then take the members of Christ, and make them the members of an harlot?[2]\* **God forbid**. 16 What? know ye not that he which is <u>joined</u> to an harlot is one body? for two, saith he, shall be one flesh.[3] 17 But he that is joined unto the Lord is one spirit.[4]* 1 Corinthians 6:15-17 *This is a rhetorical question to which the answer should be obvious. A rationally thinking Christian would not normally purposely marry a harlot; thus, the answer which immediately follows: "*God forbid.*"

Jesus used rhetorical questions very effectively, as did Paul. Rhetorical questions are figures of speech in the form of questions which are asked solely to produce an effect or to make an assertion—not to elicit a reply. That's because the reply should be apparent. There are four rhetorical questions in 1 Corinthians 6:15-17. Verses 16 and 17 are tied together in that the fourth rhetorical statement is implied in the words of the third question: *What? Know ye not ...* Thus, the fourth question includes what would also be a rhetorical question but abbreviated by Paul:

| Rhetorical Questions ([1,2,3,4]) in 1 Corinthians 6:15-17 |
|---|
| 1. Know ye not that your bodies are the members of Christ? |
| 2. Shall I then take the members of Christ, and make them the members of an harlot? |
| 3. What? Know ye not that he which is joined to an harlot is one body? |
| 4. [What? Know ye not] he that is joined unto the Lord is one spirit. |
| Answers: 1. Yes   2. No   3. Yes   4. Yes |

A Christian should know that his body is a member of Christ. That being true, a Christian should also know that he is not to be joined in a marriage with an unsaved person. God, through Paul, is giving a clear warning to avoid what can lead to potential sin. What is the character of a harlot? She assuredly is not a godly person with whom a Christian should develop an intimate relationship. A harlot, who <u>in this context</u> could be either male or female, will likely pull the godly person into unrighteous challenges and decisions. Paul also says that those who are saved are one spirit with the Lord. This statement in verse 17 should not be combined with verse 16.

Paul teaches in 2 Corinthians 6:14 that we are not to be unequally yoked with unbelievers: *Be ye not unequally yoked together with unbelievers: for what fellowship hath righteousness with unrighteousness? and what communion hath light with darkness?* This passage has broad applications to many different situations, especially with those who are not saved. However, it, *in principle*, also applies to marriage.

The word *joined* in the third rhetorical question of 1 Corinthians 6:15-17 is a key verb that must be correctly interpreted. As a student of the Word, a believer knows this doesn't mean sexual sin because of the context of the entire passage. *Joined*, in the context of verse 16, represents God's marital covenantal act of making two one flesh.

How does a reader know that? Look at the first part of the rhetorical question: *What? know ye not that he which is joined to an harlot is one body?* What comes immediately after this question? The information given directly after the question connected by the word *for* provides the information for the correct application of the first occurrence of the word *joined*: *for two, saith he, shall be one flesh.* Where and in what context are these same or similar words, *shall be one flesh*, given in the Bible and referring to a marital joining? They can be found in Genesis 2:24, Matthew 19:5, Mark 10:8, and Ephesians 5:31.

As can be seen by almost the exact words surrounding *joined* in its first usage in 1 Corinthians 6:16, each and every other recording of the words *shall be one flesh* is undeniably referring to God's one-flesh joining—marriage. Study the table on the next page.

| *What? know ye not that he which is joined to an harlot is one body?* ***for two, saith he, shall be one flesh***. 1 Corinthians 6:16 ||
| --- | --- |
| *Therefore shall a man leave his father and his mother, and shall cleave unto his wife: and they **shall be one flesh***. Genesis 2:24 | Context is marriage. |
| *And said, For this cause shall a man leave father and mother, and shall cleave to his wife: and they twain **shall be one flesh**?* Matthew 19:5 | Context is marriage. |
| *And they twain **shall be one flesh**: so then they are no more twain, but one flesh.* Mark 10:8 | Context is marriage. |
| *For this cause shall a man leave his father and mother, and shall be joined unto his wife, and they two **shall be one flesh**.* Ephesians 5:31 | Context is marriage. |

So Paul, by using these <u>same</u> interlinking words, helps to contextually define the meaning of the first part. He does this first, from the warning to not marry an unsaved person; and second, from the viewpoint of the permanence of marriage. **If** we rebel and marry an unsaved person, we will be permanently joined to that person—until one of the spouses physically dies.

It's not our souls that God joins. We are made one **flesh**. God spiritually and invisibly joins our flesh via His supernatural joining. Our state of salvation does not affect the permanence of a one-flesh joining by God. Therefore, whether we marry a saved person or one who is not saved, that joining is *what* is permanent (assuming neither we, nor the one to whom we wish to be joined, has a living one-flesh spouse).

## *But* is a signpost to indicate a change in focus.

*[What? know ye not]* is an *understood* part of the last rhetorical statement: [What? know ye not] ***but*** *he that is joined to the Lord is one*

*Spirit*. Notice that the conjunction *but* has been used. *But* is that much-used word that gives direction, and it is a signpost which points to the contextual meaning of the second occurrence of *joined*.

*But* usually indicates a change in direction—something different from what went before, or often something opposing. The function of *but* is something like the hypothetical subjunctive signpost presented in Chapter 13 (*except it be*). The word *but* should alert the reader that what comes after the conjunction is different from what came before. There's an immediate change ahead. Paul is

> The word *but* is an important signpost that should alert readers there is an immediate change ahead.

making statements of facts that every believer should know: (1) A believer should not marry an unbeliever. (2) A person who is joined in this context to another is permanently made **one flesh** through marriage; **but** (3) those who are joined unto the LORD, through salvation, are not one flesh nor are they one soul. (4) They are **one in spirit** with the LORD.

## Through Joseph and Eli we learn that sexual sins are specifically named as sins against God.

*... Now the body is not for fornication, but for the Lord; and the Lord for the body.* 1 Corinthians 6:13 Both fornication and adultery are sins for which God did not make the body. Joseph and Eli made statements that reflect the seriousness of Paul's teaching in 1 Corinthians 6:

> *And it came to pass after these things, that his master's wife cast her eyes upon Joseph; and she said, Lie with me. But he refused ... because thou art his wife: how then can I do this great wickedness, and **sin against God**?* Genesis 39:7-9

*Now Eli was very old, and heard all that his sons did unto all Israel; and how they lay with the women that assembled at the door of the tabernacle of the congregation. And he said unto them, Why do ye such things? for I hear of your evil dealings by all this people. Nay, my sons; for it is no good report that I hear: ye make the LORD's people to transgress. If one man sin against another, the judge shall judge him: but if a man **sin against the LORD**, who shall intreat for him? Notwithstanding they hearkened not unto the voice of their father, because the LORD would slay them.* 1 Samuel 2:22-25

Paul, through his rhetorical question, assumes that a Christian will know that he should not marry a harlot; however, if that rebellious choice is made; that is, if a Christian decides to marry a lost person, that would be a valid marriage. A one-flesh joining is in no way dependent upon the state of salvation of two people. Both unsaved and saved people are joined until death they do part. God recognizes marriages between both saved and unsaved people. See below:

*And Cain knew his wife; and she conceived* ...Genesis 4:17
*... and God healed Abimelech, and his wife* ... Genesis 20:17
*... He took to wife Jezebel the daughter of Ethbaal* ...1 Kings 16:31
*... his* [Pilate's] *wife sent unto him saying* ... Matthew 27:19
*For Herod himself had sent forth and laid hold upon John, and bound him in prison for Herodias' sake, his brother Philip's wife: for he had married her.* Mark 6:17
*For what knowest thou, O wife, whether thou shalt save thy husband?* ... 1 Corinthians 7:16

## Spaceship consummation slides off into outer space.

It should be clear that marriage, salvation, and sexual intimacy must be carefully defined. Covenant-marriages are valid between those who are saved and those who are lost; but, it is God, not man or man's intimacy, that makes the two one flesh. God did not make the "body" for sexual sin—fornication or adultery (nor sodomy, etc.). The two become one flesh, not soul mates when God joins a man and woman.

Souls are not joined during the act of intimacy and neither does the act of intimacy consummate a marriage. **Man not only convolutes the privilege of marital sexual intimacy, but he uplifts sexual sin to a creative act when he says intimacy makes people soul mates.**

The International Children's Bible is one of many publications which falsely teaches that sexual intimacy affects the validity of God's supernatural joining of a man and woman.

| Unscriptural teachings from International Children's Bible ||
|---|---|
| *But I tell you that anyone who divorces his wife is causing his wife to be guilty of adultery. The only reason for a man to divorce his wife is if she has <u>sexual relations</u> with another man. And anyone who marries that divorced woman is guilty of adultery.* Matthew 5:32 | *I tell you that anyone who divorces his wife and marries another woman is guilty of adultery. The only reason for a man to divorce and marry again is if his first wife <u>has sexual relations</u> with another man.* Matthew 19:9 |

The above unscriptural writing from this children's Bible expresses the same kinds of unscriptural beliefs that have led man to declare millions of God's one-flesh joinings as invalid marriages.

This has been done under the guise of religion as well as through ungodly man-made laws. Both religious and societal organizations have taken upon themselves an act only possible by God; that is, the dissolution or ending of a one-flesh marriage. Man THINKS he is the controller of a covenant-marriage as does even the church in many instances. The church does this in two ways:
- Overt acts: annulment.
- Covert acts: recognizing man's dissolution (divorce) as valid.

Chapter 14

## Man commits overt acts against God's marriage-covenant.

What is meant by overt acts is that a religious organization usurps God's authority by declaring a one-flesh marriage invalid—doing so according to man-made "church law." The Roman Catholic Church is the main organization that has declared untold numbers of marriages invalid through their annulments—more than 60,000 every year.

> *According to Roman Catholic Church law, the grounds for an annulment can be what the church considers an impediment to the union, including non-consummation of the marriage or bigamy, or where full and free consent for the marriage was not given, including cases of forced unions or emotional or mental incapacity.
> *(http://www.dailymail.co.uk/news/article-46361)

Here's how annulments can play out according to the above referenced news article titled, "Vatican overturns Kennedy wife's 10-year annulment battle." This battle was waged by Sheila Kennedy, wife of Joe Kennedy after he arranged with the Roman Catholic Church to annul their 12-year marriage declaring that theirs had never been a true marriage. In so doing, this process also declared that the children were the offspring of a marriage that had never existed. The Kennedys had two sons, and both Sheila and Joe had been willing partners to the marriage. Mrs. Kennedy remarked that the annulment had totally overlooked the fact that she felt they had a very strong marriage in the beginning and that they had two wonderful children. It shouldn't take much deep thought to realize that for there to have been two children born from this one-flesh joining, there had to have been sexual intimacy. Again, sexual intimacy is a privilege of marriage. It doesn't create a marriage. God does that.

The validation of the Kennedy's marriage—and every other one-flesh marriage—is only through the supernatural "Hand" of God. Man can add nothing to God's act of making the two one flesh. This example should make it apparent how convoluted man's usurping of God's authority over the creation and dissolution of marriage has become.

## Man commits covert acts against God's marriage-covenant.

Now let's look at the other side of the coin of marital usurpation of God's marriage-covenant by man's covert acts against God. This is by either partaking in or recognizing, as valid, a legal civil dissolution. This time the "scapegoat" becomes the government rather than the "church." "Scapegoat" is used because those not in the Catholic church point to their government's dissolution of marriage as their "proof" (scapegoat) that their marriage is no longer valid.

However, every person who buys into these deceptive practices will be held accountable by God. Because the government issues a piece of paper saying a one-flesh marriage has been dissolved, church leadership and lay people alike deem there has been a type of annulment—that the marriage no longer exists. They also, in essence, may not realize they are saying that the children belong to no one. In other words, how do you say the husband and wife are no longer part of the relationship (joining), but the children born of the joining are?

Ironically, both one-flesh spouses are called *ex-spouses* after a man-made dissolution. Yet, the children birthed from the marriage are not called *ex-children*. Neither of these coined terms (*ex-spouses* and *ex-children*) is true. The husband and wife are still husband and wife and the children are still children of this marriage.

The "church" (which should know better) and the world go along with this charade. It's quite easy for a divorced person to find a pastor, a rabbi; or, under the right circumstances of annulment, a priest to perform a ceremony between a divorced person and a third party to this relationship.

Relatives, friends, and entire church bodies come on board to support the "re-marriage" instead of sounding the alarm that God considers this relationship to be an on-going state of adultery. Of course, in man's eyes, there are always justified reasons for the "separation" and his man-made "dissolution."

*When thou sawest a thief, then thou consentedst with him, and hast been partaker with adulterers. Thou givest thy mouth to evil, and thy tongue frameth deceit.* Psalm 50:18-19

*For the LORD, the God of Israel, saith that he hateth putting away: for one covereth violence with his garment, saith the LORD of hosts: therefore take heed to your spirit, that ye deal not treacherously. Ye have wearied the LORD with your words. Yet ye say, Wherein have we wearied him? When ye say, Every one that doeth evil is good in the sight of the LORD, and he delighteth in them; or, Where is the God of judgment?* Malachi 2:16-17

There is no guidance for man-made dissolutions <u>for a one-flesh marriage</u> because there is no such thing possible by the hand of man. It's only death that brings about the dissolution of a covenant-marriage. There is Scriptural guidance for <u>separation</u>—not dissolution:

*And unto the married I command, yet not I, but the Lord, Let not the wife depart from her husband: But and if she depart, <u>let her remain unmarried</u>, or be reconciled to her husband: and let not the husband put away his wife.* 1 Corinthians 7:10-11

## Marriage is much more than sexual intimacy.

Marriage, like the birth of a baby is a miraculous creation by God. Because the husband and wife appear to look the same when they leave the wedding altar as they did before the ceremony, most people do not understand that there has been some kind of supernatural, invisible joining. Even though the fulfillment of a marriage relationship assumes the spouses will and should regularly enjoy sexual intimacy, marriage is much more than sexual pleasure. It is, of course, God's provision to replenish the earth. Additionally, both spouses are also to grow spiritually through the "sandpaper" conflicts that come from living daily with their spouse.

*So God created man in his own image, in the image of God created he him; male and female created he them. And God blessed them, and God said unto them, Be fruitful, and multiply, and replenish the earth, and subdue it: and have dominion over the fish of the sea, and over the fowl of the air, and over every living thing that moveth upon the earth.* Genesis 1:27-28

*And did not he make one? Yet had he the residue of the spirit. And wherefore one? That he might seek a godly seed.* [The warning is given again to not touch—not to try to alter or make an aberration of what God has created.] *Therefore take heed to your spirit, and let none deal treacherously against the wife of his youth.* Malachi 2:15

*Defraud ye not one the other, except it be with consent for a time, that ye may give yourselves to fasting and prayer; and come together again, that Satan tempt you not for your incontinency.* 1 Corinthians 7:5

Marriage is also meant to glorify God and to reflect His love as exemplified through the relationship of Christ and the church. In fact, marriage is the only relationship which Christ uses as an analogy of His relationship to His church:

> *Husbands, love your wives, even as Christ also loved the church, and gave himself for it; That he might sanctify and cleanse it with the washing of water by the word, That he might present it to himself a glorious church, not having spot, or wrinkle ... but that it should be holy and without blemish ... For this cause shall a man leave his father and mother, and shall be joined unto his wife ... This is a great mystery: but I speak concerning Christ and the church. Nevertheless let every one of you in particular so love his wife even as himself; and the wife see that she reverence her husband.* Ephesians 5:25-33

A covenant-marriage relationship is also meant to help perfect both the husband and wife. There is no marriage that does not have its ups and downs. However, **differences between a husband and a wife are not meant to create division but to act as sandpaper to smooth their rough edges.** When the sandpaper seems too much to bear, the LORD should be the arbiter to bring the two back into a loving relationship through forgiveness and growth in spiritual wisdom and strength. Divorce indicates that one or both spouses have a broken relationship with the LORD. God is love, and His unconditional love, charity, never fails—**if** properly extended between a husband and a wife: *Charity never faileth ...* 1 Corinthians 13:8

> Divorce means one or both spouses have a broken relationship with the LORD.

The reader by now should see that it's not sexual intimacy, but God Who "joins" a husband and a wife. Sexual intimacy has nothing to do with how God makes the two people one flesh. It is God, and only God, Who supernaturally, invisibly joins the two. The man and woman agree to be joined, but they have nothing to do with the actual joining itself and neither do pastors, priests, rabbis, justices of the peace, or laypersons. The latter ONLY officiate over the ceremony. They don't "marry" a husband and wife. God does that.

Those who partake in marriage are held to God's terms, whether they choose to observe them or not. It's an open book test. Those who refuse or neglect to study God's inerrant Word and to live by It can only hold themselves responsible. They, however, will not be excused by God for any reason on the Day of Judgment. *Know ye not that the unrighteous shall not inherit the kingdom of God? Be not deceived* ... 1 Corinthians 6:9

If the husband and wife are for some reason never sexually intimate; or, if they at some time in their lives are unable to enjoy sexual intimacy, they are still permanently one flesh. This includes those who may reach a physical stage in life where intimacy is not possible or because of a man-induced separation or divorce wherein sexual intimacy between the two has ceased.

> Lack of intimacy is not a loophole.

Hopefully, it has been made clear from the Word of God that there is no such thing as "consummating" a marriage. That is a man-made, wrongful and insidious teaching against God's Word which has promoted a loophole for man to unscripturally declare God's joining of one man and one woman as if it didn't happen when it did. This is an abhorrent act against God. The LORD totally, perfectly, and by Himself, joins the two. Man does not complete what God has created.

Chapter 14

## Is it *shall be* or *shall become* one flesh?

The word *become* indicates that something is yet to be done—a future act. A husband and wife do not later *become* one flesh. The two are made one flesh by virtue of God's joining at the altar. Study the Scriptures below to discern their accuracy in keeping with the Biblical principles regarding the joining of a man and woman:

| When God joins, the joining is immediately completed as should be indicated by the expression "they shall be." |
| --- |
| *Therefore shall a man leave his father and his mother, and shall cleave unto his wife: and they **shall be** one flesh.* Genesis 2:24 |
| *And said, For this cause shall a man leave father and mother, and shall cleave to his wife: and they twain **shall be** one flesh?* Matthew 19:5 |
| *And they twain **shall be** one flesh: so then they are no more twain, but one flesh.* Mark 10:8 |
| *What? know ye not that he which is joined to an harlot is one body? for two, saith he, **shall be** one flesh.* 1 Corinthians 6:16 |
| *For this cause shall a man leave his father and mother, and shall be joined unto his wife, and they two **shall be** one flesh.* Ephesians 5:31 |

There is another very subtle change, a *jot* and *tittle*, made in the new versions of the Bible which makes room for man to think he has something to do to complete God's joining—through consummation. They translate the marital verses as shall or will *become* one flesh, instead of they shall *be one* flesh. This changes the meaning from an action completed now (at the altar) by God to potentially an action to be completed at some future time.

The table on the next page shows how several new versions mistranslate what should be interpreted *shall be* in Genesis 2:24, Matthew 19:5, and Mark 10:8. It's God Who took the rib, and it's God Who immediately joins the two, as recorded in Genesis 2:21-24. It is shall **be** THEN, not shall later *become*, one. Continue this study by also looking in your Bible(s), (or online) to verify not only what is shown below but also that this pattern is followed in other verses such as those for 1 Corinthians 6:16 and Ephesians 5:31. In each of these verses what should be *shall be one flesh* is translated *shall become one* flesh.

| | There's a difference between *shall be* and *shall become*. |
|---|---|
| Genesis 2:24 | ... *and they shall be one flesh.* KJB<br>... *and they shall become one flesh.* NKJV<br>... *and they shall become one flesh.* NGSB<br>... *and they will become one flesh.* NIV<br>... *and they shall become one flesh.* NASV<br>... *and they shall become one flesh.* ESV<br>... *and they shall become one flesh.* HCSB |
| Matthew 19:5 | ... *and they twain shall be one flesh?* KJB<br>... *and the two shall become one flesh'?* NKJV<br>... *and the two shall become one flesh'?* NGSB<br>... *and the two will become one flesh'?* NIV<br>... *and the two shall become one flesh'?* NASV<br>... *and the two shall become one flesh'?* ESV<br>... *and the two will become one flesh?* HCSB |
| Mark 10:8 | *And they twain shall be one flesh* ... KJB<br>*and the two shall become one flesh* ... NKJV<br>*and the two shall become one flesh* ... NGSB<br>*and the two will become one flesh.* NIV<br>*and the two shall become one flesh* ...NASV<br>*and the two shall become one flesh.* ESV<br>*and the two will become one flesh* ... HCSB |
| \*Key for above Bibles: KJB: King James Bible; NKJV: New King James Version; NGSB: New Geneva Study Bible; NIV: New International Version; NASV: New American Standard Version; ESV: English Standard Version; HCSB: Holman Christian Standard Bible. | |

In the New Testament, the same Greek word is used for describing God's joining as *shall be* in Matthew 19:5, Mark 10:8, 1 Corinthians 6:16, and Ephesians 5:31 That Greek word is Strong's 2071 *esomai* which should, contextually, be interpreted: *shall be*. A different underlying Greek word, ginomai, Strong's number 1096, is usually translated: *become*:

*Who against hope believed in hope, that he might <u>become</u> the father of many nations; according to that which was spoken, So shall thy seed be.* Romans 4:18

*And said, Verily I say unto you, Except ye be converted, and <u>become</u> as little children, ye shall not enter into the kingdom of heaven.* Matthew 18:3

*But take heed lest by any means this liberty of yours <u>become</u> a stumblingblock to them that are weak.* 1 Corinthians 8:9

*That the communication of thy faith may <u>become</u> effectual by the acknowledging of every good thing which is in you in Christ Jesus.* Philemon 1:6

So again, this is another one of those subtle changes (changing *shall be* to *shall become*) which goes unnoticed by many Christians. However, it doesn't go unnoticed by God any more than did Satan's adding of the word *not* to the warning God gave for Adam and Eve.

In summary, sexual intimacy whether it's within a one-flesh marriage or between those who engage in the sin of adultery, fornication, or sodomy doesn't have any power to make two people one flesh; neither are souls joined when individuals participate in sexual intimacy. Those partaking in sexual intimacy within their one-flesh marriage are enjoying a God-given privilege. Sexual intimacy outside a one-flesh marriage is sin against God and one's own body. Two people don't *become* one flesh by consummation. They *shall be one flesh* once the vows are spoken. There is no additional act of man which completes God's work of joining a man and a woman into a one-flesh union.

> **Conflict in marriage should act as sandpaper to smooth our rough edges. It's not meant to divide a husband and a wife.**

> **Sexual intimacy has no more power to join a man and a woman into one flesh than does kissing or holding hands.**

> **Sexual intimacy does not "consummate" a marriage. Beware of using the traditions of man to create Biblical doctrine. It is God who totally creates a marriage. Intimacy is a privilege of marriage; it does not consummate a marriage. It's <u>God's joining</u> that makes two one flesh.**

# 15

# Shall We "Re-turn" To Covenant?

In this and the next chapter, a few concepts will be tied together as we take a look at two similar Scriptures with some subtle but important differences: Matthew 5:32 and Matthew 19:9. Matthew 5:32 will be examined to provide additional information to expand the study and application of fornication and its interlinking with Matthew 19:9. The principle that will be emphasized in this and the next two chapters is how we can enhance our understanding of Scripture as more evidence is recognized and applied from Scriptures. God calls this process of learning adding *precept upon* precept.

*Whom shall he teach knowledge? and whom shall he make to understand doctrine? them that are weaned from the milk, and drawn from the breasts. For precept must be upon precept, precept upon precept; line upon line, line upon line; here a little, and there a little.* Isaiah 28:9-10

We have studied the varied word usages of fornication and adultery, looked at the rule of proximity, and seen how fornication and adultery can be used both specifically and generically. It was also shown in Chapter 14 that there is no Scriptural basis for believing that a marriage must be physically consummated to make it complete. God completes the act and state of marriage before the husband and wife leave the wedding altar.

However, even with all of these available Biblical interpretation study tools, people neglect to apply them when they study the Bible. It's not enough to come to the right conclusion when dealing with Scriptural matters **if** included there are teachings which violate God's Word to get to that right answer. This is because those **wrong teachings used in arriving at the right answer often lead people astray**.

For example, on the next four pages are portions from a multi-faceted teaching on marriage which has several Scriptural errors even though the author of these writings very strongly teaches that God's perspective on marriage is absolutely one man for one woman until death they do part. He, however, gets sidetracked. He doesn't properly factor in the inerrancy of Scripture, the Jewish cultural language, the fact that sexual intimacy has nothing to do with making two people one flesh, and other related contextual information which will be explained in this chapter. Thus, as a part of some excellent teachings on marriage, he gets off on the wrong foot when trying to teach the very important exception clause in Matthew 19:9.

Carefully read the following paragraph. Can you discern erroneous statements or conclusions that could be drawn from these statements?

> **Study these quotes from the above-referenced author:**
> Judaism permitted divorce before marriage as well as after it. This is an anomaly, because until there is actual intercourse, the two have not become one flesh. Consequently, anyone who divorces an engaged spouse will *not* be held responsible by God for the future relations that that 'divorced' person will experience through a 'second marriage'. This law only applies to cultures which require a bill of divorce to break a binding marriage contract before it is consummated.

Focus on the first sentence: "Judaism permitted divorce before marriage as well as after it." Whether or not Judaism permitted divorce before marriage as well as after it should not be used to prove or disprove God's Word. It's a dangerous practice to quote sources outside the Bible, IF, when these references are quoted, they justify sin or IF they bring confusion into Biblical doctrine. It doesn't matter what numerous church fathers or renowned authors say, or what this author says. Man's writings and works must be tested <u>by God's Word</u> and not the other way around. It's God's Word that must be the standard to which we look for our theological proofs.

> Man's writings must be tested by Scripture.

Unsaved Jews who lived during Biblical times and those today had and have many beliefs that do not line up with the teachings of Jesus Christ. One of the major ones is that they do not believe that Jesus is God. Regarding marriage and divorce, what Scripture teaches is that the Jews practiced a <u>custom</u> called *espousal* (engagement) as well as an espousal divorce during the espousal period if one of the two so engaged committed fornication. Neither of these acts violated the "law of marriage" as they took place before marriage.

However, it's also clear in the New Testament that God never approves of what man calls a *dissolution of marriage* after He has joined a husband and wife together into a one-flesh union. Those who permit or partake in adulterous "marriages" ("re-marriages") are not following the teachings of the Bible.

None of us can establish Scripture. We can teach and share Biblical principles, and we can teach how to study the Word of God. We can quote Scripture; however, we don't "establish" Scripture. God and

> Man can only confirm Scripture. He doesn't establish it.

God alone has done that: *For ever, O LORD, thy word is settled in heaven.* Psalm 119:89 It is Scripture that confirms Scripture. Every Christian should look within the Word of God for his theology and proofs:

*Which things also we speak, not in the words which man's wisdom teacheth, but which the Holy Ghost teacheth; comparing spiritual things with spiritual.* 1 Corinthians 2:13

*These were more noble than those in Thessalonica, in that they received the word with all readiness of mind, and searched the scriptures daily, whether those things were so.* Acts 17:11

The remainder of the paragraph quoted from the above-mentioned author is given below. Read carefully. Do you recognize why these are **unscriptural** statements?

> **Continued discussion from above-quoted author:**
> This is an anomaly, because <u>until there is actual intercourse, the two have not become one flesh</u>. Consequently, anyone who divorces an

> engaged spouse will *not* be held responsible by God for the future relations that that 'divorced' person will experience through a 'second marriage'. This law only applies to cultures which require a bill of divorce to break a binding marriage contract <u>before it is consummated</u>. [Do you see that there is <u>error</u> concerning sexual intimacy?]

As should be clear from the teachings in Chapter 14, sexual intimacy has nothing to do with making a man and woman one flesh. The reason <u>God</u> doesn't hold the engaged spouse responsible for future relations of that "divorced" person" is because they were never married—joined by God. The above-quoted statements look at Matthew 19:9 through eyes that are focused on the unscriptural consummation theory with flawed proofs drawn from sources outside the Word of God. Thus, truths within Scripture itself are missed. The author of the above-quoted statements veers off course from the very beginning and then creates more confusion to support his unscriptural beginning foundation. He does this by also making changes in the words of Scripture in both the Greek and English. For example, he changes the wording in Matthew 19:9 from saying "*except it be for fornication*" to "not divorcing for fornication." Read another quote from the above quoted author:

> Even if we assume the participle 'divorcing' is understood here, it would read: 'not *divorcing* for fornication,' which would rule out divorce for fornication.

Why is the above quoted statement unbiblical? Consider the errors in his last statement. If the exception clause said "not divorcing for fornication," then Joseph could not have divorced Mary for what hypothetically seemed to be the sin of fornication. Additionally, as was shown in Chapter 11, fornication has some other meanings. Some of those other uses of fornication will be taught in Chapter 16, especially as they apply to the exception clauses.

## The word *fornication* plays a major part.

As was shown in Chapter 11, most new version authors change the word *fornication* (with no underlying Greek contextual evidence to do so) to a word that means unfaithfulness during a one-flesh marriage. They do this by inserting *martial unfaithfulness*, *sexual immorality,* or *immorality* for their translation of *porneia* in the exception clauses. They additionally remove the hypothetical subjunctive *except it be for* in the Matthew 19:9 exception clause. Hopefully by now, it's clear why these changes are not contextually correct.

Recall that Joseph was a just man, but he was "minded to put away" (divorce) his wife (Mary) to whom he was espoused or engaged because he initially thought she was a fornicator. If that were so, then he could have later married another wife and doing so would not have put him into a state of adultery—committ**eth** adultery. This is because Joseph and Mary had not been made one flesh by God during their espousal contract. This is true with all engagements, whether they be those of the Jewish culture or any other. Engagements are merely man-made agreements, some of which take the formality of a legal contract. To reinforce and build on the ways fornication and adultery and the two kinds of husbands and wives are used, study the table on the next page. Notice the similarities and differences between the two exception clauses. As you study these two parallel Scriptures, keep in mind context and other principles already discussed. The Scriptures immediately preceding the two exception clauses are also given.

| **Matthew 19:9 and 5:32 have similarities and some important but subtle differences. Matthew 5:31 and 19:8 are given to provide additional contextual information for the reader.** ||
|---|---|
| *It hath been said, Whosoever shall put away his wife, let him give her a writing of divorcement.* Matthew 5:31 | *He saith unto them, Moses because of the hardness of your hearts suffered you to put away your wives: but from the beginning it was not so.* Matthew 19:8 |
| *But I say unto you, That whosoever shall put away his wife, saving for the cause of fornication, causeth her to commit adultery: and whosoever shall marry her that is divorced committeth adultery.* Matthew 5:32 | *And I say unto you, Whosoever shall put away his wife, except it be for fornication, and shall marry another, committeth adultery: and whoso marrieth her which is put away doth commit adultery.* Matthew 19:9 |

Two reasons that the exception for fornication is mentioned in Matthew, especially Matthew 19:9, *could be* that (1) Jesus was speaking to the Pharisees who also recognized espousals, and their purpose in coming to Jesus was to *tempt* Him; (2) Matthew's gospel, **unlike all the other gospels**, specifically gives information about Joseph and Mary's espousal and Joseph's original intent to "put away" Mary. Even though both clauses are exceptions for fornication, there are important differences within the exception clauses as well as in the phrases that immediately follow each. Study these two clauses below. The first is from Matthew 5:32; the second, from Matthew 19:9.

*saving for the cause of fornication,* **causeth her to commit adultery**

**except** *it be for fornication, and shall marry another, committeth adultery*

## **Violating God's warning, *causeth her to commit adultery*, can create high costs and dangerous ripple effects in the lives of many innocent people.**

Focus first on the bolded phrase from Matthew 5:32, *causeth her to commit adultery*. At face value, it might seem to indicate that any time someone divorces, this sin of putting away a one-flesh spouse (*whosoever shall put away his wife*) would **cause** the other spouse to commit adultery. Even though that often happens, we know that is not always true. So is God's Word wrong? No, God's Word is never erroneous. The way we interpret and apply it often is. This is because Scriptures are often applied out of context.

The phrase *causeth her to commit adultery* is a strong **warning** to anyone who violates God's holy institution of marriage, either covertly or overtly. No one should put apart what God has joined together (Matthew 19:4 and Mark 10:9). In fact, doing so is impossible, in God's eyes. Violating God's Word by divorcing a covenant-spouse, opens each spouse and others up to a number of possible sinful alternatives and creates a huge domino effect.

First of all, both spouses may believe they are free of God's "joining." As a result of that unbiblical belief, one or both either starts dating or already was dating before the civil divorce or church annulment took place. Then the flesh takes further liberties and one or both spouses justify having a pastor, priest, etc. "re-marry" them to someone else. All involved become adulterers or adulteresses, and many others partake in approving what God hates.

Children of divorce are wrestled back and forth between two or more households and often are expected to "adjust" between newly created family members. Friends and relatives become divided—often enemies—and future generations model the aberrations that are created out of this rebellion—not withstanding the emotional damage inflicted, and the poverty and crime incubated.

However, I doubt that few, if any reading this text, as well as this author, have not at one time or another, taken part (partaken) in some way with adulterers. That's because there are those in our lives we so much love or esteem highly that we don't want to offend. Christians, however, <u>out of love</u>, are also to warn those who are living in sinful lifestyles what the Word teaches. That's what it means as written in the 18th chapter of Ezekiel. We are all "watchmen on the wall." That is, we are to warn others, or their blood will be on our hands. There's another related warning in Psalm 50:18, in which the LORD specifically pairs thieves and adulterers. Here's what He says:

*When thou sawest a **thief**, then thou consentedst with him, and hast been <u>partaker</u> with **adulterers**.* Psalm 50:18

God not only chastises those who sin but those of us who do not warn others of sin, especially when we see them committing sin and when we specifically take part (partake) with adulterers. When He says that when we see a thief we consent with him, God is saying we approve of what the thief is doing. How do we know a person is a thief? It's likely that we have seen him stealing something or know he has stolen in the past but has not repented. There must be some outward sign to tell us that a person is a thief. Thus we consent of his acts. That could be a pretty heavy weight to bear for most of us—to not consent with those who steal or have stolen.

The same is true with our consenting with adulterers, except that God adds the fact that we also *partake* with adulterers. You may or may not be familiar with the word *partake*. It means doing what others have done or by, in some way, encouraging them to continue in their sin. The sin in which He is warning us not to partake in Psalm 50:18 is adultery, a sin that God hates: *For the LORD, the God of Israel, saith that he hateth putting away ...* Malachi 2:16 God, of course, hates all sin, but here He is addressing the specific sin of adultery and is warning us against partaking in it.

*Partaker(s)* is used 31 times in the Bible, usually as a warning and with negative inferences. It may be a real eye-opener if you haven't studied the way *partake* is used. Examine the Scriptures below to learn from their contexts the depth of the meaning of *partake*. Psalm 50:18 is repeated as a point of reference.

*When thou sawest a **thief**, then thou consentedst with him, and hast been <u>partaker</u> with **adulterers**.* Psalm 50:18

*Ye **cannot** drink the cup of the Lord, and the cup of devils: ye cannot be <u>partakers</u> of the Lord's table, and of the table of devils.* 1 Corinthians 10:21

*Lay hands suddenly on no man, **neither be** <u>partaker</u> of other men's sins: keep thyself pure.* 1 Timothy 5:22

*If there come any unto you, and bring not this doctrine, receive him **not** into your house, neither bid him God speed: For he that biddeth him God speed is <u>partaker</u> of his evil deeds.* 2 John 1:10-11

*And I heard another voice from heaven, saying, Come out of her, my people, that ye be **not** <u>partakers</u> of her sins, and that ye receive not of her plagues.* Revelation 18:5

## Are the "exceptions" hypothetical (might happen), bound to (will) happen, or permissive?

An important part of what is warned, but overlooked in Matthew 5:32, is that absent the divorce, the person who is put away likely may not have committed adultery—had the divorce not happened. However, he who initiates the divorce has potentially become a catalyst to another person going astray. That's a serious sin in and of itself. The weight that is put upon the shoulders of the person who puts away a one-flesh spouse is related to what is said in Matthew 18:6-7:

*But whoso shall offend one of these little ones which believe in me, it were better for him that a millstone were hanged about his neck, and that he were drowned in the depth of the sea. Woe unto the world because of offences! for it must needs be that offences come; but woe to that man by whom the offence cometh!* Matthew 18:6-7

The heart of God's admonition in Matthew 5:32 is that when a person puts away a wife, he MAY (It's a possibility.) *cause* her to commit adultery. But is that something that <u>must</u> happen (bound to) or <u>always</u> happens? No, absolutely not. There are thousands of "put-away" spouses who choose not to sin against their marriage-covenant. Those persons are "Standards" for righteousness. They, instead, learn and exhibit a sacrificial love that few understand. They ("Standards") stand in the gap for their wayward spouses; that is, they pray for their spouses and try to woo them back home:

> There are thousands of "put-away" spouses who do not sin against their covenant spouse by dating or marrying another. They remain faithful to their vows.

*When the enemy shall come in like a flood, the Spirit of the LORD shall lift up a <u>standard</u> against him.* Isaiah 59:19

However, if the "innocent" person who is put away also chooses to date or to marry another person, she becomes an adulteress; that is, she would be fully accountable for this sin which can likewise keep her from inheriting the Kingdom of God. She would be sinning against their marriage-covenant like her "catalyst" husband who *caused* her to go astray. However, the marriage-covenant itself cannot be defiled by either spouse. It is pure and holy. It's those who sin against the marriage bed who will be judged by God:

*Marriage is honourable in all, and the bed undefiled: but whoremongers and adulterers God will judge.* Hebrews 13:4

## There's a difference between something being permissive and something being causative.

The same *principle* that holds true for Matthew 5:32, "causeth her to commit adultery," also applies to the correct interpretation of Deuteronomy 24:2: *And when she is departed out of his house, she <u>may</u>* [she might] *go and be another man's wife.*

What happens is that many fall into the trap of misinterpreting the word *may* in Deuteronomy 24:2 as God giving the wife permission to marry another spouse. This is the same erroneous principle of misinterpreting the word *causeth* in Matthew 5:32. Doing so would imply that God were forcing the put-away (divorced) person to sin. This would mean that God would be partaking in the sin of adultery. That's something He cannot do. God cannot sin.

Many readers make the former wrong assumptions when they interpret the verbs *may* and *causeth* in their more popular permissive and causative applications. However, the word *may* is also used to show contingency, possibility, or opportunity; that is, it MIGHT happen. For example, someone could say, "It may rain today." This is not giving permission but stating a possibility. The overriding principle must be the Word of God and knowing that the LORD could not be giving a covenant-wife permission to marry another husband if her one-flesh husband is living but has deserted. Likewise Jesus was not agreeing with the Pharisees in Matthew 19:7 when they implied that He commanded Moses to give a writing of divorcement. Knowing God doesn't force or encourage people to sin is evidence that there must be another interpretation of the words *may* and *causeth* in the above-mentioned Scriptures. The overriding factor, even above and beyond the meanings of these words is that God cannot conflict with His Word—the Scriptures. That would be a form of lying. We serve a God ... *that cannot lie.* Titus 1:2

In Deuteronomy 24:2, the word *may* is stating what might happen if the husband puts her away. It means there is a possibility that she will (she might) "re-marry" another husband. As noted above, there are many spouses who are put away—divorced—and never commit adultery. They, instead, keep their love alive for their wayward spouses and pray and intercede for them to return to the marriage relationship.

> The word *may* can be permissive or causative depending on its context.

Compare Deuteronomy 24:2 and Matthew 5:32 by studying them below. Interpret *may* and *causeth* with the synonym *might*:

| *May* <u>can</u> indicate a possibility, or it <u>can</u> be permissive. Causeth <u>can</u> mean *might cause*. | |
|---|---|
| And when she is departed out of his house, she *may* [might] go and be another man's wife. Deuteronomy 24:2 | ... *whosoever shall put away his wife, saving for the cause of fornication, causeth* [might cause] *her to commit adultery* ... Matthew 5:32 |

## God's message is to <u>re</u>-turn to covenant.

Some readers may still have their doubts thinking that it is God who was giving permission for the divorced spouse to marry another in Deuteronomy 24:2. Such an interpretation violates the "law of marriage" God established in Genesis 2:21-24. Others may argue that interpreting *causeth* as *might cause* is wrongly adding to the Word of God. However, what is really driving such interpretations is following the guideline, "interpreting Scripture with Scripture" and focusing on context but this time focusing on the overall context of God's sinless character. God cannot violate His own laws and precepts.

There are several interlinking Scriptures which provide additional supporting information. For example, as mentioned before, Jesus in Matthew 19:8, stated that <u>Moses</u> *allowed*—not commanded—the writing of divorcement because of the hardness of man's heart. However, also notice that there was no mention by Jesus of permission for a "re-marriage." Instead, He clearly stated that any "re-marriage" (that didn't fall under the exception for fornication) was adultery. Equally as important in the correct interpretation of

Deuteronomy 24:4 is information given in Jeremiah 3:1. This is an example where important contextually related interlinking information is given in a different book of the Bible:

| Jeremiah 3:1 clarifies the contextual interpretation of Deuteronomy 24:4. ||
|---|---|
| *Her former husband, which sent her away, may not take her again to be his wife, after that she is defiled; for that is abomination before the LORD: and thou shalt not cause the land to sin, which the LORD thy God giveth thee for an inheritance.* Deuteronomy 24:4 | *They say, If a man put away his wife, and she go from him, and become another man's, shall he return unto her again? shall not that land be greatly polluted? but thou hast played the harlot with many lovers; yet return again to me, saith the LORD.* Jeremiah 3:1 |

This should be an exciting time for readers who haven't previously connected interlinking precepts in Deuteronomy 24:4, Matthew 19:8, and Jeremiah 3:1. That will become evident with more study.

## Interpretation of Scripture must be based not on isolated facts but on the entire Word of God.

Before delving into the specifics of Jeremiah 3:1, the reader is reminded that God has not made man a puppet and that Scriptures must not be taken out of context. Man *can* choose between good or evil: *And if it seem evil unto you to serve the LORD, choose you this day whom ye will serve ... Joshua 24:15* As mentioned previously, God has allowed millions of people, in both Bible times and today, to divorce, murder, and steal. He, however, does not approve of these acts and lifestyles.

There's a huge gulf between <u>allowing</u> something because of hard heartedness and <u>giving approval</u> to it. God does not approve of evil, sinful choices, but He allows man to sin; to reject Him, or to obey

Him. However, **it's only the regenerated who can "hear" the voice of the LORD and can truly follow Him**. That foundation must be firmly laid as a reference before interpreting Deuteronomy 24:1-4.

God clearly gave His laws and precepts to His chosen nation Israel. Israel, however, chose to turn against God. He <u>allowed</u> her to do this, BUT there were consequences to Israel for rebelling against God's ways. It's what is called in this book God's *punitive judgment*; that is, He *allows* man to choose evil ways but in so doing there is a judgment on man even before physical death. That punitive judgment is God allowing people to live in sinful lifestyles. Very few people who are living in sinful lifestyles see their sins as they are reflected through Scriptural examples of God's punitive judgment.

> There's a huge difference in the concept of God allowing man to sin and God approving of the same rebellion.

*<u>Because</u> they had not executed my judgments, but had despised my statutes, and had polluted my sabbaths, and their eyes were after their fathers' idols. Wherefore <u>I gave them also statutes that were not good</u>, and judgments whereby they should not live; And I polluted them in their own gifts, in that they caused to pass through the fire all that openeth the womb, that I might make them desolate, to the end that they might know that I am the LORD.*
Ezekiel 20:24-26

God allowed Israel to choose to do evil, but there was an expensive price to pay. Study two additional examples from Hosea 4:

*My people ask counsel at their stocks, and their staff declareth unto them: for the spirit of whoredoms hath caused them to err, and they have gone a whoring from under their God. They sacrifice upon the tops of the mountains, and burn incense upon the hills, under oaks and poplars and elms, because the shadow thereof is good: <u>therefore your daughters shall commit whoredom, and your spouses shall commit adultery</u>. I will not punish your daughters when they commit whoredom, nor your spouses when they commit adultery:*

*for themselves are separated with whores, and they sacrifice with harlots: therefore the people that doth not understand shall fall.* Hosea 4:12-14

*My people are destroyed for lack of knowledge*: [Many people quote only this part of this verse; however, the meaning—the correct interpretation—is in what follows] *because thou hast rejected knowledge* [God's Word], *I will also reject thee ... seeing thou hast forgotten the law of thy God, I will also forget thy children.* Hosea 4:6

> Those who live in a lifestyle the Word says is sin are rejecting God.

These same kinds of misunderstood warnings are also given in the New Testament. Study the examples below:

*And with all deceivableness of unrighteousness in them that perish; <u>because</u> **they received not the love of the truth**, that they might be saved. And **for this cause** God shall send them strong delusion, that they should believe a lie: That they all might be damned who believed not the truth, but had pleasure in unrighteousness.* 2 Thessalonians 2:10-12

*Professing themselves to be wise, they became fools ... Wherefore God also gave them up to uncleanness through the lusts of their own hearts, to dishonour their own bodies between themselves: **Who <u>changed</u> the truth of God into a lie** ... **For this cause** God gave them up unto vile affections ... And even as they did not like to retain God in their knowledge, God gave **them over to a reprobate mind**, to do those things which are not convenient; Being filled with all unrighteousness, fornication, wickedness ... inventors of evil things ... Without understanding, covenantbreakers, without natural affections ... Who knowing the judgment of God, that they which commit such things are worthy of death, not only do the same, but have pleasure in them that do them.* Romans 1:22-32

Do you see that God labels people who persist in sinful lifestyles as reprobates? *For this cause* (hard-hearted rebellion) *God gave them up unto vile affections; God gave them over to a reprobate mind* permitting them to continue in the sinful lifestyle practices they chose.

<u>They chose</u> to reject the Word of God; and thus, by their own hard-hearted choices, they became entangled in sinful acts, and God's

punitive judgment (as it's called in this book) sets in. This is evidenced by a continued rejection of His Word. (Two important sins listed in Romans 1:31, covenant-breakers and unnatural affections, are removed from most new Bible versions. These omissions will be discussed in Chapter 22.)

## Man deceives only himself when he thinks a piece of paper can dissolve <u>WHAT</u> it is that God has joined together.

Study the illustration below. These two documents (one from Old Testament days; the other, from today) both reflect actions of man who has been turned over to a reprobate mind.

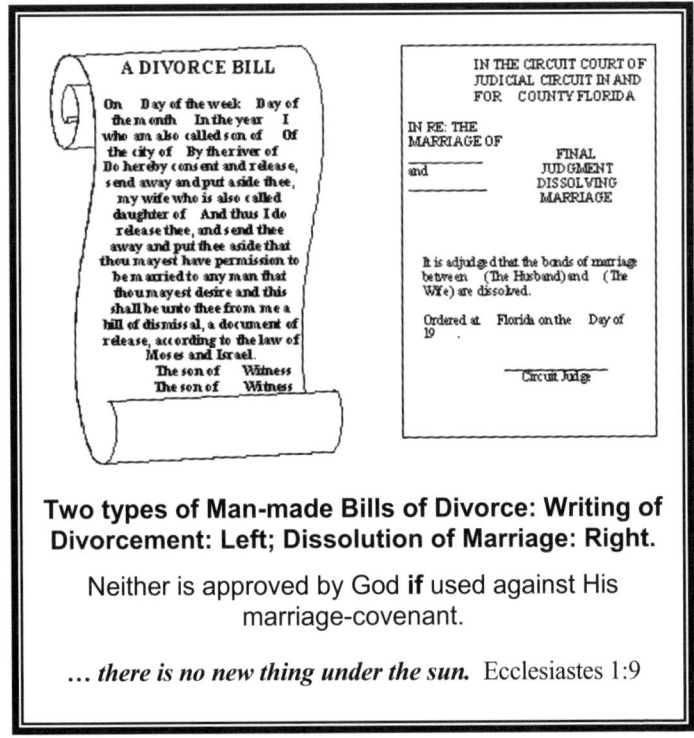

**Two types of Man-made Bills of Divorce: Writing of Divorcement: Left; Dissolution of Marriage: Right.**

Neither is approved by God **if** used against His marriage-covenant.

*… there is no new thing under the sun.* Ecclesiastes 1:9

Man is "allowed" to do those things which God hates including his efforts to put asunder (to dissolve) what the LORD has permanently joined until physical death dissolves—the covenant of marriage.

God, through Moses, *allowed* the *Writing of Divorcement* because of man's hardened heart. God is *allowing* the same today with man's ungodly modern legal document, the *Dissolution of Marriage*. You've heard it said, "There's nothing new under the sun." Is that not true with how man is still trying to achieve the same thing today as was being done in Biblical times? The people are different; the "instrument" is called by a different name, but the heart of man is the same.

The "old" (Writing of Divorcement) has become the "new" (Dissolution of Marriage). Both become an instrument against God when they are used to try to dissolve a one-flesh marriage; that is, when they are used to declare that God's supernatural, permanent joining is no longer valid.

## Jeremiah 3:1 is a powerful interlinking Scripture.

Jeremiah 3:1 is a Scripture that interlinks several vital teachings between the Old and New Testaments on marriage and divorce. This includes Deuteronomy 24:1-4, Matthew 5:27-32, 19:3-9, and Mark 10:2-12. Perhaps that's why Jeremiah 3:1 is such a highly attacked, but unnoticed, Scripture. It's one in which the pure words of the LORD are rewritten into untruths from which many try to create loopholes to divorce and "re-marry." Study Jeremiah 3:1 below:

***They say****, If a man put away his wife, and she go from him, and become another man's, shall he return unto her again? shall not that land be greatly polluted? but thou hast played the harlot with many lovers; yet return again to me, saith the LORD.* Jeremiah 3:1

To understand some of the important information in Jeremiah 3:1, it will be broken into four parts for purposes of teaching:

> Part 1: ***They*** *say,*
>
> Part 2: *If a man put away his wife, and she go from him, and become another man's,*
>   *shall he return unto her again?*
>   *shall not that land be greatly polluted?*
>
> Part 3: *but*
> *thou hast played the harlot with many lovers;*
> *yet return again to me,*
>
> Part 4: *saith the **LORD**.*

What is a big difference between parts one and four if you consider the highlighted text? It should be apparent that there are two different referenced people. In part one, it is *they*. In part four, it is the *LORD*. Both are different, and both are saying something different. It's what: (1) *They say* and (4) *saith the LORD*.

Notice the first two words in Jeremiah 3:1, (*They say*) are at the beginning of the verse to show what immediately follows is what some unnamed people say. These unnamed people are <u>not</u> the LORD:

*If a man put away his wife, and she go from him, and become another man's, shall he return unto her again? shall not that land be greatly polluted?*

Where else is this same hearsay conversation recorded? It's in Deuteronomy 24:4 which is part of many misapplied words:

*24:1 When a man hath taken a wife, and married her, and it come to pass that she find no favour in his eyes, because he hath found some uncleanness in her: then let him write her a bill of divorcement, and give it in her hand, and send her out of his house.*
*2 And when she is departed out of his house, she may go and be another man's wife.*
*3 And if the latter husband hate her, and write her a bill of divorcement, and giveth it in her hand, and sendeth her out of his house; or if the latter husband die, which took her to be his wife;*
**4 Her former husband, which sent her away, may not take her again to be his wife, after that she is defiled; for that is abomination before the LORD: and thou shalt not cause the land to sin,** *which the LORD thy God giveth thee for an inheritance.* Deuteronomy 24:1-4

Review the two Scriptures below as they were given earlier in the chapter. Perhaps the comparison now takes on more meaning:

| Jeremiah 3:1 and Deuteronomy 24:4 are statements from "they say." ||
|---|---|
| *Her former husband, which sent her away, may not take her again to be his wife, after that she is defiled; for that is abomination before the LORD: and thou shalt not cause the land to sin, which the LORD thy God giveth thee for an inheritance.* Deuteronomy 24:4 | *They say, If a man put away his wife, and she go from him, and become another man's, shall he return unto her again? shall not that land be greatly polluted? ...* Jeremiah 3:1 |

God is quoting what others said. What *they say* may or may not be true. What is true must be evaluated by other contextual Scriptural information. The last part of Jeremiah 3:1 should make it evident that the first part must be read with discernment. A discerning reader should recognize that there are many things in the Bible said by others (they say) with which God disagrees or are taken out of context.

Deuteronomy 24:4 says: *Her former husband, which sent her away, may not take her again to be his wife, after that she is defiled; for that is abomination before the LORD ...*

There are some important truths missed in Deuteronomy 24:4. One is that if the wife who is put away marries another, she is defiled. To marry another when you have a living one-flesh spouse is an "abomination before the LORD." It is adultery. Then there is a statement that few today probably notice at the end of verse 24:4: ... ***and thou shalt not cause the land to sin, which the LORD thy God giveth thee for an inheritance.*** God states that sin defiles the land upon which the sinner lives. This is telling the reader that he is not to cause the land to sin by defiling it with hard-hearted adultery. Even though it is possible for those with hardened hearts to repent, the reality is that most who choose to become caught in the web of adultery do not repent. If you doubt this statement, please carefully read, study, and meditate on what God warns in Proverbs 5 and 6. Proverbs 6:32 gives the price most pay for the sin of adultery:

*But whoso committeth adultery with a woman lacketh understanding: he that doeth it destroyeth his own soul.* This applies equally to women who choose to become caught in the web of adultery.

Deuteronomy 24:1-4 is quoted in part in the two questions recorded in Jeremiah 3:1—those that come AFTER the introductory words of verse one: *They say.*

*If a man put away his wife, and she go from him, and become another man's, shall he return unto her again? shall not that land be greatly polluted?*

These two questions do not express God's perspective on marriage. They are, instead, to what the Pharisees alluded when they said that Moses commanded the Writing of Divorcement: ... *Why did Moses then command to give a writing of divorcement, and to put her away?* Matthew

19:7 Jesus corrected the Pharisees' wrong statement telling them that Moses suffered or allowed the writing of divorcement because of man's hardened heart. God is doing the same in Jeremiah 3:1.

## God's Word does not give conflicting messages. It's man's wrongful interpretation that gives conflicting messages.

Many point to Deuteronomy 24:4 to try to prove that a divorced person should not return to his covenant spouse. Deuteronomy 24:4 could sound like it confirms a conflicting message—that a "put-away" spouse cannot reconcile with the covenant spouse IF these words are incorrectly translated or taken out of context.

However, 1 Corinthians 7:11 should be considered. It states there are only two choices if someone is put away. Divorcing a covenant wife is a separation, not a dissolution. We know that because God tells us that only death ends a covenant-marriage. Thus, one-flesh spouses who are separated or legally divorced are given one of two options:

1. To remain in an unmarried state.
2. To return to the covenant spouse.

*And unto the married I command, yet not I, but the Lord, Let not the wife depart from her husband: But and if she depart, let her remain unmarried, or be reconciled to her husband: and let not the husband put away his wife.*
1 Corinthians 7:10-11

Is the Old Testament teaching a conflicting message? No, definitely not. Recall that we must not apply Scripture out of context and must learn to compare Scripture with Scripture. So what does the rest of

Jeremiah 3:1 say? God switches <u>from</u> reporting what others have said and misapplied <u>to</u> what He says in Part 3: *but thou hast played the harlot with many lovers; yet return again to me ...*

The word *but* is a "turn" word—it indicates change. What comes next is God's answer to what "They say": ***but*** *thou hast played the harlot with many lovers;* ***yet return*** *again to me,* **saith the LORD**. *Thou hast played the harlot with <u>many</u> lovers* means you (hard-hearted people) have done the same thing in your relationship to me (the LORD). This is the same message Jesus gave in the conflict with the Pharisees over what Moses allowed. *They* said it. *They* pursued it—putting away.

God was telling the Israelites that they were to return to Him, their spiritual husband. Likewise, those in physical marriage-covenants are to return to their covenant spouses. Similarly with the covenant of salvation, the LORD is not say-

> To say we are not to return to a covenant spouse would be like saying sinners cannot return to the LORD.

ing that when we sin we cannot repent and re-turn to Him. How horrible that would be because we all sin and come short of the glory of God. We are, instead, to confess sin, forsake it, and return to the LORD as He commands in His summary statement in Jeremiah 3:1: ***<u>yet return again to me</u>****, saith the LORD.*

## God's covenants are not dissolved because of man's sin.

Some additional contextual information may help to clarify the vital interlinked and contextual teachings in Jeremiah 3:1. Israel, as a nation, was God's spiritual wife through a covenant which the LORD made with the nation of Israel.

*Now when I passed by thee, and looked upon thee, behold, thy time was the time of love; and I spread my skirt over thee, and covered thy nakedness: yea, I sware unto thee, and entered into a **covenant** with thee, saith the Lord GOD, and thou becamest mine.* Ezekiel 16:8

The fact that the Israelites became exceedingly wicked and unfaithful did not change the fact that they were God's spiritual wife. As such, they were accountable to the terms of their spiritual marriage-covenant with God. They, however, were given the choice to be faithful to God or to rebel with sinful lifestyles, practices, and beliefs. They chose to rebel but that didn't change the terms of God's spiritual marriage-covenant with them. He is still waiting for Israel to return unto Him. Israel also modeled that same kind of unfaithfulness with their physical wives. The same principle which applies to the nation of Israel's spiritual idolatry also applies to a covenant-marriage between a man and a woman. Even though the Israelites (as millions today) divorced their physical covenant wives, God says all are still, YET, their wives.

> Sin and unfaithfulness do not alter the marital joining.

*Yet ye say, Wherefore? Because the LORD hath been witness between thee and the wife of thy youth, against whom thou hast dealt treacherously: **yet** is she thy companion, and the wife of thy covenant.* Malachi 2:14

It's impossible for man to dissolve God's covenant of marriage. This fact is reinforced many times in this text. This permanently created, universal, unchanged Truth rings consistently throughout the Bible. It is summed up in the physical love story of the Old Testament prophet Hosea whose wife Gomer became an adulteress. Yet, the LORD commanded Hosea to buy back and love his adulteress wife:

*Then said the LORD unto me, Go yet, love a woman beloved of her friend, **yet an adulteress**, according to the love of the LORD toward the children of Israel, who look to other gods, and love flagons of wine.* Hosea 3:1

Hosea's wife, like the nation of Israel and many covenant spouses today, committed adultery. She even married another man; however, God's direction was the same to Hosea as it is to every spouse today—to be faithful to one's covenant spouse. Even though Gomer had become an adulteress, no matter how deep the hurt and pain she had inflicted upon her faithful husband, Hosea was instructed not only to return, but to love her—unconditionally.

> God's message to Israel, to Hosea, and to every one is to return to covenant.

## Doctrinally flawed Bible translations give deadly messages to their readers.

Before we leave the message of God's command to return to one's covenant spouse, it's important to understand the significance of the correct contextual interpretation and application of the command given though the LORD in the last clause in Jeremiah 3:1: ... *yet return again to me, saith the LORD.*

Study examples of the unscriptural, man-made doctrine that is being taught through several versions of the Bible in Jeremiah 3:1. These are illustrated in the table on the next page. The King James Bible is given first as a point of reference. The new versions shown give a horribly skewed picture of this very important teaching that God has preserved through Jeremiah.

| | Jeremiah 3:1 |
|---|---|
| | ***They say***, *If a man put away his wife, and she go from him, and become another man's, shall he return unto her again? shall not that land be greatly polluted? but thou hast played the harlot with many lovers;* **yet return again to me, saith the LORD**. KJB |
| Bible* | Jeremiah 3:1 |
| NIV | *"If a man divorces his wife and she leaves him and marries another man, should he return to her again? Would not the land be completely defiled? But you have lived as a prostitute with many lovers--would you now return to me?" declares the LORD.* |
| ESV | *"If a man divorces his wife and she goes from him and becomes another man's wife, will he return to her? Would not that land be greatly polluted? You have played the whore with many lovers; and would you return to me? declares the LORD.* |
| HCSB | *If a man divorces his wife and she leaves him to marry another, can he ever return to her? Wouldn't such a land become totally defiled? But you! You have played the prostitute with many partners-can you return to Me? [This is] The bracketed text has been added for clarity. the Lord's declaration.*\*\* |
| ICB | *"Now a man might divorce his wife. And she might leave him and marry another man. Should her first husband come back to her again? If he went back to her, the land would become completely unclean. But you have acted like a prostitute with many lovers. And now you want to come back to me?" says the Lord.* |

*KJB: King James Bible; NIV: New International Version; ESV: English Standard Version; HCSB: Holman Christian Standard Bible; ICB: International Children's Bible

\*\*What is quoted above from HCSB is how Jeremiah 3:1 appears in that Bible, including the brackets [ ] and the words in and after the brackets.

**God's command to return to a marriage-covenant in Jeremiah 3:1 interlinks (1) the LORD's spiritual marriage to the nation of Israel, (2) Hosea's physical marriage-covenant to Gomer (to return), and (3) God's covenant-based salvation. They all have similar principles.** However, what is being taught about the covenant of marriage has gone horribly awry. This is, in part, fed by false doctrine developed from teachings such as those recorded through the new versions of the Bible shown on the previous page. They replace a vital truth that God has preserved about returning to a covenant spouse. How do they do that? First of all, they start at the beginning of Jeremiah 3:1 by removing "*They say*." These are two very important words which identify who it is that is responsible for saying a deserted spouse cannot return. God is quoting what others have said. By removing these words, it sounds like God is appearing to be the one saying that a divorced person cannot return to his spouse. Instead, it was what others had been saying and misapplying.

> It's vital to know whose doctrine is being promoted: God's or man's.

This deadly error is promoted through teachings by pastors as well as those who are saved and those who are not saved. Many who do not want to reconcile with their covenant spouses quote from these flawed teachings to create a loophole for divorce and "re-marriage." Here's what "they say" even today: "You cannot return once there has been a divorce and especially if one of the spouses has "re-married." These sayings blatantly conflict with what is taught throughout Scripture.

## *Yet return again to me, saith the LORD*

***If** thou wilt return, O Israel, saith the LORD, **return** unto me: and **if** thou wilt put away thine abominations out of my sight ...* Jeremiah 4:1

*Even from the days of your fathers ye are gone away from mine ordinances, and have not kept them. Return unto me, and I will **return** unto you, saith the LORD of hosts. But ye said, Wherein shall we return?* Malachi 3:7

*But and if she depart, let her remain unmarried, or **be reconciled** to her husband: and let not the husband put away his wife.* 1 Corinthians 7:11

Again, what God is consistently and repetitively teaching in Jeremiah 3:1 comes after the "turn word" *but.* It is then that God clarifies His teaching on returning to covenant. Repentant sinners, IF they are to return, must first repent—and then abandon the sinful relationship. That is how they return to the LORD—to their covenant relationship: <u>**yet**</u> **return again to me, saith the LORD.** Jeremiah repeats this message to return in several of his other writings. For example: *If thou wilt return, O Israel, saith the LORD,* ***return*** *unto me: and* ***if*** *thou wilt* <u>*put away*</u> *thine abominations out of my sight ...* Jeremiah 4:1

In Jeremiah 3:1, the underlying Hebrew text, like the correct English translation, records the concluding statement of the LORD. It is not a question challenging the need to return. It is a declarative command that must not be removed or wrongly translated. It is to return to the LORD—to re-turn to covenant relationship.

If this were a secular court of law, those who make statements as in Jeremiah 3:1, as given in the above-quoted new Bible versions, might be called witnesses for the Plaintiff. They would be stating, under oath, what they are swearing they "heard" the Defendant, God, say:

| As part of a jury, would you make the decision that the Defendant or the Respondent is guilty of perjury? ||
|---|---|
| Defendant: God | Plaintiffs: New Bible Versions |
| ***... yet return again to me, saith the LORD.*** Jeremiah 3:1 KJB | *would you now return to me?" declares the LORD.* NIV |
| | *and would you return to me? declares the LORD.* ESV |
| | *can you return to Me?* HCSB |
| | *now you want to come back to me?" says the Lord.* ICB |

As you read the *Plaintiffs'* testimony as shown above, it leads the "jury" to believe it is almost ridiculous for a person to think that he can or should return to covenant. These *witnesses* are implying that if you sin, why would you think you should or could repent and return.

Please be aware of too quickly reading over the statements made by the new version authors. They are the model from which thousands of Christians quote. They feel they have Biblical evidence to **change God's command** from "return to Him" to having Him ask the question: "Would you return to me?" Thus, God's message in Jeremiah 3:1 has been almost totally mutilated. The incorrectly translated texts make God's Word sound like the LORD is not waiting for repentant sinners to return to Him, or that divorced spouses should not reconcile. In fact, it really sounds like they cannot return. That would be a serious matter if when we sin we could not turn back to the LORD through repentance; or if we become separated from our spouse for whatever the cause that we think we could not reconcile because of false teachings. All those in covenant-marriages who are separated from their spouse are wrongly being told, through new Bible version doctrines, the opposite of what God is teaching. The Hebrew underlying text and the consistent contextual message that God teaches is to return to covenant: "Yet return." See page 352.

## There is a price to pay for being a false witness.

These are serious doctrinal changes to God's Word. What have these authors, and those who teach and quote from these flawed statements, done? They have <u>changed the testimony</u> of **the** Witness: the Word: Jesus—God Himself. Changing the testimony of a witness, even in man's court, can become a criminal offense. Few people, however, consider the even more serious consequences of changing the Word of God or of adopting teachings, beliefs, and lifestyles from doctrinally inaccurate texts. They are "tampering" with God's testimony.

*...which keep the commandments of God, and have the <u>testimony</u> of Jesus Christ.* Revelation 12:17 *... and of thy brethren that have the <u>testimony</u> of Jesus: worship God: for the <u>testimony</u> of Jesus is the spirit of prophecy.* Revelation 19:10 *... I saw under the altar the souls of them that were slain for the word of God, and for the <u>testimony</u> which they held.* Revelation 6:9

*For I* [Jesus Christ] ***testify***
*unto every man that heareth the words of the prophecy of this book,*

*If **any man** shall add unto these things, God shall add unto him the plagues that are written in this book:*

*And if **any man** shall take away from the words of the book of this prophecy, God shall take away his part out of the book of life, and out of the holy city, and from the things which are written in this book. He which testifieth these things saith,*

*Surely I* [Jesus] *come quickly. Amen. Even so, come, Lord Jesus.* Revelation 22:18-20

God's Word provides direction for living and the key to eternal life. Marriage and divorce are major issues in many peoples' lives. Knowing the Truth on these foundational issues is a matter of spiritual life and death as are many other Scriptural matters. That's why God is very clear that no one should tamper with His Word. Doing so could "cause" someone to make a wrong decision, especially that of remaining in the sin of adultery which, according to Scripture, would keep that person from inheriting the Kingdom of God.

## NIV, like all new versions, must change thousands of God's words with each new version.
(Review the Derivative Copyright Law, page 178.)

Each new version gets further away from Truth and doctrinally changes more of God's Word. Many of the Scripture changes are focused attacks on God's perspective on marriage. Below are two examples out of hundreds to illustrate major errors by the authors of the NIV between their 1984 and 2011 versions:

| NIV 1984 | NIV 2011 | KJB |
|---|---|---|
| **Malachi 2:16** | **Malachi 2:16** | **Malachi 2:16** |
| *"I hate divorce,"* says the LORD God of Israel ... | *"The <u>man</u> who hates and divorces his wife,"* says the LORD, the God of Israel ... **God is removed as hating divorce.** | For the LORD, the God of Israel, saith that **he hateth putting away** ... |

NIV 2011 removes the fact that God hates divorce. The authors shift from God hating divorce to man who hates his wife. This totally changes the meaning and infuses words and meanings that are not in their underlying Hebrew text. It's one of many examples of <u>man writing his own theology</u>.

| NIV 1984 | NIV 2011 | KJB |
|---|---|---|
| **Romans 7:3** | **Romans 7:3** | **Romans 7:3** |
| So then, if she marries another man while her husband is still alive, she is called an adulteress ... | So then, **if she has sexual relations with another man** while her husband is still alive, she is called an adulteress ... | So then if, while her husband liveth, she be married to another man, she shall be called an adulteress ... |

The NIV authors totally restructure the definition of an adulterous marriage in their 2011 version. <u>They change the focus from divorcing and "re-marrying" to sexual relations</u>. It's the sin of "re-marriage" that is being avoided by most clergy in their teachings and counsel and one that is being removed from Bibles. Yes, both are sins called *adultery*, but the sin of marrying another when there is a living spouse is the aspect of adultery that isn't being clearly taught and is what these authors change here.

www.onlinebaptist.com/home/topic/14519-what-about-the-new-niv-2011:
NIV has changed 40% of the verses from their 1984 version, **have removed 32,863 words, and added 34,469 different words**. They add to and subtract from their underlying Hebrew and Greek texts.

# 16

## For What Cause?

Beware. This chapter can be overwhelming if you haven't studied the materials already presented, **especially the rule of proximity introduced in Chapter 12.** This study is a continuation of Chapter 15, but the focus is ultimately on a word that is often overlooked in one of the exception clauses, the word *cause*. Before *cause* is studied, it's important to make sure there is an understanding of the word *except* in Matthew 19:9. By now, its meaning and application should be clear. For example, a small child can be instructed that he can have everything except for _____. If he has been trained to obey, he will understand that whatever the stated exception is, it is something that is not included in what he may have. Simply put, that is the essence of the exception clauses—there is something which is excluded from the rest of the verse or statement.

## What is the context? Who is the audience?

Even though both Matthew 5:32 and Matthew 19:9 are giving the same overall message in each exception clause—an exception for fornication—there are important differences between the two verses. Contextual information within each verse <u>and</u> in other verses for each of these clauses can help provide additional important insight for deeper understandings. The context of Matthew 5:32 is from a teaching Jesus gave, the *Sermon on the Mount*, with the <u>on-going purpose</u> of training His disciples for ministry although there were "multitudes" who heard this teaching. (See also Mark 3:13-14 and Luke 6:20-49.)

Matthew 19:9 has a very different purpose, mainly because of the audience to whom Jesus was speaking. It was the Pharisees who were addressed, but they were not there to learn from Jesus. They came with an adversarial motive. In fact, they came *tempting* Jesus as was discussed in Chapter 7. The Pharisees, like man today, were adept at quoting the law and then creating loopholes to get around it.

This game playing is equally as insidious today. Yet, pastors and lay people alike seem to not recognize it as such. Thus, these teachings bear repetition. The Pharisees were focused on grounds for divorce. They were trying to trap or maneuver <u>Jesus the Word</u> into giving a reason to put away a wife "for every [any] cause." Conversely, Jesus' focus, <u>as should be ours</u>, was the institution of marriage—its creation and its terms: ... *let not man put asunder.* Matthew 19:6 He clearly and explicitly told the Pharisees what would happen if they put away one spouse and married another. They would commit adultery. It's true that man should not commit adultery; however, as was the practice of the Pharisees then and many today, the law simply stated was misused by those with wicked hearts. They tried to create loopholes to divorce their covenant wives. Jesus not only knew why they were questioning Him, He also knew that <u>divorce often leads to the sin of adultery—or adultery often is the sin that leads to the desire to divorce a spouse</u>.

So there is a contrast that must be recognized between the two audiences. The biggest contrast is in the **heart** of each of the two groups being addressed then **and** today. Jesus, in teaching His disciples—those who came with a heart to learn—not with a purpose to *tempt* Him—gave a message that applies to the heart of man.

***But*** *I say unto you, That whosoever looketh on a woman to lust after her hath committed adultery with her already in his <u>heart</u>.* Matthew 5:28.

In Matthew 5:27, Jesus, as part of His teachings to train His disciples for ministry (Review Matthew 5:1.), began this teaching with a statement from the Old Testament quoting what had been said:

<u>Ye have heard</u> *that it was* <u>said by them</u> *of old time, Thou shalt not commit adultery.* Matthew 5:27

This same pattern of reference to what others had said was repeated four verses later. However, Scripture was being quoted by others out of context: *It hath been said ...* Matthew 5:31.

In Chapter 15, it was shown how God differentiates in subtle ways between what He is teaching and what others have said. This was illustrated through the words in Jeremiah 3:1: "They say." There is a similar pattern in the *Sermon on the Mount* as Jesus spoke to His disciples: *Ye have heard that it was said <u>by them</u> ... **It** <u>hath been said</u>, Whosoever shall put away his wife, let him give her a writing of divorcement.*

The word *it* was not referring to Jesus' giving approval to what had been said. The word *it* in Matthew 5:31 is like the words *"They say"* in Jeremiah 3:1 when God was referring to what had been said in Deuteronomy 24:1. Neither God nor Jesus agreed with the practice of putting away a **covenant wife**. After all, Jesus and God are One. They cannot disagree. The misuse of the Writing of Divorce was allowed but not approved by God. He set the record straight on that in His teaching in Jeremiah 3:1. Notice there is a like pattern of words in both Matthew 5:31 and Jeremiah 3:1 (*"It hath been said"* and *"They say"*) to tell the reader that these were things other people were saying:

| The same pattern of teaching is used by God in the Old Testament as is used by Jesus in the New Testament: ||
|---|---|
| ... *as we* [God and Jesus] *are one.* John 17:22 ||
| ***They say***, ["They say" ... was not God's doctrine.] *If a man put away his wife, and she go from him, and become another man's, shall he return unto her again? shall not that land be greatly polluted?* ***but*** *[God now speaks] thou hast played the harlot with many lovers; <u>yet return</u> again to me,* **<u>saith the LORD</u>**. Jeremiah 3:1 | ***It*** <u>hath been said</u>, *Whosoever put away his wife, let him give her a writing of divorcement:* ***But I say*** *unto you, That whosoever shall put away his wife, saving for the cause of fornication, causeth her to commit adultery: and whosoever shall marry her that is divorced committeth adultery.* Matthew 5:31-32 |

Embedded in Matthew 5:32 is Jesus' teaching for those who had "ears to hear"—His disciples and all who had or have a right heart to hear. *He that hath an ear, let him hear what the Spirit saith ...* Revelation 2:7

***But** I say unto you, That whosoever shall put away his wife, saving for the **cause** of fornication, causeth her to commit adultery: and whosoever shall marry her that is divorced committeth adultery.* Matthew 5:32

## "... saving for the cause of fornication, causeth ..."

Perhaps you've done what I did for many years. I overlooked two words which seemed like they meant the same thing in Matthew 5:32, *cause* and *causeth*. They, however, are quite different which is revealed when they are carefully studied. C*ause* is a noun; *causeth* is a verb, and it's "saving for the cause of fornication." *Cause* is used fifty times in the New Testament; causeth, only five times.

Even more astounding to me (Yes, I mean *astounding!*) was *how* different the meanings of each of these words *cause* and *causeth* are. Study the table below to see if you can discern why I'm so excited about this contextual "discovery" of the differences between *cause* and *causeth*. Focus on the underlined words in the left column.

| ***Cause** and *causeth* are two very different words.* | |
|---|---|
| *... saving for the **cause** of fornication ...* Matthew 5:32 | *... causeth her to commit adultery ...* Matthew 5:32 |
| *When any one heareth the **word** of the kingdom ...* Matthew 13:19 | *... God, which always causeth us to triumph ...* 2 Corinthians 2:14 |
| *... by my mouth should hear the **word** of the gospel ...* Acts 15:7 | *... causeth through us thanksgiving to God.* 2 Corinthians 9:11 |
| *... thou hast kept the **word** of my patience ...* Revelation 3:10 | *... causeth the earth and them ... to worship ...* Revelation 13:12 |
| *... these which hear the **word** of God, and do it.* Luke 8:21 | And he causeth all ... to receive a mark ... Revelation 13:16 |
| *... And the **word** of the Lord was published throughout all the region.* Acts 13:49 | *Causeth* is used as a verb. *Cause* is used as a noun. However, there is a much more important contextual difference between the two words. |
| *... rightly dividing the **word** of truth.* 2 Timothy 2:15 | |

It should be evident that all the underlined terms are the same word, except for Matthew 5:32. The underlined word in Matthew 5:32 is *cause*. However, both Matthew 5:32 and <u>all</u> the other underlined words have been translated from the same Greek word, *logos*, Strong's 3056. *Logos* means the written or spoken Word of God and is even at times specifically a synonym or name of Jesus:

*In the beginning was the **Word**, and the **Word** was with God, and the **Word** was God. And the **Word** was made flesh, and dwelt among us* ... John 1:1, 14.

These are significant facts. *Logos* refers to the written or spoken Word of God, or Jesus Himself, and is used some 300 times in the Bible. However, for some reason, the translators were inspired to choose the word *cause* in their translation of ... *saving for the <u>cause</u> of fornication*, even though the <u>underlying word</u> for *cause* in Matthew 5:32 is the same as when *logos* is translated *word*. Now study the pattern of the word <u>usage</u> in the left column above: cause <u>of fornication</u>, word <u>of the kingdom</u>, word <u>of the gospel</u>, word <u>of my patience</u>, word <u>of God</u>, word <u>of the Lord</u>, and the word <u>of truth</u>. These are prepositional phrases. They begin with a preposition (of) and end with a noun, called the object of the preposition. A noun or a pronoun that follows a preposition completes its meaning. Here's what each of the prepositional phrases indicate:

> The Greek word for *cause* is *logos*.

What the Word says about fornication in Matthew 5:32.
What the Word says about the kingdom in Matthew 13:19.
What the Word says about the gospel in Acts 15:7.
What the Word says about patience in Revelation 3:10.
What the Word says about God in Luke 8:21.
What the Word says about the Lord in Acts 13:49.
What the Word says about truth in 2 Timothy 2:15.

Chapter 16

How is saying "for the <u>cause</u> of fornication" in Matthew 5:32 different from saying "except it be for fornication" in Matthew 19:9? There's a reason why the Holy Ghost inspired what is translated *cause* in the Matthew 5:32 exception clause. It *could* have been influenced (1) by the specific audience Jesus was addressing and (2) by the purpose for the teaching to this audience. Recall that the LORD was training His disciples in the *Sermon on the Mount* (Matthew 5-7). In contrast, He was responding to a confrontational issue with the Pharisees in 19:9.

Applying the above-noted usage patterns to *cause* in Matthew 5:32, *for the <u>cause</u> of fornication*, could indicate a broader meaning—what the Word of God says about fornication. Here's a unique situation where the underlying Greek gives some very important related or supporting information. That information could support a broader range of meanings for fornication in Matthew 5:32. This is because of the unconventional use of the underlying Greek word for *cause—logos* and the pattern of usage which occurs in the translation of logos.

## The word *cause* in Matthew 5:32 is uniquely used.

There are several Greek words, other than Strong's 3056 which are translated *cause* in the New Testament; however, none of those others has the underlying Greek word which refers to the written or spoken Word of God (*logos*). Study the table below. Not only are *cause* and *causeth* different parts of speech but they have two very different underlying Greek counterparts. These words *cause* (a noun) and *causeth* (a verb) are enclosed in rectangles. Notice that the Greek

263

For What Cause?

words from which these two words are translated are different. The Greek word underlying *cause* is logos/*logou*; that for *causeth* is poiei. (Greek words have different endings depending upon how they are used in the sentence.)

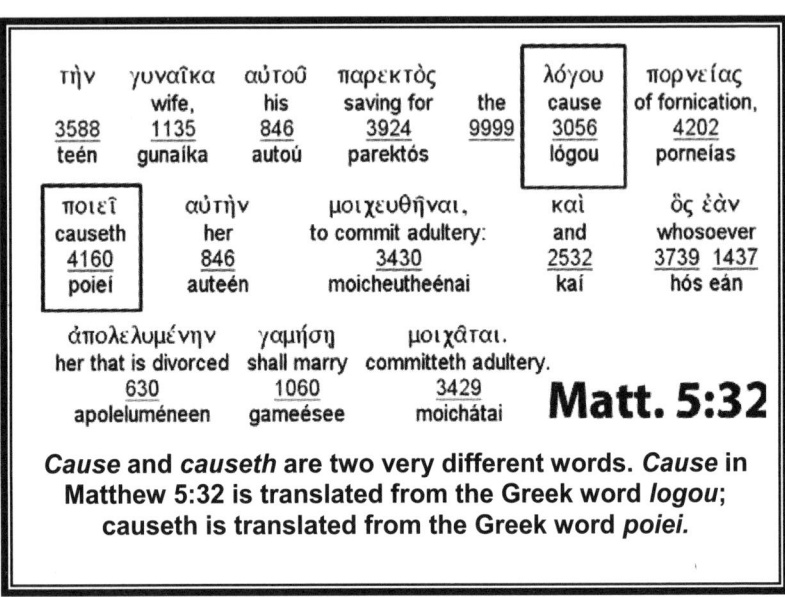

### It all has to do with the heart.

It has been shown that there are differences between the two exception clauses because of (1) the audiences addressed, (2) the addition of the word *cause*, and (3) contextual information surrounding Matthew 5:32. Based on these factors **and** Jesus' reference to the Old Testament, the meaning of fornication in 5:32 may be reflecting the generic application of fornication. Jesus specifically mentioned the Old Testament twice in Matthew 5:27-31: ... *by them of old time* ... and *It hath been said* ... (verses 27 and 31).

In principle, the inclusion of the word *cause* in the Matthew 5:32 exception clause is reflective of the teaching in the gospel of James. He taught the difference between the **word** of faith and the **acts** of faith. James, in his epistle, modeled the essence of the *Sermon on the Mount: But wilt thou know, O vain man, that faith without works is dead?* James 2:20. That is, it's what we do in our flesh that reveals what's in our heart; it's the *works* of the Word. It's what would be the difference between an act of fornication and the word (*cause*) of fornication.

Another illustration may help to show the difference between the word of fornication (*cause of fornication*) and an act or deed of fornication (*except it be for fornication*). The Greek word for *act, deed*, or *works* is *ergo* (Strong's 2041). *Ergo* is not the word the Holy Ghost inspired Matthew to record in 5:32. He, instead, wrote the more inclusive word *logos* "which being interpreted is" *cause* with its broader meaning. It is the logos or Word of fornication—what the Word says about fornication. An **act or deed is narrower** in scope than is a reference to the Word of God. An act or deed is *what* is manifest through the flesh of man—his lifestyle: a specific application. Study 1 Corinthians 5:1-2:

*1 ... there is fornication among you, and such fornication ... 2 that he that hath done this deed might be taken away from among you.* 1 Corinthians 5:1-2

Study the Scriptures on the next page. See how *word* and *deed* are differentiated. This is an application of the "rule of proximity." Proximity tells the reader that words used in the same verse or in one located close to that verse take on their specific meanings. They are not inclusive; that is, they do not include definitions of other words also included in that same verse. The "rule of proximity" was introduced in Chapter 12. Specifically here, the principles behind this rule tell the reader that *word* and *deed* have different meanings because of their proximity to one another. The context also helps to show that *deed* and *word* have different meanings:

| **The Rule of Proximity:** **Word (*logoo*) and *deed* (*ergoo*) are differentiated.** |
|---|
| ... *a prophet mighty in deed* [ergoo] *and word* [logo] ... Luke 24:19 |
| ... *to make the Gentiles obedient, by word* [logo] *and deed* [ergoo]. Romans 15:18 |
| *And whatsoever ye do in word* [logoo] *or deed* [ergo] ... Colossians 3:17 |
| ...*in word* [logoo], *neither in tongue; but in deed* [ergoo] *and in truth.* 1 John 3:18 |

Yet, more important for this teaching is that there is a contextual difference between what is included in the word *fornication* in Matthew 5:32 because of the inclusion of the word *cause* in the exception clause. Likewise, there is a difference between the *cause* (word) of fornication in Matthew 5:32 and the act or deed of fornication in Matthew 19:9. Even though both verses are speaking of the same sin, *fornication*, each focuses on a different aspect of fornication—the one, a specific usage; the other, generic or what the Word includes about fornication, especially in the Old Testament. This, in principle, again is what the New Testament writer James taught. That is, we can *know* what is written in the Word of God, but it is how we live, as shown through our deeds (our lifestyles), that "proves" if we **know** God.

What often gets lost in all the rhetoric about the correct meaning of the exception clauses is the underlying substance behind Jesus' teaching <u>to His disciples</u> in Matthew 5. It was important for them to learn more than the "letter of the law." That was the focus of the Pharisees. The disciples needed to understand how sin is related to the heart of man and not just that sin is a violation of God's law. That is evident in how Jesus expanded in His teaching on the sin of divorcing one's wife in Matthew 5. He was not only getting to the heart of sin in verses 27-32 but especially to the heart of man and the dangers of not being faithful to one's spouse, of overlooking the seriousness of harboring unforgiveness toward one's spouse, and the dangers of even the act of looking at another person with lust.

> It's what's in the heart of man that was the focus of Jesus' teaching in the exception clause in Matthew 5:32.

The resolution for those with hardened hearts, such as exhibited by the Pharisees and others who didn't want to learn to live in love with their wives, was to get rid of them by simply giving them a piece of paper—a Writing of Divorcement. After all, those doing this may have thought: "It's because of her that I'm unhappy; it's because of her that I'm not successful; it's because of her that I'm not sexually fulfilled; it's because of her that I don't have more friends."

Whatever the "cause" may have been, Jesus taught that divorcing one's spouse cannot be reduced to a man-made piece of paper. Putting away one's wife is something much worse, even potentially worse than cutting off one's hand or plucking out one's eye. (Review the teaching on this in Chapter 5, page 46-47.) Putting away one's wife is a sin that is embedded in the heart and often leads to eternal death:

*But I say unto you, That whosoever shall put away his wife, saving for the cause of fornication, causeth her to commit adultery: and whosoever shall marry her that is divorced committeth adultery.* Matthew 5:32

*Know ye not that the unrighteous shall not inherit the kingdom of God? Be not deceived: neither fornicators ... nor adulterers ... shall inherit the kingdom of God.* 1 Corinthians 6:9-10

## The logos in the New Testament reinforces the Word from the Old Testament.

The New Testament is a fulfillment of the Old Testament. Jesus quoted from and alluded to the Old Testament many times. That pattern is present in the *Sermon on the Mount* and especially surrounding the teachings on adultery, divorce, and "re-marriage" in Matthew 5:27-28 and 31-32.

In Matthew 5:32, notice the conjunction **but** at the beginning of the verse—what has often, in this text, been called a "turn" word. **But** is a word which indicates change; that is, something different follows from what went before. The word *but* is used to introduce something contrasting with what has already been mentioned in verse 31. That contrast is (1) to what the Pharisees had promoted about marriage (to put away a wife by giving her a Writing of Divorcement) and (2) what the word (*cause*) says about fornication:

> The conjunction *but* is a signpost that indicates a change in thought. It tells the reader to take notice.

*31 It hath been said, Whosoever shall put away his wife, let him give her a writing of divorcement: 32 **But** I [Jesus] say unto you, That whosoever shall put away his wife, saving for the cause of fornication, causeth her to commit adultery: and whosoever shall marry her that is divorced committeth adultery.* Matthew 5:31-32

Study the illustration below which was introduced in Chapter 13 for Matthew 19:9. This is the same grammatical structure also used by Matthew in 5:32. The word *wife* again applies to two different kinds of wives, except that now, we need to factor a potential additional category of those who are put away (divorced). This includes

> Unlawful marriages could be included in the fornication exception.

not only putting away because of fornication during an espousal, it *could* also be broadened to include unlawful marriage relationships, especially those mentioned in the Old Testament in Leviticus 18 and elsewhere in the Old Testament and in the New Testament. These, such as incest and sodomite "marriages," could come under a special inclusive or generic category of fornication because of the addition of the word *cause* and the reference Jesus made: *"Ye have heard that it was said by them of old time ..."* Matthew 5:27

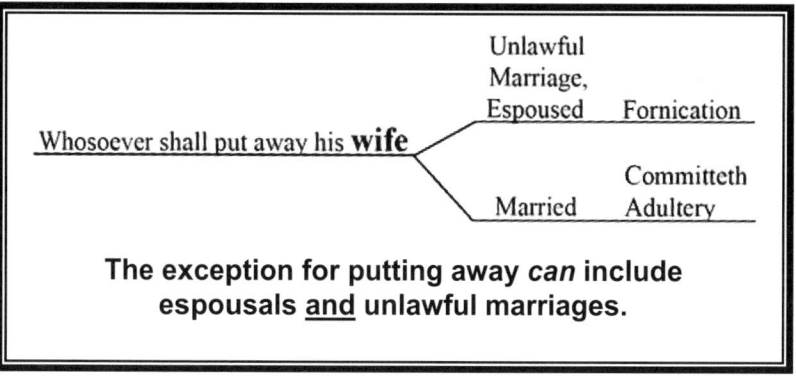

**The exception for putting away *can* include espousals <u>and</u> unlawful marriages.**

The exception clauses are hypothetical and are written to let the reader know there is an exception to something and that exception is for fornication. Now the question becomes what fornication can or might include contextually. The Word or Scriptures from the Old Testament record what might be included. Those from the "old time" include some of the following:

- A sin God would consider to be fornication.
- A sin God would consider to be fornication, and those involved in this sin call themselves husbands and wives.
- A sin God would consider to be fornication, and those involved in this sin call themselves husbands and wives; but if they divorce, they would be free to enter into a one-flesh marriage and would not commit adultery.

One such example that would fit these exception parameters is what has been taught thus far in the Matthew 19:9 exception clause—those who are espoused. However, the addition of the word *cause*, included in Matthew 5:32, indicates that this exception is different; and thus, it *could* serve as a broader-based reference.

What is included in the Word of God about fornication that *could* contextually apply but not just for the Jewish espousal? That is, what does the **Word** of God say are examples where a man could divorce his wife and marry another wife and not put himself into a state of adultery and which would not violate any Scriptures? That would include, in addition to those who were espoused or engaged, those of "*old time*" (as mentioned in Matthew 5:27) who are in Biblically illegitimate marriages. These could include incestuous relationships listed in Leviticus 18:6-22 and any other forbidden marriage relationship such as sodomy. **Those in covenant-marriages are <u>not</u> included**

> Illegitimate marriages must be considered.

**in the exception for unlawful marriages;** that is, in *except it be for the cause of fornication*. Even though adulterous "marriages" are sinful relationships, adultery is specifically named as adultery, not fornication, in New Testament Scriptures. The "rule of proximity" provides a guideline to indicate that marital adultery would be excluded from the fornication exception because both fornication and adultery are used in the same verse. That being the case, they do not refer to the same sin. They are used in contrast one to the other.

If a truly single person (one who doesn't have a living one-flesh spouse) leaves (divorces) any unscriptural marriage relationship and marries someone who doesn't have a living one-flesh spouse, neither party would enter into a state of adultery. Those who are truly single are those who have not previously been joined into a covenant-marriage or have, but their spouse has died. Incestuous and sodomite "marriages" are also in violation of God's "law of marriage." Leaving these relationships and marrying another person, assuming the parameters of God's law are met, would not put people into a state of adultery. However, without the vital exception clauses, anyone who puts away a wife (even one for incest or sodomy) and marries another would commit adultery, and anyone who was espoused could not break his espousal. That would say there would be no way to get out of a sinful "marital lifestyle" or, under the Jewish man-made tradition, out of an espousal. Those in same sex marriages and those in incestuous relationships

> The exception clause, included only by Matthew, has important information.

would be destined to never be able to repent from those sins and thus enter into a covenant-marriage. They could never be saved. Therefore, it's essential to understand that the word *wife* which precedes the exception clause, *whosoever shall put away his wife,* has more than one meaning, especially as it applies to what the Word (*cause*) says about the sin of fornication:

> ***But*** *I say unto you, That whosoever shall put away his wife, saving for the **cause** of fornication, causeth her to commit adultery: and whosoever shall marry her that is divorced* [put away] *committeth adultery.* Matthew 5:32

Study the Matthew 5:32 illustration of the exception clause below. It pictures the exclusion of "unlawful" wives listed in the right column from the remaining part of the verse (*causeth her to commit adultery, and whosoever shall marry her that is divorced committeth adultery*). Those in the right column **are those who would be exempted from committing adultery** if they divorce and marry someone who isn't married:

| Matthew 5:32 exceptions: **Whosoever shall put away his wife:** | |
|---|---|
| These could be included in the "saving for the cause of <u>fornication</u>"*<br><br>Marital adultery is specifically named as *adultery* in several New Testament verses. These would not be exceptions. | except for a "wife"*:<br><br>• from an espousal or betrothal<br>• from incestuous relationship**<br>• from a sodomite relationship**<br><br>**These are contrary to God's "law of marriage." See also page 271—truly single persons. |
| *If these enter a covenant-marriage, they will not commit adultery because they have never been made one flesh by God. ||
| *Leviticus 18:6-22; 20:11-17; Deuteronomy 27:20-23; Deuteronomy 22:30; Jude 7; 1 Corinthians 5:1; 1 Corinthians 7:2; Matthew 19:9; Matthew 14:3-4; Mark 6:17; Romans 1:28-31; et al. ||

The exception clause could serve to exempt those who are espoused, those in incestuous or sodomite "marriages," and those in adulterous "marriages" who are fornicators—never been made one-flesh by God. The remainder of the verse applies to those who ARE in a covenant-marriage. If those in covenant-marriages divorce **and** marry another, or if a put-away covenant spouse marries another person, each of those involved in these relationships committ**eth** adultery.

Whether the above discussion about the application of *cause* to the Word of God is accepted or not, even absent any exception clause, those who are filled with the Spirit of God would know that they should not remain in any sinful lifestyle. It's the same kind of spiritual logic that helps a spirit-filled person understand that the expression "causeth her to commit adultery" does not mean that this always happens. It is up to the person who is put away to flee the sin of adultery. If a divorced person enters into an adulterous relationship, he will be held fully accountable for his own sinful choice.

## The introductory words differ between the two exception clauses.

There's one more difference between the two exception clauses—the introductory words used in Matthew 5:32 and Matthew 19:9: *saving for* and *except it be for*. The reason for this difference in English is because the underlying Greek text from which each of the two Scriptures is translated are from different words. Even though they mean about the same, for some reason, different Greek words were recorded.

However, each complements the other. *Saving for* is from the Greek word *parektos* which means outside of, apart from, except for, with the exception. In Matthew 19:9, the clause begins with *ei me* which also means *except for*. Even though *parektos* is a different word than that used to start the exception clause in Matthew 19:9 (*ei me*), the two words contextually mean the same. They indicate an exception follows. Compare the two exception clauses as shown below:

> saving <parektos> for the cause <logos> of fornication <porneia>
> except <ei me> it be for <epi> fornication <porneia>
>
> **Both exception clauses are simplified on one line showing different Greek words for the English translations: *saving* and *except*.**

## Study three omissions or changes by authors of the new versions in the exception clause from Matthew 5:32.

The exception clauses provide a means to legally separate from sinful relationships which is what the Word states would need to be done to inherit the kingdom of God: *He that covereth his sins shall not prosper: but whoso confesseth and <u>forsaketh</u> them shall have mercy.* Proverbs 28:13

The exception clause would not include marital adultery; that is, what is Biblically called *adultery*. It's the sin that is committed by those who are in a one-flesh marriage but are sexually unfaithful. The resolution to unfaithfulness within a covenant-marriage is to repent, seek, and extend forgiveness. Sexual sin with someone outside a covenant-marriage is sin; however, it is not a *cause* to divorce. Jesus and other New Testament writers tell us that divorcing a one-flesh spouse <u>and</u> marrying another spouse, no matter the *cause*, is adultery, not fornication.

> There is a pattern of changes in the new versions which isn't supported by their Greek text.

Both the underlying Greek text for the New Versions (Nestle Aland) and the Greek text that is used for the King James Bible (Textus Receptus) are the same for the exception clause in Matthew 5:32. However, there is a pattern of changes and omissions among most new versions of the Bible. They:

- Leave their Greek word *logos* (cause) untranslated.
- Do not translate parektos as *saving for*.
- Incorrectly translate the Greek word for fornication, *porneia*.

As shown in Chapter 11, the authors of the new versions incorrectly substitute *martial unfaithfulness*, *sexual immorality*, or *immorality* for *fornication*. See the table below. **The KJB is shown for comparison:**

| New versions incorrectly translate Matthew 5:32. saving <parektos> for the cause <logos> of fornication <porneia> ||
|---|---|
| Bible* | **Exception clause from Matthew 5:32** |
| KJB | ... ***saving* for the *cause*** *of fornication* ... |
| NKJV | ... *except sexual immorality* ... |
| NGSB | ... *except sexual immorality* ... |
| NIV | ... *except for marital unfaithfulness* ... |
| NASV | ... *except for the cause of unchastity* ... |
| ESV | ... *except on the ground of sexual immorality* ... |
| HCSB | ... *except in a case of sexual immorality* ... |
| *Key for above Bibles: KJB: King James Bible; NKJV: New King James Version; NGSB: New Geneva Study Bible; NIV: New International Version; NASV: New American Standard Version; ESV: English Standard Version; HCSB: Holman Christian Standard Bible ||

| **Unscriptural teaching from International Children's Bible\*** |
|---|
| *But I tell you that anyone who divorces his wife is causing his wife to be guilty of adultery. The only reason for a man to divorce his wife is if she has sexual relations with another man. And anyone who marries that divorced woman is guilty of adultery.* Matthew 5:32 |
| \*The tag line for this Bible is "The Version Children Can Read and Understand." **This should sound an alarm that parents must carefully assess children's Christian literature, especially Bibles.** |

*Fornication* applies equally to either a husband or a wife in both exception clauses. Transgression of God's laws applies to both the husband and the wife—to both male and female: *There is neither Jew nor Greek, there is neither bond nor free, there is neither male nor female: for ye are all one in Christ Jesus.* Galatians 3:28

Several examples have been given of Bibles which change the exception clause to read *marital unfaithfulness*. That's one reason why it's so dangerous for Christians to study Biblical doctrine from Bibles in which their text has not been contextually correctly rendered. No one should be "renewing" his mind with incorrectly translated Scriptures.

To recap: The LORD has a purpose for every word. Neglecting to translate the word *cause* in Matthew 5:32 is an example of changing the Word of God which is a grievous sin against God. No one should partake in re-writing the Word. A plausible explanation has been given for the interpretation of the word *cause* (logos) in *saving for the cause of fornication*. Because of other contextual information in Jesus' training His disciples in the *Sermon on the Mount*, "saving for the cause," potentially expands the meaning of *fornication* from its more specific focus of an act of fornication in Matthew 19:9 to an inclusive one in Matthew 5:32. Yet, neither exception clause is in opposition to the other. They agree. It also does not mean that Matthew 19:9 could not include other fornicative sins such as those discussed.

## There's a difference between an exception and an escape.

The "exception clauses" are not escape clauses for those in one-flesh marriages; that is, they are not included as an escape from a God-ordained/God-created marriage. They *could* be called an "escape clause" for those relationships that violate God's marriage laws, and they also allow for an espousal divorce, the Jewish practice included in Matthew 1:18-19.

As you move forward with additional principles, it's important to not forget those that have already been established. It's assumed that what has already been taught still applies. That's the way it works with all Bible topics; that is, **not every passage or book of the Bible contains the entire doctrine on that subject**. As a general rule, it's the whole counsel of God that must be considered—the context of the entire Bible must be the foundation rather than isolated words or Scriptures.

The next chapter *What Is A Divorce?* will include some reinforcing repetition along with some additional important clarifying information. It should help to solidify some of the concepts mentioned in this chapter and remove any confusion about how God looks at divorce and why His spiritual wife Israel was given a Writing of Divorcement and put away. Do you know not only why this happened but where and how God has that answer "treasure-housed" in the Scriptures? The next chapter provides further information and study on this topic.

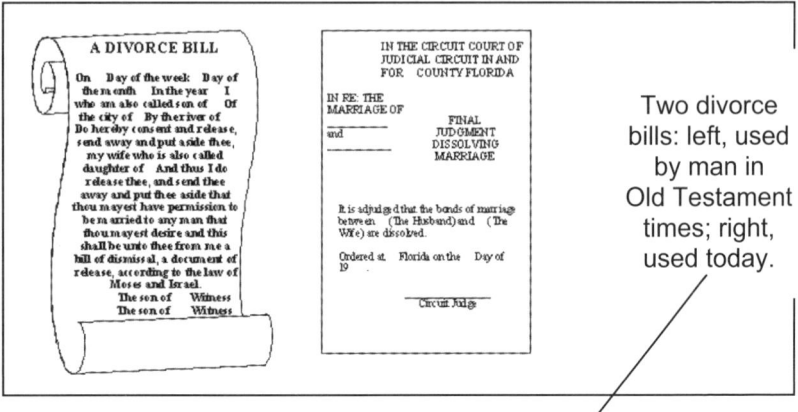

Two divorce bills: left, used by man in Old Testament times; right, used today.

**Paul feared that those to whom he had ministered would be pulled astray with other versions of the gospel.
He also gives an additional warning twice
to those who preach another gospel.**

*But I fear, lest by any means, as the serpent beguiled Eve through his subtilty, so your minds should be corrupted from the simplicity that is in Christ. For if he that cometh preacheth another Jesus, whom we have not preached, or if ye receive another spirit, which ye have not received, or **another gospel**, which ye have not accepted, ye might well bear with him.* 2 Corinthians 11:3-4

*I marvel that ye are so soon removed from him that called you into the grace of Christ unto **another gospel**: 7 Which is not another; but there be some that trouble you, and would **pervert the gospel of Christ**. 8 But though we, or an angel from heaven, <u>preach any other gospel</u> unto you than that which we have preached unto you, <u>let him be accursed</u>. 9 As we said before, so say I now again, <u>If any man preach</u> **any other gospel** unto you than that ye have received, <u>let him be accursed</u>.* Galatians 1:6-9

# 17

# What IS A Divorce?

Beware of confusion over the word *divorce*. It, like the word *wife*, is multifaceted and must be contextually and properly interpreted. Man's understanding of divorce is a dissolution that is the result of a court action when one spouse petitions the court by filing a lawsuit against the other. When the judge brings down his "stroke of death" on the marriage, the striking of the gavel means that he has dissolved the relationship between the Petitioner-spouse and the Defendant-spouse. This is how the **world and most churches wrongly** interpret what the court has adjudicated. That's because this is how the secular and church environments define a divorce. They consider it a dissolution. However, the Word of God has specific teachings that may prove helpful in properly understanding what the Bible says about divorce as it applies to marriages.

## What Is A Divorce?

There are three categories of divorces from a Biblical perspective. The first is the divorce allowed because of fornication during the Jewish espousal contractual period such as that which *could* have been used to dissolve the espousal **contract** between Joseph and Mary. That is what is recorded in the first chapter of Matthew's writings about Joseph's initial thought to divorce Mary during their espousal. This would have been for the cause of fornication. The second category would be a divorce from a Biblically "unlawful" marriage, such as sodomite and incestuous relationships. These are man-made legal procedures for man-made legal relationships. Such "divorces" would be considered dissolutions because the divorce in these instances **dissolves** a man-made **contractual** arrangement, not a one-flesh joining by God. These divorces dissolve contracts, not covenants.

The third category of divorce is between covenant spouses—those marriages which are created by God. However, when a covenant spouse separates himself from his one-flesh spouse—even when accompanied by man's legal divorce document, called a dissolution of marriage—it is **not** a dissolution. Why isn't it a dissolution? After all, a court decree states that it is a dissolution. See below:

> **"The court has jurisdiction of the subject matter and of the parties. The marriage between John Doe and Mary Doe is dissolved because it is irretrievably broken."**

The judicial system, however, is deceived. They do not have jurisdiction over God's covenant of marriage any more than does man have jurisdiction over God's covenant of salvation. Scripture states very clearly and repetitively that **God creates** the covenant of marriage through His supernatural joining, and **God dissolves** marriage when one of the spouses physically dies. What **man** says and thinks he does through his instrument of dissolution is what God says is impossible. The rap of a judge's gavel on the bench and a piece of paper called a dissolution of marriage cannot dissolve *what* God has created—until death; that is, *what* He has joined together.

This third category of divorce, that against a covenant-marriage, is an integral part of both the Old and New Testaments. The difficulty with this divorce lies in recognizing and contextually correctly applying it today. Two Old Testament examples which help to clarify this confusion are God's spiritual wife Israel and Hosea's physical wife Gomer. These two are closely related because:

1. They were both covenants created and sanctioned by God.
2. They both involved wives who became unfaithful.
3. **They both involve divorces but neither was a dissolution.**

Israel was God's chosen nation. He "took" her as His spiritual wife. This spiritual marriage to Israel is a model of God's unilateral side of the marriage-covenant which also applies to a physical marriage. Review the teaching in Chapter 12 about the unilateral and bilateral aspects of a marriage-covenant. **It's the terms and the joining of the marriage-covenant that God unilaterally sets.** These cannot be altered by man. Only God has jurisdiction over covenant-marriages.

He, alone, unilaterally creates them, and "adjudicates" them:

*Now when I* [God] *passed by thee* [the nation of Israel], *and looked upon thee, behold, thy time was the time of love; and I spread my skirt over thee, and covered thy nakedness: yea, I sware unto thee, and entered into a covenant with thee, saith the Lord GOD, and thou becamest mine.* Ezekiel 16:8

In a physical prototype, Hosea married Gomer. This is also the prototype for all covenant-marriages today. It's what God creates and in which man becomes a part and usually over which a member of the clergy officiates (or a justice of the peace, etc.).

*The word of the LORD that came unto Hosea ... And the LORD said to Hosea, Go, <u>take</u> unto thee a wife ... So he went and <u>took</u> Gomer.* Hosea 1:1-3

The Biblical "language of marriage" should be familiar because of what has been presented thus far, especially the description written by Matthew of the relationship between Joseph and Mary.

*Then Joseph being raised from sleep did as the angel of the Lord had bidden him, and <u>took</u> unto him his wife.* Matthew 1:24

God's wife and Hosea's wife were to remain faithful to their spouses. However, each refused to do that. They became caught up in the lust of their flesh—sin. Israel went after other gods;

> The Bible teaches there are spiritual marriages and physical marriages.

worshipped them, sacrificed to them; adopted pagan practices and man-instituted beliefs. Gomer went after other men. Both she and Israel became what God says were whores and harlots. They "departed" from the LORD.

These were grievous sins against God. Sin creates a separation between the transgressor and God. This is what happened with Israel (as well as her sister-nation Judah). Because of their sin, **they separated themselves** from God, their spiritual husband. Gomer, because of her harlotry, separated herself from her physical husband Hosea. These separations are also what is spoken of in the Bible as a *divorce*, as *putting away*, and as *dealing treacherously* against a wife. Read carefully:

*The LORD said also unto me* [Jeremiah] *... Hast thou seen that which backsliding Israel hath done? she is gone up upon every high mountain and under every green tree, and there hath played the harlot. And I* [God] *said after she had done all these things, Turn thou unto me. But she returned not. And her treacherous sister Judah saw it. And I saw, when for all the causes whereby backsliding Israel committed adultery I* [God] *had **put her away, and given her a bill of divorce**; yet her treacherous sister Judah feared not, but went and played the harlot also. And it came to pass through the lightness of her whoredom, that she defiled the land, and committed adultery with stones and with stocks.* Jeremiah 3:6-9

So it was Israel's sin (like Gomer's sin and like man's sin today) that separated her from God and from which she was told, pleaded with, and begged to re-turn. Israel refused; she is still playing the harlot. Yet, God's covenant was not dissolved. It is still in place today, even as are the covenants of those spouses who are a part of God's physical marriage-covenant. Even though husbands and wives <u>can</u> choose not to honor that commitment, *Marriage is honourable in all, and the bed undefiled but whoremongers and adulterers God will judge.* Hebrews 13:4

*Go and proclaim these words toward the north, and say, **Return**, thou backsliding Israel, saith the LORD; and I will not cause mine anger to fall upon you: for I am merciful, saith the LORD, and I will not keep anger for ever. Only acknowledge thine iniquity, that thou hast transgressed against the LORD thy God, and hast scattered thy ways to the strangers under every green tree, and ye have not obeyed my voice, saith the LORD. **Turn**, O backsliding children, saith the LORD; **for I am married unto you** ...* Jeremiah 3:12-14

## God will not repent for us.
## We must decide to hate our sin
## and remove ourselves from it.

Israel committed adultery. God divorced her, BUT she is yet (still) His wife. This may sound as if it means that people can divorce in a like manner. This, however, is where a deeper understanding of the contextual nature of how God "defines" divorce is vital. Divorce **within a covenant-marriage** is a separation—not a dissolution. That's why the Scripture tells us that whosoever divorces **and** marries another spouse committ**eth** adultery. The divorce has no effect on the validity of the marriage-covenant. Likewise, God is waiting for His deserting spouse Israel to return, for her to repent and re-turn to Him. Repentance within a covenant-marriage means that those who go astray from covenant put aside the sin and re-turn to covenant love:

> Covenant divorce is a separation.

*Therefore I will judge you, O house of Israel, every one according to his ways, saith the Lord GOD.* ***Repent, and turn yourselves from all your transgressions****; so iniquity shall not be your ruin.* ***Cast away from you*** *all your transgressions, whereby ye have transgressed; and make you a new heart and a new spirit: for why will ye die, O house of Israel? For I have no pleasure in the death of him that dieth, saith the Lord GOD: wherefore* ***turn yourselves****, and live ye.* Ezekiel 18:30-32

*Then said the LORD unto me* [Hosea]*, Go yet, love a woman* [His covenant wife Gomer] *beloved of her friend, yet an adulteress, according to the love of the LORD toward the children of Israel, who look to other gods, and love flagons of wine.* Hosea 3:1

Gomer, Israel, and all who sin, must choose to come out of sin and re-turn\* to God: *If ye love me, keep my commandments.* John 14:15

\*The term *re-turn* (without the quotes and with dash), like *re-marriage* without quotes and with dash, is used to emphasize the re-turn to covenant-marriage.

Chapter 17

*And this have ye done again, covering the altar of the LORD with tears, with weeping, and with crying out, insomuch that he regardeth not the offering any more, or receiveth it with good will at your hand. Yet ye say, Wherefore? Because the LORD hath been witness between thee and the wife of thy youth, against whom thou **hast dealt treacherously**: yet is she thy companion, and the <u>wife of thy covenant</u>. And did not he make one? Yet had he the residue of the spirit. And wherefore one? That he might seek a godly seed. Therefore take heed to your spirit, and let none deal treacherously against the wife of his youth. For the LORD, the God of Israel, saith that **he hateth putting away: for one covereth violence with his garment**, saith the LORD of hosts: therefore take heed to your spirit, that ye **deal not treacherously**. Ye have wearied the LORD with your words. Yet ye say, Wherein have we wearied him? When ye say, Every one that doeth evil is good in the sight of the LORD, and he delighteth in them; or, Where is the God of judgment?* Malachi 2:13-17

*They say, If a man put away his wife, and she go from him, and become another man's, shall he return unto her again? shall not that land be greatly polluted? but thou hast played the harlot with many lovers; **yet return again to me**, saith the LORD.* Jeremiah 3:1

*And I saw, when for all the causes whereby backsliding Israel committed adultery I had put her away, and given her a bill of divorce; yet her treacherous sister Judah feared not, but went and played the harlot also. And it came to pass through the lightness of her whoredom, that she defiled the land, and committed adultery with stones and with stocks.* Jeremiah 3:8-9

*... **Return**, thou backsliding Israel, saith the LORD; and I will not cause mine anger to fall upon you ... Only acknowledge thine iniquity, that thou hast transgressed against the LORD thy God, and hast scattered thy ways to the strangers under every green tree, and ye have not obeyed my voice, saith the LORD. **Turn**, O backsliding children, saith the LORD; **for I am married unto you** ...* Jeremiah 3:12-14

*And unto the married I **command**, yet not I, but **the Lord**, Let not the wife depart from her husband: But and if she depart, let her remain unmarried, or be reconciled to her husband: and let not the husband put away his wife.* 1 Corinthians 7:10-11

There is a Scripture in Isaiah which supernaturally pulls this all together. It is framed through two rhetorical questions and God's declarative answer. The LORD uses rhetorical questions throughout the Old and New Testaments through many of the writers who recorded the Scriptures. Already presented have been some of the rhetorical statements made by God and Jesus through the pens of Jeremiah, Matthew, and especially Paul in his contrast between being joined in a marriage to a harlot and being joined in spirit to the LORD (Review Chapter 14.). Now, for another rhetorical example, study that which was written by the prophet Isaiah. Compare and contrast the structure of Isaiah 50:1 and Jeremiah 3:1.

| God's rhetorical statements must be carefully read and contextually discerned. ||
|---|---|
| *Thus saith the LORD, [1]Where is the bill of your mother's divorcement, whom I have put away? or [2]which of my creditors is it to whom I have sold you? Behold, for your iniquities have ye sold yourselves, and for your transgressions is your mother put away.* Isaiah 50:1 | *They say, If a man put away his wife, and she go from him, and become another man's, shall he return unto her again? shall not that land be greatly polluted? but thou hast played the harlot with many lovers; yet return again to me, saith the LORD.* Jeremiah 3:1 |

What is God saying here? It may appear to some undiscerning readers that God has given the [1]bill of divorce as a dissolution and that He has [2]sold the harlot Israel to creditors. However, God's two rhetorical questions must be read in context with His declarative statement—His answer to the questions which immediately follows. It's because of iniquities and transgressions that **man** sells himself to the works of Satan: *Behold, for **your** iniquities have **ye sold yourselves**, and for **your** transgressions is your mother put away.* This is God's *punitive judgment*. He permits man to choose—to live righteously or in sinful lifestyles: *Know ye not, that to whom **ye yield yourselves** servants to obey, his servants* *ye are to whom ye obey; whether of sin unto death, or of obedience unto righteousness?* Romans 6:16

Here's how some of the new versions create false statements from Truths that God speaks. They paraphrase God's Words and change the meaning of what He says. Below is what is recorded in the NIV and NASV for Isaiah 50:1 (in the right column). The same verse is given as it appears in the King James Bible in the left column:

| Study Isaiah 50:1 with its rhetorical questions and God's answer. ||
|---|---|
| *Thus saith the LORD, Where is the bill of your mother's divorcement, whom I have put away? or which of my creditors is it to whom I have sold you? Behold, <u>for your iniquities</u> have <u>**ye sold yourselves**</u>, and for <u>your</u> transgressions is your mother put away.* KJB | *This is what the LORD says: "Where is your mother's certificate of divorce with which I sent her away? Or to which of my creditors did I sell you? Because of your sins **you were sold**; because of your transgressions your mother was sent away.* NIV |
| What are the key words which totally change the meaning for whom it is that sold them? Ye sold *yourselves*. The answer is **not** that they were sold, but <u>they sold themselves</u>. It was their choice to turn from God. God did not send them away. **Their** sins sent them astray. | *"Where is the certificate of divorce, By which I have sent your mother away? Or to whom of My creditors did I sell you? Behold, **you were sold** for your iniquities, And for your transgressions your mother was sent away.* NASV |

Those who are in a covenant-marriage and seek a civil court for the dissolution of a marriage or go to a church for an annulment have put themselves away—they have <u>sold themselves</u> unto unrighteousness. It's not God who has done this. They have sold themselves over to a lifestyle of sin. What should be understood from this additional teaching is how God, through the words written in the Bible, shows us how He looks at divorce. Readers must be careful not to misinterpret God's statement that He put Israel away and gave her a bill of divorce after she committed adultery. This is a covenant, **not** a contract. This divorce and all **covenant** divorces **are not dissolutions. They are separations**. Conversely, the courts consider marriage a contract. That's why judges wrongly "think" they can dissolve a covenant-marriage. They are deceived. Men can dissolve **adulterous "marriages" because they are not covenants,** but they have absolutely no authority from God to "touch" His covenants. They are sinning by doing so and so is everyone who partakes in such a blasphemous act. Men **can** violate the terms, but they **cannot** dissolve *what* it is that God joins together through His covenant of marriage. God's covenant principles are an integral part of the entire Bible starting with the recording of the creation of the marriage-covenant in Genesis:

*And Adam said, This is now bone of my bones, and flesh of my flesh ...* Genesis 2:23 *Yet ye say, Wherefore? Because the LORD hath been witness between thee and the wife of thy youth, against whom thou hast dealt treacherously:* ***yet is she*** *thy companion, and* ***the wife of thy covenant****.* Malachi 2:14 *And they twain shall be one flesh: so then they are no more twain, but one flesh.* Mark 10:8

The Bible is a miraculous book written over a period of 1,500 years by at least 40 different authors all from different backgrounds; yet, incredibly their writings complement one another which prove the Bible is truly the work of the miraculous "Hand" of God:

*Knowing this first, that no prophecy of the scripture is of any private interpretation. For the prophecy came not in old time by the will of man: but holy men of God spake as they were moved by the Holy Ghost.* 2 Peter 1:20-21

*Even from the days of your fathers ye are gone away from mine ordinances, and have not kept them.* ***Return unto me****, and I will return unto you, saith the LORD of hosts.* ***But*** *ye said, Wherein shall we return?* Malachi 3:7

# 18

## What *Kind* Of Wife... Is An Exception?

There has been much said about the Jewish espousal and the two different kinds of husbands and wives. They will be addressed again in this chapter, but there will be some additional information about wives that will be added to what you already know. It's also important to understand that the relationship between Matthew 19:9 (and 5:32) and the practice of the Jewish betrothal/espousal are contextually tightly interwoven throughout both the Old and New Testaments. Thus, there will also be several examples to study from both Testaments which reflect these Jewish linguistic wife-husband patterns. The word *wife* is a **key word in structurally** tying many teachings together. It is used 407 times but not always in the context of its most recognized association—that of a woman who is married. That familiar usage is beautifully portrayed through the Proverbs 31 wife where she is called a *virtuous woman*. The value of this **help meet** is recorded to be far above the price of rubies. Study Proverbs 31:10-31.

This seemingly simple word, however, is really quite complex. How many different **ways** can you think of in which *wife* is addressed in the Bible? One thing is for sure, if you came up with more than one kind, you must have considered context. It is through this additional word study of *wife* that perhaps you will see how important context is. Every word is carefully placed and is included for a given purpose:

*The words of the LORD are pure words: as silver tried in a furnace of earth, purified seven times. Thou shalt keep them, O LORD, thou shalt preserve them from this generation for ever.* Psalm 12:6-7

Some of the different **ways** *wife* is used in the Bible are summarized below. You may not have realized that in this book five different examples have already been mentioned:

- A married wife: Matthew 1:24.
- An engaged wife: Matthew 1:19.
- The bride of Christ which is the church, the body of believers; believers are engaged, not married, to Christ: 2 Corinthians 11:2, Revelation 19:7, and 21:9.
- God's spiritual wife Israel: Ezekiel 16:8.
- The relationship between a married husband and wife which is to be a reflection of Christ and His relationship to the church: Ephesians 5:23-31.
- A sixth structural use is found in the expression "to wife." This usage hasn't been specifically taught so far. It means *to marry someone* and is used 46 times. It, like the five uses above, reflects the Jewish Biblical language: Genesis 12:19.

## The dual nature of *wife* is used throughout the Bible.

There are many times that someone who studies the Bible must understand the Jewish espousal language in order to correctly interpret Scripture. This language is not outdated as many have been wrongly taught. The words in the Bible have been carefully and specifically recorded to accurately reflect (1) the underlying languages and (2) contextual idiosyncrasies. They express unique Jewish practices which existed within the Greek-speaking environment into which Jesus was born, raised, and in which He taught. Review the illustration below. Its purpose is to help summarize visually what has been discussed thus far. In the first diagram, *Mary* is illustrated as being both an espoused and a married wife; in the second, the dual nature of wife is shown as it is used in Matthew 19:9.

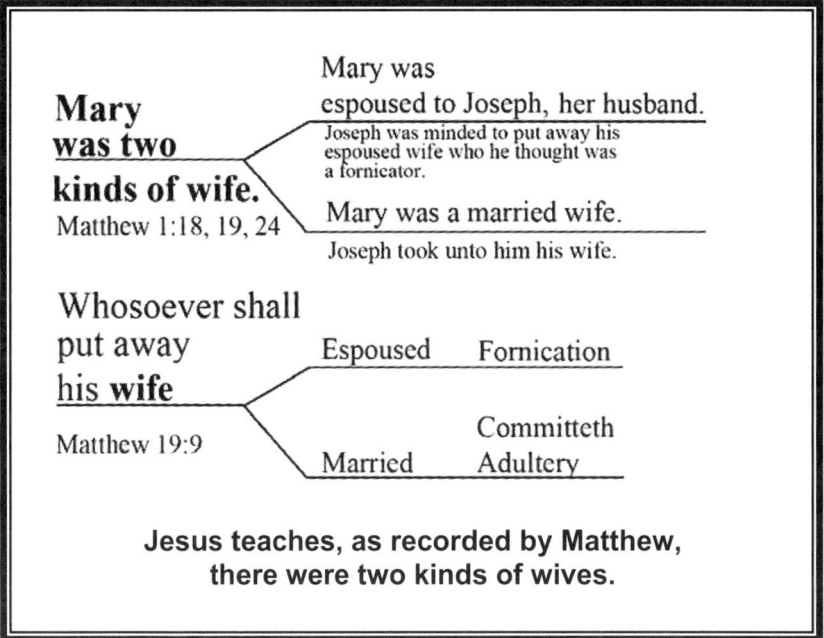

## What Kind Of Wife Is An Exception?

The word *fornication* must also be interlinked with an espoused wife. Even though *fornication* <u>can</u> include Biblically unlawful marriages, the New Testament teachings focus on:

1. Covenant marriages (marrying and putting away a Biblically joined husband or wife).
2. Espoused husbands and wives.

The Jewish language expressions are used not only in the first book of the New Testament but in the last book and throughout the entire Bible. They provide a depth of understanding that is missed when these words are replaced by modern, paraphrased translations and teachings which do not consistently rely upon the Scriptures. Study the following 14 examples from both Testaments. Notice not only the subtle references to engaged wives (and husbands) but also other Jewish expressions such as "to wife" and "married to a wife."

1. *Why saidst thou, She is my sister? so I might have <u>taken</u> her to me **to wife**: now therefore behold thy wife, <u>take</u> her, and go thy way.* Genesis 12:19:
This was a conversation between Abram and Pharaoh who was saying that he might have married (*to wife*) Abram's wife Sarai because he thought she was Abram's sister rather than his wife. (She was really also Abram's half sister.)

> The word *take* has different meanings depending on the context.

It's important to read all of Genesis 12 to understand the context. The underlined word *take* in this Scripture doesn't mean *to marry* (as it does in Matthew 1:20). That's because the context is different. Abram and Sarai were already married.

2. *And what man is there that hath **betrothed a wife**, and hath not **taken** [married] **her** ...* Deuteronomy 20:7:
The words *not taken* mean "had not married." This should be evident because of other contextual information. *Betrothed a wife* means the man has an engaged wife whom he has not married.

3. *If a man be found lying with a woman **married to an husband** ...* Deuteronomy 22:22:
Some new Bible versions record this: "If a man is found sleeping with another man's wife ..." That removes the vital Biblical language and incorrectly translates what is written in the underlying Hebrew text.

4. *If a damsel that is a virgin **be betrothed unto an husband**, and a man find her in the city, and lie with her ... because he hath humbled **his neighbour's wife** ...* Deuteronomy 22:23-24:
The reader should be able to determine by reading the first part of Deuteronomy 22:23 (the context) that the expression "his neighbour's wife" is speaking not of a married wife but an engaged wife. It is wrong to remove God's Biblical language which runs throughout the Bible like the threads that hold together a tapestry. The table on the next page shows what some of the other versions of the Bible substitute for the first part of verse 23: *be betrothed unto an husband*.

They replace *be **betrothed** unto an **husband*** which removes not only important Jewish/Hebrew facts, but it also hinders interlinking of Scriptures. These authors also aren't faithful to the text from which they are translating. They are incorrectly translating the underlying Hebrew text. Using words such as *engaged* is infusing Gentile paraphrasing rather than *reflecting* Jewish/Hebrew Biblical idioms.

## The Hebrew should be translated as it has been preserved, word-for-word, as much as possible: Deuteronomy 22:23.

| לְאִישׁ | מְאֹרָשָׂה | בְתוּלָה | | נַעַר (נַעֲרָה) | יִהְיֶה | כִּי |
|---|---|---|---|---|---|---|
| unto an husband, | be betrothed | a virgin | that is | a damsel | | If |
| 376 | 781 | 1330 | 9999 | 5291 | 1961 | 3588 |
| lᵃiysh | mᵃoraasaah | bᵉtuwlaah | | naᵃraah | yihᵃyeh | Kiy |

**Hebrew is written right to left.**

| |
|---|
| *If a damsel that is a virgin **be betrothed unto an husband** ...* KJB |
| *If there is a girl who is a virgin engaged to a man* ... NASV |
| *If a man happens to meet in a town a virgin pledged to be married* ... NIV |
| *If there is a betrothed virgin, and a man meets her* ... ESV |
| *If there is a young woman who is a virgin engaged to a man* ... HCSB |
| *A man might meet a virgin in a city* ... ICB |
| Bible Key: KJB: King James Bible; NASV: New American Standard Version; NIV: New International Version; ESV: English Standard Version; HCSB: Holman Christian Study Bible; ICB: International Children's Bible |

5. ... *for more are the children of the desolate than the children of the **married wife**, saith the LORD.* Isaiah 54:1:
Some authors change "of the married wife" to "of her who has a husband." "Her who has a husband," doesn't reflect the important Biblical language. By including the phrase, "married wife," the "kind" of wife is specified, and the text then also accurately reflects the Hebrew text from which the English is translated. Even though the context would indicate that this is a married wife, man does not have the right to create Scripture and then remove the interlinking examples ("jots" and "tittles") given throughout the Bible.

6. *18 ... When as his mother Mary was **espoused** to Joseph, before they came together, she was found with child of the Holy Ghost. 19 Then Joseph **her husband**, being a just man, and not willing to make her a publick example, was minded to put her away privily. 20 But while he thought on these things, behold, the angel of the Lord appeared unto him in a dream, saying, Joseph, thou son of David, fear not to **take** unto thee **Mary thy wife** [engaged]: for that which is conceived in her is of the Holy Ghost.* Matthew 1:18-20:
Similar language patterns are also used in the New Testament which

reflect these Biblical linguistic expressions. The word *take*, in verse 20 above, means to "marry." A reader knows this if he understands the Biblical language and the several contextual language clues. Matthew, in verse 18, writes that Mary was espoused to Joseph. In verse 19, her espoused husband was going to divorce her (put her away). Joseph could have done this *if* Mary had committed the sin of fornication. A Jewish espoused husband did not ordinarily break his espousal contract; but, according to Matthew 1:19, he could break it if the reason were for fornication. Joseph, however, had no cause to divorce his espoused wife. Mary was a chaste woman of God.

> Biblical expressions reflect the underlying text.

7. *But I say unto you, That whosoever shall put away his **wife**, **saving for the cause of fornication**, causeth her to commit adultery: and whosoever shall marry her that is divorced committeth adultery.* Matthew 5:32

8. *And I say unto you, Whosoever shall put away his **wife**, **except it be for fornication**, and shall marry another, committeth adultery: and whoso marrieth her which is put away doth commit adultery.* Matthew 19:9:

Consider why each of the above exception clauses contextually refers to one of the two different kinds of Jewish wives—those who were espoused. Both Jesus a Jew and the Jewish Pharisees understood the dual nature of the word *wife*. It was a part of their cultural heritage. As mentioned previously, New Testament Scriptures focus on two different kinds of husband and wife relationships: covenant marriages (marrying and putting away Biblically joined husbands and wives) and espoused husbands and wives. There rarely is any mention or emphasis about divorcing from other sinful relationships; that is, from incestuous and sodomite relationships, even though these are also lifestyles God abhors. The New Testament emphasis is on adulterous marriages and situations referenced which distinguish between married and espoused wives (and husbands). **This could be vital, significant evidence to restrict Matthew 5:32, but especially 19:9, to these two relationships: espousals and covenant-marriages.**

The Bible **reflects a Jewish culture within a Gentile-dominated world** and that influence must be preserved and taught today. The importance of a word-for-word translation in Matthew's recorded exception clauses (and for all Scripture) is absolutely essential. It gives contextual continuity for understanding the **embedded linking of the espousal and marital language expressions**, and it is what the LORD has preserved in His law for us to study and obey—not from which to paraphrase and create loopholes.

9. ... *when he had **married a wife** ...* Matthew 22:25
10. *And another said, I have **married a wife**, and therefore I cannot come.* Luke 14:20:
Some new Bible version authors change "married a wife" to expressions such as "after he had married" or "the first one married." In so doing, they remove important embedded teachings, especially the reinforcement of Biblical language idioms. These are expressions which reflect what the Jewish culture recognized—that there were two different kinds of wives: *espoused* and *married*. In so doing, these authors dishonor the text from which they translate.

11. Art *thou **bound unto a wife**? seek not to be loosed. Art thou loosed from a wife? seek not a wife.* 1 Corinthians 7:27:
The expression "bound unto a wife" should by now take on a fuller

meaning. It is reflective of the distinction between the two different kinds of wives. "Bound unto a wife" carries the same meaning as does the expression "What therefore God hath joined together." It means *married to a wife*. It doesn't mean, "Are you espoused to a wife?" *Bound unto a wife* is another signpost, but here it should alert the reader of the differences between the two kinds of Biblically expressed Jewish wives.

12. *... for I have **espoused** you to one **husband**, that I may present you as a chaste virgin to Christ.* 2 Corinthians 11:2:
This Scripture was discussed in Chapter 10. It is not speaking of a married husband. It is referring to an espoused one. The highlighted words, *espoused* and *husband* should give the text depth of meaning. It is another reinforcement of the dual nature of the Jewish espousal and marriage language. If a Gentile person is engaged, he would not be called a husband, but readers who understand the Jewish espousal language know that this is an engaged husband, not a married one, and it embeds the reason for the specifically chosen words *espoused* and *husband*. Again, Gentiles do not "espouse a husband." How much clearer could it be that this is Biblical linguistics?

13. *Let us be glad and rejoice, and give honour to him: for the marriage of the Lamb is come, and **his wife** [engaged] hath made herself ready.* Revelation 19:7:
This is another Scripture that was discussed in Chapter 10, but adding the additional information from this chapter should help to reinforce the previous teaching. A wife comes **to the wedding altar,** not as a married wife, but as an engaged wife. The *wife* referenced here is the "spiritual" body of Christ. It is made up of individual believers. It's

the body of Christ who is espoused or engaged to Jesus (individually and corporately); but, as in keeping with the Biblical Jewish influenced espousal-marriage expressions, the church is called His *wife*. The body of Christ is an engaged wife until after the marriage ceremony—The *Marriage Supper of the Lamb*. Whether we be Jews or Gentiles, when we understand the Biblical language so expressed, we know this is an espoused wife who is to be joined to her espoused Husband [the LORD] in marriage.

14. *For we are members of his body, of his flesh, and of his bones. For this cause shall a man leave his father and mother, and shall be **joined unto his wife**, and they two shall be one flesh. This is a great mystery: but I speak concerning Christ and the church.* Ephesians 5:30-32:
The expression "joined unto his wife" again reflects Biblical language distinctions. It doesn't say, "shall ... leave his father and mother, and shall be married" as most Gentiles would express this. It says "shall be joined [married] unto his [espoused] wife."

God's "law of marriage," with His creation powers and permanent joining, is the same for all Jews and Gentiles. It doesn't matter whether there has been a formal engagement or not or whether those so joined are Jewish or Gentile. It's a supernatural joining by God of a man and woman. After the vows are given, they are married. The husband is "bound or married unto a wife." They are one flesh, not during an espousal, not before the wedding ceremony, and not because of any kind of sexual sin. It is *what* therefore God hath joined together. It is an espoused or non-covenant **wife**, not a covenant wife, who is the "subject" of the exception for fornication in the exception clauses.

# 19

# *There Is A Unique Biblical Blessing For Those Who Have Been "Put-away"!*

Incredible amounts of money are often invested in wedding ceremonies where two people are made one flesh by God. The fanfare, the music, the bride's dress are all focal parts of weddings. However, many who exit the wedding altar starry-eyed and happy do not remain that way. Something causes a breakdown in the relationship, and one or both spouses seek a legal, man-made divorce. Because there are more than a million divorces every year, it's no secret that God's once perfect earth is filled with wounded, hurting people. What are they to do? Perhaps there's a message in the book of Matthew that has been overlooked.

After teaching on the permanency of marriage, as recorded in Matthew 19:4-6, Jesus, in an extended conversation with His disciples, also talked about what <u>could be</u> a "eunuch solution" to extreme marriage challenges. This is not the commonly taught interpretation of this passage; however, it is one that perhaps should be examined:

*For there are some eunuchs, which were so born from their mother's womb: and there are some eunuchs, which were made eunuchs of men: and there be eunuchs, which have made themselves eunuchs for the kingdom of heaven's sake. He that is able to receive it, let him receive it.* Matthew 19:12

In this one Scripture, there are three different examples of the word *eunuchs*. There are eunuchs:

1. Which were so born from their mother's womb.
2. Which were made eunuchs of men.
3. Which have made themselves eunuchs for the Kingdom of Heaven's sake.

Perhaps you've never seriously studied this teaching recorded only in the gospel of Matthew. The definition of eunuch that most people think of is a male who has been castrated so as to divest him of the capability of sexual arousal. This was something practiced in Biblical times, especially in Old Testament days when a male servant was to be in charge of overseeing concubines for his master. This castration was to assure that the male servant would not become sexually involved with one of the concubines. That is a common definition of a *eunuch*. But is this really the focus of Jesus teaching? The Bible contains hundreds of figures of speech. Are these three kinds of eunuchs figures of speech or are they simply teachings about eunuchs? Could it be that the first two are factual and the last one a metaphor, a phrase that ordinarily designates one thing but it is used to illustrate something different than its normal use? Could it be that the first two are used in contrast to the last kind of eunuch which is metaphoric? It's important not to isolate Matthew 19:12 but to interpret its meaning within the context with which it is given. Much wrong theology is created when Scriptures are applied out of the context in which they are given. Perhaps that is true here.

## Two different writers record the same incident but with different facts.

The following statement was made in Chapter 16: "This is the way it works with all Bible topics; that is, not every passage or book of the Bible contains the entire doctrine on that subject ... **the context of the entire Bible must be the foundation rather than isolated words or Scriptures.**" This teaching about eunuchs is a strong example to further support the above statements about the importance of cross-referencing when studying the Bible. This is another way of saying it's important to always consider context. Context may come not only from the immediate verse but often from several other Scriptures.

Some readers may not understand how the eunuch discussion could be related to marriage as it rarely is taught that way. Let's consider this unconventional approach. First review and factor in some of the guidelines given on page eight as aids to help in properly interpreting Scripture: Who was it to whom Jesus made these statements? Where did He make them and why? Matthew doesn't give the answers to all these questions. The gospel writer Mark provides some details that Matthew, for some reason, was not led to include; and Matthew gives some details that Mark, for some reason, was not led to include. Neither writer, however, gives conflicting information; the one supplements the other. Compare the two accounts below:

| Matthew and Mark both record different aspects of the same events between Jesus and the disciples and Pharisees. | |
|---|---|
| Matthew 19:8-12 | Mark 10:2, 9-12 |
| 8 *He saith unto them [Pharisees], Moses because of the hardness of your hearts suffered you to put away your wives: but from the beginning it was not so.* | 2 *And the Pharisees came to him, and asked him, Is it lawful for a man to put away his wife? tempting him.* |
| 9 *And I say unto you, [Pharisees] Whosoever shall put away his wife, except it be for fornication, and shall marry another, committeth adultery: and whoso marrieth her which is put away doth commit adultery.* | 9 *What therefore God hath joined together, let not man put asunder.* |
| | Mark does not include the extended teachings given by Jesus to the Pharisees nor that about the eunuchs given to the disciples. |
| Mark lets us know that there is some kind of break between verses 9 and 10. | |
| 10 *His <u>disciples</u> say unto him, If the case of the man be so with his wife, it is not good to marry.* | 10 *And in the house his disciples **asked him again** <u>of the same matter</u>.* |
| 11 ***But** he [Jesus] said unto them, All men cannot receive this saying, save they to whom it is given.* *Jesus was not agreeing with them. He didn't even address their off-base remark. He instead gave a deeper teaching: | 11 *And he saith unto them,* [the disciples] *Whosoever shall put away his wife, and marry another, committeth adultery against her.* |
| 12 ***For** there are some eunuchs, which were so born from their mother's womb: and there are some eunuchs, which were made eunuchs of men: and there be eunuchs, which have made themselves eunuchs for the kingdom of heaven's sake. He that is able to receive it, let him receive it.* | 12 *And if a woman shall put away her husband, and be married to another, she committeth adultery.*<br><br>Mark and Matthew both recorded different aspects of what Jesus and the disciples said. |

The table above contains a lot of information. It's essential to carefully study these two accounts and understand that putting Matthew and Mark together sequentially is important to gain some insight about Jesus' teaching on eunuchs. An immediate, and obvious, noticeable difference should be the exception clause since it has been the forefront of so many teachings in this book. Mark did not include an exception clause; Matthew did. Not only did Matthew include the exception clauses once, but twice and with some significant differences between the two clauses. Mark did not include the eunuch teaching of Jesus to His disciples, but he lets the reader know that the disciples asked Jesus to explain a <u>second</u> time why it is not lawful for a man to divorce his wife. Jesus gave His answer straight-forwardly and in simple terms. If anyone divorces and marries another, he commits adultery. Matthew tells us that the disciples were so astounded by the reality of the permanence of marriage that they made an extreme irrational statement to which Jesus did not even respond. This was His pattern when people made statements or asked questions that were misleading or out of context.

Let's take a closer look at the intermingling of these two accounts. It's only from Mark's account that we find that the disciples, in a private conversation with Jesus, questioned Him again about it being lawful to divorce a wife. They, however, unlike the Pharisees, were not tempting Jesus but were reassuring themselves of something that people from all ages have a hard time accepting. *And in the house his disciples **asked him again** <u>of the same matter</u>.* Mark 10:10

Mark writes that Jesus answered the disciples' question with the same basic information He gave to the Pharisees, but He did not include the exception clause: *And he saith unto them, Whosoever shall put away his wife, and marry another, committeth adultery against her. And if a woman shall put away her husband, and be married to another, she committeth adultery.* Mark 10:11-12

Only Matthew records the disciples' astonishment, and perhaps almost a loss of words, for what they were trying to grasp. This was something that they and Jesus knew few would receive: "Listen" to their response given by Matthew: *His disciples say unto him, If the case of the man be so with his wife, it is not good to marry.* Matthew 19:10

Jesus, of course, **did not agree with the disciples' response.** He had taught that marriage was established from the beginning of recorded time; and among other things, marriage is vital to replenish the earth. Jesus most certainly did not teach to do away with marriage, but He taught about doing away with divorcing a covenant spouse.

Some people, even some religions, take the disciples' statement out of context: "It is good not to marry." What is true is that getting married is a very serious matter; however, that does not mean it's not good to marry. Jesus didn't even comment on their remark. He, instead, abruptly turned to a seemingly totally different set of examples. He didn't belabor what He had so clearly already repeatedly taught. Jesus gave a totally different response, perhaps to give them even more food for thought. He gave them three meanings of a eunuch to consider:

*And I [Jesus] say unto you, Whosoever shall put away his wife, except it be for fornication, and shall marry another, committeth adultery: and whoso marrieth her which is put away doth commit adultery. His disciples say unto him, If the case of the man be so with his wife, it is not good to marry.* **But he said unto them**, *All men cannot receive this saying, save they to whom it is given.* **For** *there are some eunuchs, which were so born from their mother's womb: and there are some eunuchs, which were made eunuchs of men: and there be eunuchs, which have made themselves eunuchs for the kingdom of heaven's sake. He that is able to receive it, let him receive it.* Matthew 19:9-12

Notice again the key word—*but*. It indicates an abrupt turn in thought. Jesus was saying that not everyone will "receive" His teaching on marriage; that is, not everyone will honor God's "law of marriage":

*All men cannot receive this saying* [teaching], *save* [except] *they to whom it is given.* The latter means only those who have a "heart" after God will receive the Truth of what Jesus taught.

> All cannot, or do not, "receive" the Word of God because they have a heart that is hardened by sin.

It also means that all men cannot receive it because they harden their hearts against *what* it is that God has joined together. This is much the same in principle as is the desire of God that all men would be saved and receive the Truth of the gospel, **but** we know that all are not saved; many there are who reject Truth:

*For this is good and acceptable in the sight of God our Saviour; Who will have all men to be saved, and to come unto the knowledge of the truth.* 1 Timothy 2:3-4

If one's heart is not right, not even the entire Bible will present enough proofs against putting away a spouse and marrying another. However, those whose hearts are directed by the Holy Spirit will have understanding and will pay whatever price is necessary to remain faithful to their covenant spouses, and by analogy, to God:

*But he said unto them, All men cannot receive this saying, save they to whom it is given ... He that is able to receive it, let him receive it.* Matthew 19:11-12

## How Is the eunuch teaching structurally united with the statement made by the disciples?

Study the three verses given below to see how they are all tied together. Note that verse 12 is not an isolated teaching about the physical aspect of eunuchs:

| The eunuch teaching is not a disjointed addition; it's a vital part of the overall teaching *let not man put asunder.* ||
|---|---|
| Matthew 19:10-12<br>*10 His disciples say unto him, If the case of the man be so with his wife, it is not good to marry.*<br><br>*11 **But** he said unto them, All men cannot receive this saying* [teaching], *save they to whom it is given.*<br><br>*12 **For** there are some eunuchs, which were so born from their mother's womb: and there are some eunuchs, which were made eunuchs of men: and there be eunuchs, which have made themselves eunuchs for the kingdom of heaven's sake. **He that is able to receive it, let him receive it**.* (The word *for* connects 11 and 12.) | The word *but* (verse 11) tells the reader Jesus is turning the tables on their wrong train of thought: all men will not receive this teaching; and as an example, He continues with the examples of eunuchs.<br><br>The word *For* at the beginning of verse 12 is a key way of tying this all together and then the summary statement of all that Jesus had taught on this topic is given: **He that is able to <u>receive</u> it, let him <u>receive</u> it.**<br>God lets man choose whether to "receive" Him or to live in sin. |

## There are many eunuchs today for the sake of the Kingdom of Heaven.

The internal evidence shows that the eunuch teaching is related (1) to the statement made by the disciples and (2) to Jesus' overall teaching summed in His statement in Mark 10:11-12:

*And he saith unto them,* **[the disciples]** *Whosoever shall put away his wife, and marry another, committeth adultery against her. And if a woman shall put away her husband, and be married to another, she committeth adultery.*

## Chapter 19

The only other mention of *eunuch* in the New Testament is in Acts 8:34-39 and that context and teaching are totally unrelated to this conversation with the disciples. So it seems that it would be necessary to redefine this special contextual use of *eunuch* to align with Jesus' teaching—the all-important context:

*... and there be eunuchs, which have made themselves eunuchs for the kingdom of heaven's sake.* Matthew 19:12

Another potential Biblical application of the above *eunuchs* that is closely related to the topic which the LORD was discussing is that of being faithful to one's covenant spouse, even when the other spouse has divorced and married someone else. The metaphoric example is when the put-away spouse, male or female, upholds the "standard" that God has established in His Word. This term *Standard*, mentioned earlier in this book, is coined from a teaching from Isaiah 59:19:

*So shall they fear the name of the LORD from the west, and his glory from the rising of the sun. When the enemy shall come in like a flood, the Spirit of the LORD shall lift up a **standard** against him.*

A Standard has a unique way of being a eunuch for the Kingdom of Heaven's sake. This faithful spouse who chooses to make himself a eunuch because of desertion by the other spouse, foregoes the companionship of marriage and the pleasure of sexual intimacy. He does this not only for the sake of the Kingdom of Heaven but to not jeopardize his relationship with the LORD. Additionally, he holds within his heart a true love for his spouse no matter what the surrounding circumstances may be. (Be aware to recall that *male* and *female*, *he* and *she*, etc. are usually contextually generic.)

Whether this faithful spouse is called a eunuch for the sake of the Kingdom or a Standard, this lifestyle is a reality that thousands of other faithful spouses experience because they have chosen to give this kind of sacrificial love. They have a special calling on their lives. That calling is something that cannot be forced upon them. It comes from a special kind of love buried deeply within their hearts that cannot be taught or explained. A Standard does not date or in any way show inordinate affections toward another of the same or opposite sex. He or she remains holy and pure before God and serves the LORD. When, and if possible, each Standard reconciles with his own wayward spouse; that is, when and if that opportunity presents itself.

> A Standard has no desire to date and doesn't entertain inordinate affections.

There are, however, those who are <u>forced</u> to become "marital" eunuchs who do not "re-marry." They do not "re-marry" <u>but</u> for the wrong reason. They have been made eunuchs by a civil divorce but have become "imprisoned." Imprisoned, when they become filled with anger and bitterness and some even wish their spouse would die. How tragic this is. They are ignorantly living in the bondage of unforgiveness. They do not continue to love their wayward spouse; neither do they pray for their salvation and for reconciliation.

## Standing in the Gap

Sadly, instead of encouraging those who stand in the gap for a lost mate (a Standard for righteousness), friends, relatives, and even some pastors criticize them. Standards are often encouraged to not only date but to even "re-marry" someone else. Standards are often posed unbiblical questions or statements by others such as:

- He has committed adultery so you have a right to find someone else. Get on with your life.
- Why would you want him back?
- God wouldn't expect you to live alone the rest of your life.
- God will bring you another wife/husband.

Maybe you have, at some time, discouraged a person from continuing to stand in the gap for his wayward spouse. This may have been when talking with or ministering to a person who is civilly divorced (been given a legal divorce decree) from a one-flesh mate. Perhaps you need to repent and ask forgiveness for "partaking" in what God hates. These are examples of calling good evil and evil good.

*Woe unto them that call evil good, and good evil; that put darkness for light, and light for darkness; that put bitter for sweet, and sweet for bitter! Woe unto them that are wise in their own eyes, and prudent in their own sight!*
Isaiah 5:20-21

*Woe* is a word used many times in both the Old and New Testaments. It often expresses grief that is associated with death. God, however, uses it more often to threaten judgment. Jesus also used "Woe" as a warning when addressing the wicked scribes and Pharisees and those who

> A marriage Standard remains totally faithful to her spouse and to the marriage-covenant through which she and her husband have been joined.

practice shallow and corrupt religion. He specifically addressed the Pharisees eight times in Matthew 23 beginning with the statement, "Woe unto you."

A word of caution is important here, especially if there has been a separation because of a pattern of physical abuse—domestic violence. If that be the case, discernment must be used when deciding whether or not to live with a physically abusive spouse after a reconciliation. Has there been a change of heart? Has there been true repentance?

*Now I rejoice, not that ye were made sorry, but that ye sorrowed to repentance: for ye were made sorry after a godly manner, that ye might receive damage by us in nothing. For godly sorrow worketh repentance to salvation not to be repented of: but the sorrow of the world worketh death.* 2 Corinthians 7:9-10

To not live together could be the wise decision for the spouse or children if there is some kind of safety issue or abuse. In such cases, there is the Biblical option in 1 Corinthians 7:11. That directive instructs the deserted spouse to remain in a married state or to return to the husband or wife:

> Discernment must be exercised before returning to a physically abusive spouse.

*But and if she depart, let her remain unmarried,\* or be reconciled to her husband: and let not the husband put away his wife.* \*This is an unmarried state in that they do not "re-marry" another spouse. 1 Corinthians 7:11

## Virgins who remain chaste
## for the cause of the Kingdom are also eunuchs.

Others called to be eunuchs <u>could</u> include those who forego marriage to serve the LORD. These include both males and females. Paul speaks of these so-committed Christians in 1 Corinthians 7:32-35:

*But I would have you without carefulness. He that is unmarried <u>careth for the things that belong to the Lord</u>, how he may please the Lord: But he that is married careth for the things that are of the world, how he may please his wife. There is difference also between a wife and a virgin. The unmarried <u>woman careth for the things of the Lord</u>, that she may be holy both in body and in spirit: but she that is married careth for the things of the world, how* *she may please her husband. And this I speak for your own profit; not that I may cast a snare upon you, but for that which is comely, and that ye may attend upon the Lord without distraction.* 1 Corinthians 7:32-35

Individuals who choose to remain celibate and not marry should not be criticized and surely should not be demeaned as when people say, "She's an old maid." Paul, however, is not saying there is anything wrong with marriage. He certainly isn't implying that it is "good not to marry" (as will be discussed in Chapter 20). God instituted marriage, and it is needed:

- To replenish the earth.
- To provide an environment for two people, a husband and wife, to become perfected—holy—while *serving* one another; to die to the flesh as each is molded by ministering one to the other in the fear of the LORD. See Ephesians 5:21-33.
- To glorify the LORD through the marital relationship.

We should encourage young people who decide to make serving the LORD their main focus in life. The LORD may have unforeseen blessings in store for those who choose that pathway in life. Isaiah 56:4-5 informs us that God holds a special place in His heart for those people who are willing to forego some of the otherwise pleasures of this life for the Kingdom of Heaven's sake:

*For thus saith the LORD unto the eunuchs that keep my sabbaths, and <u>choose the things that please me, and take hold of my **covenant**</u>; Even unto them will I give in mine house and within my walls a place and a name better than of sons and of daughters: I will give them an everlasting name, that shall not be cut off.* Isaiah 56:4-5 God has established both a covenant of salvation and a covenant of marriage with important similarities.

Every faithful disciple of Christ needs to do what he can to encourage and help victims of civil divorce who choose to obey what God has said about marriage; that is, those who refuse to enter into adulterous relationships. They, instead, choose to be true Standards for righteousness, honoring God's perspective for marriage by keeping their love for their wayward spouse alive. That means they have "eyes" only for their one-flesh spouse. All Christians should join in praying with and ministering to Standards and to the wayward spouse by encouraging him to repent <u>and</u> to return in love to his covenant spouse.

Churches, instead of creating "singles" ministries to include those who are or should be Standards, should consider who these people are in the LORD and actively teach what Scripture says about faithfulness to one's covenant spouse. **They are not singles**; they are as married as all other covenant-spouses. Their spouse, however, may have been caught in the web of a spiritual war. Churches should also help Standards to handle their additional life challenges. For example, some churches have a once-a-month out-reach program to provide help with home maintenance and car repairs. They reach out with food and help with childcare.

Remember that men are oft-times less apt to tell others they are hurting and have needs with which they need assistance. The church should not neglect serving both male and female Standards. They should not grow weary in praying and uplifting Standards—even if it takes more than 15-20 years of standing beside faithful Standards and by **continually encouraging the wayward spouse to re-turn.**

# 20

## *Desertion Is Not Dissolution: It's A Call To WAR.*

P aul makes the statement in 1 Corinthians 7:15 that if the unbeliever deserts the marriage, the faithful spouse is not under *bondage* to the one who leaves. Some wrongly

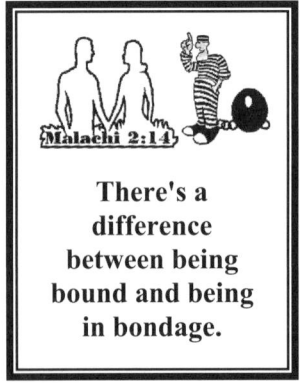

**There's a difference between being bound and being in bondage.**

conclude that the Bible really means, in such a situation, the two "are no longer bound" or married. These people wrongly believe if they are married to an unbeliever and the unbeliever leaves, the covenant has been dissolved and the believer is free—as free as if they had never been married. "This," they say, "is because the other person deserted the marriage." That interpretation is not Biblical. Read carefully what is recorded in 1 Corinthians 7:15:

*But if the unbelieving depart, let him depart. A brother or a sister is not <u>under bondage</u> in such cases: but God hath called us to peace.* 1 Corinthians 7:15

Please read carefully. It's not the word *bound* but *bondage* that is recorded in this Scripture. What Paul is addressing in this passage is that the deserted spouse is not in bondage to the unfaithful spouse.

Nothing is said to indicate that the one-flesh union God created is or can be dissolved because either the husband or wife has left. If the unbeliever chooses to leave, both spouses are still bound to the marital covenant. The deserted spouse has an obligation—a commitment to pray and intercede for the lost mate; to continue to love—until death they do part. However, if the unbelieving partner departs and doesn't want to have anything to do with the faithful spouse, or ONLY wants to "visit" his spouse for sex and then return to someone with whom he is having an affair, the faithful spouse is not under that kind of **bondage** to the wayward spouse.

Gather some of the context from the previous verses. These Scriptures are addressing a separation from an unsaved spouse. First, there is the warning that just because one spouse is saved and the other is not is no cause to separate from the lost spouse.[1] However, **"but if"** the lost spouse is determined to leave, or there must be a separation because of a safety issue, the saved spouse should not feel in turmoil or bondage to the lost spouse[2]:

[1] *But to the rest speak I, not the Lord: If any brother hath a wife that believeth not, and she be pleased to dwell with him, let him not put her away. And the woman which hath an husband that believeth not, and if he be pleased to dwell with her, let her not leave him.* 1 Corinthians 7:12-13

[2] *But if the unbelieving depart, let him depart. A brother or a sister is not under bondage in such cases: but God hath called us to peace.* 1 Corinthians 7:15

A separation can never dissolve a one-flesh marriage. Even though there may be a separation, the two are still (yet) married (bound). To interpret the passage any other way would contradict other verses in 1 Corinthians 7 and the whole of Scripture on marriage, beginning with Genesis 2:21-24:

*And the LORD God caused a deep sleep to fall upon Adam and he slept: and he took one of his ribs, and closed up the flesh instead thereof; And the rib, which the LORD God had taken from man, made he a woman, and brought her unto the man. And Adam said, This is now bone of my bones, and flesh of my flesh: she shall be called Woman, because she was taken out of Man. ... and they shall be one flesh.* Genesis 2:21-24

*But and if she depart, let her <u>remain</u> unmarried, <u>or</u> be <u>reconciled</u> <u>to her husband</u>: and let not the husband put away his wife.* 1 Corinthians 7:11

*The wife is bound by the law as long as her husband liveth;* ***but if*** *her husband be dead, she is at liberty to be married to whom she will; only in the Lord.* 1 Corinthians 7:39

It is important that the deserted spouse not hold bitterness and unforgiveness toward her wayward spouse and if possible to let him know that the love and commitment until death hasn't changed. Keeping alive a sacrificial love under these conditions may not be easy, but obedience is the framework in which Jesus defines a deeper spiritual love expected of every believer regardless of the circumstances: ... *If a man love me, he will keep my words ... This is my commandment, That ye love one another, as I have loved you.* John 14:23; John 15:12

> Freedom from bondage does not mean a person is no longer married.

To understand the depth of love that should be exhibited for a spouse, regardless of the circumstances, review 1 Corinthians 13:4-8. This is a love called *charity* that:

- *Suffereth long and envieth not.*
- *Vaunteth not itself and is not puffed up.*
- *Doth not behave itself unseemly.*
- *Seeketh not her own and is not easily provoked.*
- *Thinketh no evil and rejoiceth not in iniquity.*
- *Beareth all things.*
- *Believeth all things.*
- *Hopeth all things, endureth all things.*
- *Never faileth.*

## There's a difference between being bound and being under bondage.

One major influence on those who believe that desertion by one of the spouses is grounds for a divorce, or that such an act dissolves the marital bond, is spawned through erroneous Bible translations such as are found in some translations of 1 Corinthians 7:15. This coupled with the fact that many do not study all the Scriptures on marriage seems to be a combination that influences many Christians and others to adopt sinful behaviors. Study three versions of 7:15 below. Directly below the English translations is a section of the underlying Greek text from which 1 Corinthians 7:15 has been taken:

| **Three versions of 1 Corinthians 7:15 which depict different messages about the permanency of covenant-marriages:** |||
|---|---|---|
| *But if the unbelieving depart, let him depart. A brother or a sister is not under **bondage** in such cases: but God hath called us to peace.* KJB | *But if the unbeliever leaves, let him do so. A believing man or woman is not **bound** in such circumstances; God has called us to live in peace.* NIV | *But if the unbelieving partner desires to separate, let it be so; in such a case the brother or sister is not **bound**.* RSV |
| It's death, not desertion, which dissolves a covenant-marriage. |||
| Bibles: KJB: King James Bible; NIV: New International Version; RSV: Revised Standard Version |||

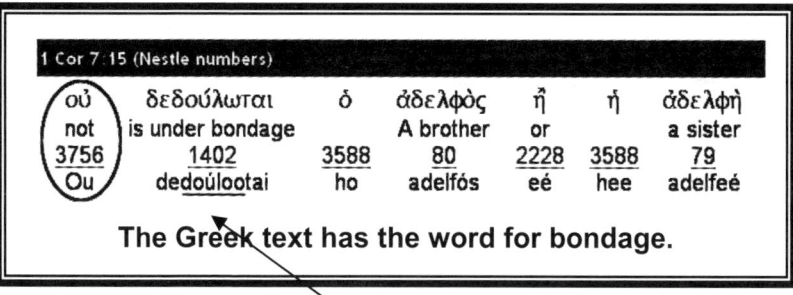

The Greek text has the word for bondage.

The underlying Greek word from which the English word *bondage* is translated in 1 Corinthians 7:15 is *douloo*, which means *bondage*. The Greek text also includes the adverb *not* (circled above); thus, the sentence should be translated *not under bondage. A brother or a sister is not under **bondage** in such cases*.

## Desertion Is Not Dissolution. It's A Call To WAR.

It should be obvious that the word *bound,* instead of *bondage,* is wrong in the NIV and RSV. Why obvious? It's because of context and the many other Scriptures with which these statements disagree. The only thing that frees a person from the marital bond is the physical death of one of the covenant spouses. Secondly, there's no supporting evidence in the immediate or surrounding verses or in the concluding statement in 1 Corinthians 7:39 to back up the contradiction in the NIV and RSV between 7:15 and 7:39 and several other verses.

> Sin cannot dissolve a marriage-covenant.

*The wife is <u>bound</u> by the law as long as her husband liveth; but if her husband be dead, she is at liberty to be married to whom she will; only in the Lord.* 1 Corinthians 7:39

The underlying Greek text is given on the previous page for 1 Corinthians 7:15 so the reader will see that the Greek words that are in this text have not been accurately translated by the authors of the NIV and RSV. Why should a person care what is in the underlying text <u>in such instances</u>? Normally that's not necessary. However, many people innocently feel their NIV and RSV can be depended upon to give them accurate doctrine. This is one of many instances to show those who read from these texts that there should be alarm.

If a person believes the statements made by these two new versions, as quoted on page 317, he can come to the wrong conclusion about his marriage. He could wrongly believe that if his spouse deserts the home, that spouse has committed an act which dissolves the marriage. That, of course, is not true.

Every person must get to the place in his dependence upon God to know that it's God's Words, not man's, that are eternal life: ... *the words that I* [Jesus] *speak unto you, they are spirit, and they are life.* John 6:63 Man doesn't have God's permission or the wisdom to usurp God; to substitute thousands of synonyms for God's Words in a quest to author a copyrighted version of Scripture. Review pages 178 and 256.

*Every word of God is pure: he is a shield unto them that put their trust in him. Add thou not unto his words, lest he reprove thee, and thou be found a liar. Proverbs 30:5-6*

The word "bondage" in 1 Corinthians 7:15 does not mean that either spouse is free from the marital bond if serious conflict arises. The two are bound (joined together), but they are not under bondage. There's a big difference between being bound or married and being under bondage to another person. **Bondage generally refers to sin or oppression.** Study the Scriptures below:

| **Contextual evidence proves a husband and wife are not under bondage. They, however, are still bound.** |
|---|
| *But and if she depart, let her remain unmarried, or be **reconciled to her husband**: and let not the husband put away his wife.* 1 Corinthians 7:11 |
| *For what knowest thou, O wife, whether thou shalt save **thy husband**? or how knowest thou, O man, whether thou shalt save **thy wife**?* 1 Corinthians 7:16 Marriage doesn't save the unbeliever, but it can put him in an environment where he can be influenced by a godly wife's actions and prayers. It's only personal obedience that works to sanctify each person. Salvation is the work of the Holy Spirit. |
| *The wife is bound by the law **as long as her husband liveth**; but if her husband **be dead**, she is at liberty to be married to whom she will; only in the Lord.* 1 Corinthians 7:39 |
| There is no Biblical evidence that any one-flesh spouse becomes what many incorrectly call an "ex-spouse," no matter what kind of sin the other spouse might commit, and there's no term "ex-spouse" in God's Word. **It's man, not God who "x's" out spouses!** |

The underlying Greek word for *bound* is *deo*. It is used in 1 Corinthians 7:27 in the context of marriage. Through God's supernatural miracle, two are joined, knit, bound (deo) together. No matter what the sin, the husband and wife are bound until physical death separates them. God has never recorded that sin dissolves the **bond** of marriage, whether that sin is adultery, desertion, or any other sin.

Marriage is not a state of slavery or bondage (douloo). We, instead, are joined or bound in marriage which is a reflection of Christ's sacrificial love for the church. The Greek word for *joined* or *married, bound* (*deo*), is not used in 1 Corinthians 7:15 because the context there is speaking of bondage. Deo (bound or married) is used in 1 Corinthians 7:27 where the context **is** speaking of marriage. Compare the Greek for the two verses below; 15 on the left, and 27 on the right:

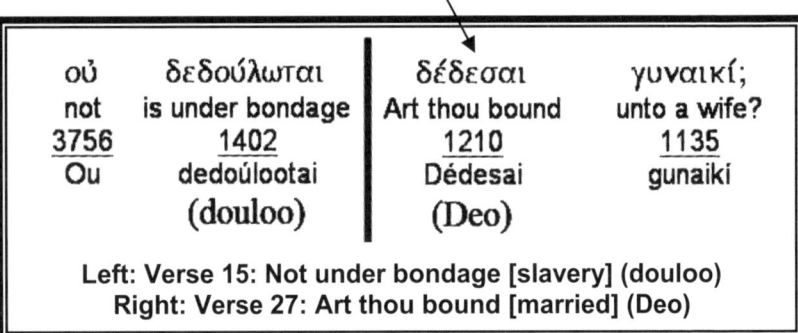

Left: Verse 15: Not under bondage [slavery] (douloo)
Right: Verse 27: Art thou bound [married] (Deo)

When the word *bondage* in 1 Corinthians 7:15 is changed to words meaning "no longer bound" as done in the RSV and NIV, God's Word is changed which, if believed, can create a deadly unbiblical loophole for those who do not honor their covenant of marriage.

## Bound or married—different but the same; yet, their differences must be retained.

As a review, recall the engagement custom of the Jewish people. They could have an engaged wife, as with Mary in Matthew 1:18, or a married wife, as recorded in Matthew 1:24, after Joseph married her. These two kinds of wives are contrasted within Matthew 5:32 and 19:9. This Jewish espousal-marriage language is again embedded in 1 Corinthians 7:27: *Art thou bound unto a wife ...?* However, the NIV authors incorrectly recorded the word *married* for *bound* in verse 27 in their paraphrased version of that verse. This does two things. It (1) removes the teaching as recorded using Biblical language idioms and (2) changes the Word of God by not translating what is in the underlying text. There are strong reasons why the word *bound* is used in verse 27. It accurately records the fact that this is a wife that is bound to a husband in marriage, not engaged; and it is the word that the Holy Ghost inspired Paul to record. It is the same word *bound* (Greek *deo*) also recorded in 1 Corinthians 7:39. *The wife is **bound** ...* **The Greek word for *marry* is not found in 1 Corinthians 7:27:**

| The NIV authors incorrectly translate the Greek text, diffusing the Biblical language in 1 Corinthians 7:27. ||
|---|---|
| *Art thou bound unto a wife ...?* KJB | *Are you married ...?* NIV |

Even though today, we would say, "Are you married?" and even though *bound* means *married*, in this context, that's not what Paul recorded BECAUSE CONTEXTUALLY THE WORD MARRIED DOESN'T CORRECTLY REFLECT THE UNDERLYING TEXT NOR DOES IT REINFORCE THE ESPOUSAL BIBLICAL IDIOMS.

The Greek word for *marry* inserted by the NIV and RSV authors is from a different Greek word than is that for *bound*. There is an important cultural difference preserved when the correct translation is made. It's the kind of exactness ("jots" and "tittles") that brings deeper meaning, accuracy, and interconnectivity to God's preserved Words. This is missed with dynamic equivalency or paraphrasing in which many of the revealed Biblical treasures are glossed over and idiosyncrasies of the Jewish culture, reflective of the meanings for the time in which the Bible was recorded, are removed.

```
δέδεσαι         γυναικί;
Art thou bound  unto a wife?
   1210            1135
  Dédesai         gunaiki
   Deo

    1 Corinthians 7:27
```

```
The     wife    is bound
9999    1135      1210
        Guneé   dédetai
                  deo

    1 Corinthians 7:39
```

## Marriage and bondage are not the same.

This is no game that we are playing with life. The differences between being bound in marriage and under bondage are two very different things. WHAT therefore God hath joined (bound) together is beautiful. How can any believer conclude that something so beautiful and miraculous that God creates—marriage—is bondage? Everything He creates is good; however, when a person fills his mind with and follows corrupted doctrine, God's creation can take on the attributes depicted in the graphic on the first page of this chapter—a war—a war between good and evil. That war is Satan waging war on individuals and families. It's not WHAT God has bound together, but sin in people's lives and man-created doctrinal error that makes them come under what they feel is a state of bondage or that marriage is bondage.

The picture most do not recognize is that the wayward spouse is "off to war." This is, however, an unrecognized war. He is in the bondage of the war between the flesh and the spirit—a **different kind of war** for which a wayward spouse has "volunteered" to serve because he has chosen to sin. Few are equipped to win this kind of lustful war between the flesh and the spirit, and few there are who are rescued from it. Yet, MANY tempt the flesh with flirting and private meetings with friends and work associates of the opposite sex. They feed the sinful flesh by watching seductive TV programming; texting inappropriate messages, and viewing easily accessible pornography on the Internet:

> There's a spiritual war that many are in the midst of, but they don't recognize it.

*Let not thine heart decline to her ways, go not astray in her paths. For she hath cast down many wounded: yea, many strong men have been slain by her. Her house is the way to hell, going down to the chambers of death.* Proverbs 7:25-27 Recall that nouns and pronouns *her*, *she*, and *men* are generic. They **usually** apply equally to both men and women.

Even though a relationship may seem impossible to mend, the faithful spouse should continue to forgive, to pray, and to intercede on behalf of the wayward spouse so that he might be pulled out of the fire of eternal separation from the LORD.

*Then came Peter to him, and said, Lord, how oft shall my brother sin against me, and I forgive him? till seven times? Jesus saith unto him, I say not unto thee, Until seven times: but, Until seventy times seven.* Matthew 18:21-22

*And the servant of the Lord must not strive; but be gentle unto all men* [Men here, as a generic noun, can include men, women and a wayward spouse.], *apt to teach, patient, In meekness instructing those that oppose themselves; if God peradventure will give them repentance to the acknowledging of the truth; And that they may recover themselves out of the snare of the devil,* **who are taken captive by him at his will**. 2 Timothy 2:24-26

*... And others save with fear, pulling them out of the fire ...* Jude 1:23

## She innocently said, "I thought I was sinning."

It's vital for every believer to learn to apply Biblical guidelines. Many people are losing the skills to analyze Scripture and to think contextually. That's a major reason why so much error is creeping into many Bibles, into thousands of pulpits, and into most homes. It is slipping in unnoticed by most who have let this happen. **Laymen and clergy, instead of recognizing doctrinal errors, are being lulled into acceptance of wrong interpretations; and, even worse, acceptance of unbiblical doctrine about marriage and divorce.**

For example, one young woman spoke up in a seminar saying that she was confused and in turmoil about praying for her lost husband to return to their home. This is because she had learned false doctrine from the Bible from which she was studying. Her Bible, the NIV, said that it was **not good** for her to marry; thus, she wrongly feared that she was sinning because she had gotten married and now was further complicating things because she was praying for her husband to return home. She loved the LORD, and her heart's desire was to serve Him and follow His teachings as they are recorded in the Bible.

> Paraphrased words incorrectly translated brought turmoil.

What a blessing that I was able, through the seminar teachings, to show her how her Bible had changed God's Word and had led her to believe an egregious untruth. She was under the bondage of deception created because she relied upon the Bible from which she had studied so diligently for many years. This was a type of emotional oppression caused by doctrinal error in her Bible. The teaching included in this chapter made a huge positive impact on her understanding of marriage; and today, many years later, she has remained faithful to her marriage-covenant and continues to pray and intercede for her husband. Here's what she had incorrectly learned from her NIV Bible:

*Now for the matters you wrote about: It is good for a man <u>not to marry</u>.* 1 Corinthians 7:1 NIV

Before even proceeding, and without any proof from underlying Greek texts or a huge theological discourse, the reader should know that the LORD did not have Paul record that it isn't good to marry. It's through the institution of marriage that God instructed man to be fruitful and multiply:

*So God created man in his own image ... and God said unto them, Be fruitful, and multiply, and replenish the earth, and subdue it: and have dominion over the fish of the sea, and over the fowl of the air, and over every living thing that moveth upon the earth.* Genesis 1:27-28

Here is the correct translation of 1 Corinthians 7:1:

*Now concerning the things whereof ye wrote unto me: It is good for a man <u>not to touch</u> a woman.* 1 Corinthians 7:1

On the next page is the Greek text from which 1 Corinthians 7:1 is translated. The underlying Greek text says that it is good for a man not to <u>touch</u> a woman.

Desertion Is Not Dissolution. It's A Call To WAR.

| It is | καλὸν good | ἀνθρώπῳ for a man | γυναικὸς a woman. | μὴ not | ἅπτεσθαι· to touch |
|---|---|---|---|---|---|
| 9999 | 2570 | 444 | 1135 | 3361 | 680 |
| | Kalón | anthroópoo | gunaikós | meé | háptesthai |

The Greek text in 1 Corinthians 7:1 doesn't have any word in it for the word *marry*; yet, the NIV authors incorrectly insert *marry* for the word *touch*.
**They** bring doctrinal error into God's Word.

The word *touch* is translated from the Greek word *haptesthai*. Notice that the Greek word for the English word *marry* is nowhere in 1 Corinthians 7:1. In contrast, the Greek text from 1 Corinthians 7:28 has the word for *marry*. It is *gameesees* (Strong's 1060): *But and if thou marry, thou hast not sinned.* The two Greek words *haptesthai* (to touch)

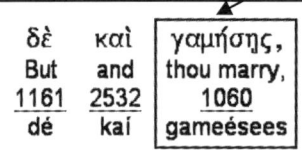

**1 Corinthians 7:28: The Greek word for *marry* is different than that for *touch*.**

and *gameesees* (marry) are very different in spelling and in meaning. Compare the text at the left with that above to see each word's Greek counterpart: *marry* and *touch*. Paul is warning in 1 Corinthians 7:1 that everyone should flee sexual sin. Sexual sin can lead to eternal spiritual death. The change to God's Word by the NIV and other authors not only gives an unscriptural message about marriage, it also **removes** a warning against a serious sexual sin that man is to flee; that of fornication. There seems to be no fear of God: *Ye shall not add unto the word ... neither shall ye diminish ought from it.* Deuteronomy 4:2

Those who are single are to remain celibate and not to commit fornication. That's the contextual meaning of "not to touch" in 1 Corinthians 7:1 which is clear when the context provided in verse two is read. Verse 2 contextually defines "not to touch" as *fornication*:

*1 Now concerning the things whereof ye wrote unto me: It is good for a man not to touch a woman. 2 Nevertheless, **to avoid fornication**, let every man have his own wife, and let every woman have her own husband.* 1 Corinthians 7:1-2

Compare the correct translation from the King James Bible with the erroneous translation from the NIV below:

| Compare the two translations for 1 Corinthians 7:1-2: ||
|---|---|
| King James Bible | New International Version |
| *7:1 Now concerning the things whereof ye wrote unto me: It is good for a man not to touch a woman.* | *7:1 Now for the matters you wrote about: It is good for a man not to marry.* |
| *7:2 Nevertheless, to avoid fornication, let every man have his own wife, and let every woman have her own husband.* | *7:2 But since there is so much immorality, each man should have his own wife, and each woman her own husband.* |

Not touching a woman is another way of saying not to become intimate before marriage. Touching can be the first step which often leads to passionate feelings which can turn into fornication. It is fornication, not covenant-marriage, which is to be avoided.

The LORD, through Paul, is addressing pre-marital sin. How can the reader determine that? It's by word usage. If Paul were addressing sexual sin by those who are in a covenant-marriage, he would have recorded the word *adultery*. He, instead, used the word *fornication* and tells readers that sexual intimacy belongs between a husband and wife. As a review, this is another place where the rule of proximity can be applied. Even though the word *adultery* is not specifically written, it should be obvious that Paul is drawing a contrast between those who are married and those who are not; and by implication, a contrast between *fornication* and *adultery.* If you are confused on the difference between *fornication, adultery,* and *immorality,* review Chapter 11. There are doctrinal errors in both verses one and two in the NIV: "It is good for a man not to marry" in verse one and the use of "immorality" in verse two. Needless to say the young woman from the above-mentioned seminar had a heavy burden lifted by learning what was recorded in her NIV was false doctrine.

> Touching someone and marrying are very different actions.

Another Bible mentioned earlier that has gained some popularity is Lamsa's version of the Bible which **he calls**, The Holy Bible from Ancient Eastern Manuscripts. It, too, contains doctrinal error in 1 Corinthians 7:1. Lamsa also includes many errors about marriage and the deity of Jesus Christ elsewhere in his Bible translation. Here's how he <u>erroneously</u> paraphrases 1 Corinthians 7:1-2:

*1 Now concerning the things which you wrote to me. It is proper for a husband not to have intimacy with his wife at times. 2 Nevertheless, because of the danger of immorality, let every man hold to his own wife, and let every woman hold to her own husband.*

The errors above should be easily discernible. Lamsa greatly changes verse one. This verse is not speaking about marriage and neither is it the subject of not having intimacy with one's spouse. His confusion of *immorality, adultery,* and *fornication* in this verse and verse two should be apparent. This is also true, in several other Scriptures, including Matthew 5:32 and 19:9 as shown previously in other chapters of this book:

**Additional <u>Erroneous</u> Translations by Lamsa:**
*But I say to you that whoever divorces his wife, except for fornication, causes her to commit adultery; and whoever marries a woman <u>who is separated but not divorced</u>, commits adultery.* Matthew 5:32

*But I say to you, Whoever leaves his wife <u>without a charge of adultery</u> and marries another commits adultery; and he who marries a woman thus separated commits adultery.* Matthew 19:9

It's hoped that, by this time, the reader can see the importance of considering the whole counsel of God; that is, comparing Scripture with Scripture. This is so that he can recognize when something is awry with a statement, whether it be spoken by a pastor, or a layperson, or rendered in a mistranslated Scripture.

There are many Scriptures that we may not understand. However, after studying the above examples and others in this book, readers should know that there are some real dangers in relying on spiritual life-and-death issues from authors who make unscriptural statements. That's why the LORD tells us to flee teachings with false doctrine and encourages us in 2 Timothy 2:15 to *study* as workmen so that we can *rightly divide* (correctly interpret) God's written Word.

Before leaving this topic, study the illustration of 1 Corinthians 7:1-2 on the next page. This should pull together many of the teachings already presented in this book and help the reader see the importance of the many teachings focused on HOW to study and interpret Scripture with Scripture.

Desertion Is Not Dissolution. It's A Call To WAR.

```
καλὸν     ἀνθρώπῳ   γυναικὸς    μὴ      ἅπτεσθαι·     The Greek word is
good      for a man  a woman.    not     to touch      for touch; that for
2570      444        1135        3361    680           marry is nowhere
Kalón     anthroópoo gunaikós    meé     háptesthai    in verse one or two.

² διὰ       δὲ          τὰς      πορνείας    ἕκαστος    τὴν    ἑαυτοῦ
  to avoid  Nevertheless,        fornication, every man         his own
  1223     1161                  4202        1538      3588    1438
  diá      dé                    porneías    hékastos  teén    heautoú

                                 ἑκάστη      τὸν       ἴδιον    ἄνδρα    ἐχέτω.
                                 every woman           her own  husband  let have
                                 1538        3588      2398     435      2192
                                 hekástee    tón       ídion    ándra    echétoo
```

*Greek word is for fornication not adultery.*

**The Greek text, in 1 Corinthians 7:1-2, has no word for *marry* or *immorality***

The Greek is shown above once more to reinforce the dangers of dynamic equivalency and unreliable translations. If the Scriptures in English are unreliable; that is, if they have doctrinal error, then all the talk one can come up with about the underlying Hebrew or Greek, or whether the text is translated from a new or old manuscript, is a mute issue. It's not God's inerrant Word if it has these kinds of doctrinal errors. How do I make that kind of statement? Please consider the Scriptures and warnings below:

*The words of the LORD **are pure words**: as silver tried in a furnace of earth, purified seven times; Thou shalt keep them, O **LORD, thou** <u>shalt preserve them</u>* [His Words] *from this generation for ever.* Psalm 12:6-7

<u>Every</u> *word <u>of God</u> is pure: he is a shield unto them that put their trust in him. **Add** thou **not** unto <u>his</u> words, lest he reprove thee, and thou be found a liar ... all liars, shall have their part in the lake which burneth with fire and brimstone: which is the second death.* Proverbs 30:5-6; Revelation 21:8

# 21

# Paul's Teachings Are Taken Out Of Context.

The apostle Paul wrote many of the books of the New Testament. He uses analogies in several of his writings, including some of those which teach precepts about marriage. They are often overlooked or taken out of context. His use of *comparative teaching* is a technique wherein he uses seemingly unrelated examples to illustrate what he is teaching. It's a type of teaching that can be observed by studying Romans 7:2-3 where he uses truisms about marriage as a metaphor or figure of speech to illustrate that when we are saved, we die to the old (sinful) self and to the law. The principle that applies to marriage is that when we are physically dead we are no longer joined to our one-flesh spouse. Likewise, it's when we die to the old self—to old patterns of sinful living—and walk in faith and in the spirit as a new man in Christ that we exhibit our rightful relationship to Christ. Review Romans 7:1-3 below. Notice the word *for* which is a word often used to help the reader know that what went before is related to what comes after:

*1 Know ye not, brethren, (for I speak to them that know the law,) how that the law hath dominion over a man as long as he liveth? 2 **For** the woman which hath an husband is bound by the law to her husband so long as he liveth; but if the husband be dead, she is loosed from the law of her husband. 3 So then if, while her husband liveth, she be married to another man, she shall be called an adulteress: but if her husband be dead, she is free from that law; so that she is no adulteress, though she be married to another man.*
Romans 7:1-3

Romans 7:2-3 are two verses that are not normally debated directly. They are very clear and repetitive; however, sadly what does happen is that some pastors totally avoid Romans 7:2-3 by skipping over it when they teach on marriage and divorce or when they are teaching through the book of Romans. Others "silently" avoid these verses in other ways. In fact, several years ago after I had gathered the funds to purchase several one-minute spots on a Christian radio station, I met with their marketing executive and shared with him that I wanted to read two Scriptures to be aired a given number of times per week with no additional commentary. He stated that I would need a good lead in and closing which he would be happy to help write. He had some great ideas for these. I then opened up my Bible and read him the Scriptures I wanted to have aired: Romans 7:2-3.

There, however, was a response for which I was totally unprepared. It was a sudden silence as he heard the words that I read. There was no more eye contact as he looked down at the floor, loosened his tie, backed his chair away from the conference table and said: "I will need to get someone else to handle your account." He quickly left the room. After a period of perhaps 20 minutes, he returned telling me that there wasn't anyone who could help with the request to air my radio spot. I was shocked. He was unmovable in this decision. I left shaking my head in unbelief. (I later found that this man was himself in an adulterous "marriage.") This is only one of many like incidents shared to help you realize that I know teaching the topics in this book will be met with much opposition. Please understand, however, I have a responsibility to share, as best I can, what the Holy Spirit has taught me based on the Scriptures.

> He suddenly gave a response for which I was totally unprepared. He loosened his tie and backed away from the conference table and then abruptly got up and left the room.

In this chapter, we will look at four additional Scriptures recorded by Paul that are taken out of context. They are misapplied and often used as loopholes to justify adulterous marriages: 2 Corinthians 5:17, Romans 8:1, 1 Corinthians 7:20 and 7:24.

## "My marriage occurred before we became Christians so God doesn't hold us accountable for it. I am under no condemnation."

These statements often arise when someone has married, divorced, and married again (maybe several times), and then this person gets saved. He then incorrectly concludes that his original one-flesh marriage is not valid because it took place when he wasn't saved and that he's under no condemnation from the LORD for having now "remarried." The way these two Scriptures are quoted in part and applied out of context to justify this Loophole are shown below:

> "I'm a new creature in Christ—old things are passed away; all things have become new. I'm under no condemnation because I am in Christ Jesus." These statements, paraphrased from 2 Corinthians 5:17 and Roman 8:1, are applied out of context.

These statements *can* be true. However, they *can* be false <u>when</u> they, as above, are applied out of context and not quoted in their entirety. They are from two Scriptures that have some important similarities and key words. As you look at them properly quoted below, can you see how each of these is a type of hypothetical statement—that is when all of the words that belong in these verses are quoted? Here are the two Scriptures as they should be written and quoted:

*Therefore if any man be in Christ, he is a new creature: old things are passed away; behold, all things are become new.* 2 Corinthians 5:17

*There is therefore now no condemnation to them which are in Christ Jesus, who walk not after the flesh, but after the Spirit.* Romans 8:1

These two verses have some similarities. Can you see what they are?

| Two Scriptures which have like structures and teachings ||
|---|---|
| 2 Corinthians 5:17 | Romans 8:1 |
| *Therefore if any man be **in Christ**, he is a new creature: old things are passed away; behold, all things are become new.* | *There is therefore now no condemnation to them which are **in Christ Jesus**, who walk not after the flesh, but after the Spirit.* |

First of all, each of these Scriptures is patterned like hypothetical statements in that they include a condition, and a condition that must be met. If the condition is met, then the conclusion is that the person can know that he is saved. Each verse contains the words *in Christ*. It must be clear what it means to be *in Christ*. Those who are *in Christ* are saved. Paul gives the characteristics of someone **who is in Christ**. What are five things he lists in these two Scriptures?

| Paul gives characteristics of those who are saved. ||
|---|---|
| 2 Corinthians 5:17 | Romans 8:1 |
| He is a new creature. Old things are passed away. All things are become new. | They walk not after the flesh. They walk after the Spirit. |

Those who are *in Christ* have become a new creature. But how? Their old lifestyle no longer dominates their life. They exhibit a new lifestyle. They walk after the Spirit, not after the flesh. Becoming a new creature, however, doesn't happen by osmosis. It's true that Jesus paid the price for our sin "debt." By His own shed blood, He provides the gift of salvation. But we also have our part. There must be a clean-up process in our lives called *sanctification*. This is closely tied to repentance. Repentance says we must stop living in sinful lifestyles. It's all predicated on the conditional word IF used directly or implied.

> Scripture says what it means to be "in Christ."

Does being *in Christ* mean that we never have sinful thoughts or sin? No, it's that we do not live daily in a lifestyle of repetitive sin. Spiritual growth is a process. Can this analysis of what it takes to be *in Christ* pass the test of context? Yes, there are many Scriptures which tell a believer he must walk in righteousness. A good contextual commentary on 2 Corinthians 5:17 is Ephesians 4:22-32. I urge you to read this passage in its entirety. Ephesians 4:22-24 summarizes what happens IF a person *is* a new creature:

*That **ye put off** [stop participating in] concerning the former conversation* [lifestyle] *the old man, which is corrupt according to the deceitful lusts; And be renewed in the spirit of your mind; And that **ye put on** the new man, which after God is created in righteousness and true holiness.* Ephesians 4:22-24

Answer this question. If a person is in Christ will he live in a lifestyle of adultery? If he is living in adultery, has he become a new creature? Has he put away past sinful lifestyle practices?

## Romans 8:1 helps to clarify what it means to be saved.

Studying the Bible can become such a wonderful experience when we learn to apply guidelines and don't get pulled off base by taking things out of context. Ephesians 4 (above) is very clear as is Romans 8:1 to reinforce what has been discussed about living a sanctified lifestyle. However, all the words in Romans 8:1 must be included. ***There is therefore now no condemnation to them which are in Christ Jesus***, *who walk not after the flesh, but after the Spirit.* Romans 8:1

What frequently happens is that many do not understand that the first clause of Romans 8:1 is structured as a conditional statement: "There is therefore now no condemnation to them which are in Christ Jesus." Ask the questions: How do we know there is no condemnation? What is the condition for those for whom there is no condemnation (for those who are **in Christ Jesus**)? The answer is given in the remaining part of the verse. We know we are in Christ Jesus **if** we walk not after the flesh (in sin), but after the Spirit (in holiness). **Condemnation**

**comes because of unrepentant sin;** that is, sin for which there has been no repentance. The condition to not be under condemnation is what Paul teaches in 2 Corinthians 5:17 to *be in Christ*. We must change IF we are a new creature. Old things (walking after the flesh) are passed away. We <u>now</u> walk differently—after the Spirit:

| Paul's hypothetical statement: Romans 8:1 ||
|---|---|
| Hypothesis: IF | Fulfillment |
| *There is therefore now no condemnation to them which are in Christ Jesus ...* | *... <u>who walk</u> **not** after the flesh, ... but after the Spirit.* KJB |

Sadly, here's where a big problem emerges. Entire books, songs, some ministries, and many of the new versions of the Bible quote only the first half of Romans 8:1—that in the left side of the table above. Study the table below to see what is being changed:

| The fulfillment of Romans 8:1 is omitted from most new versions of the Bible. |
|---|
| *There is therefore now no condemnation to them which are in Christ Jesus,* ***who walk not after the flesh, but after the Spirit.*** KJB |
| *Therefore, there is now no condemnation for those who are in Christ Jesus.* NIV |
| *There is therefore now no condemnation to those who are in Christ Jesus.* NKJV |
| *There is therefore now no condemnation to them that are in Christ Jesus.* NASV |
| *There is therefore now no condemnation for those who are in Christ Jesus.* ESV |
| *There is therefore no condemnation to them who walk in the flesh after the Spirit of Jesus Christ.* LAMSA Readers, beware of this wording. The flesh and Spirit war <u>against</u> one anther. You <u>either</u> walk in the flesh or in the Spirit. Study Galatians 5:16-19 on page 339. |
| *So now, those who are in Christ Jesus are not judged guilty.* ICB |
| NIV: New International Version; NKJV: New King James Version; NASV: New American Standard Version; ESV: English Standard Version; Lamsa: The Holy Bible ICB: International Children's Bible |

People are led astray because the sanctification part of God's Word is missing in their theology—and even worse, their scissors have cut deeply into the flesh of Jesus. The main <u>interlinking</u> part has been removed as shown above. God's standard to walk in righteousness is gone. There is something very wrong with this man-made false grace. It masks sin. Because of this many wrongly think they do not have to flee their old sinful lifestyle and live a new life in holiness. The requirement to walk according to the spirit **is not a works-based salvation; it is a repentance-based salvation.**

Again, the strong proof is in the context. It would be difficult to seriously study the entire eighth chapter of Romans and not understand for whom there is no condemnation and how Romans 8:1 should be interpreted. It's those who walk **not** after the flesh, but after the Spirit who are **in Christ Jesus—who are saved.** They are the ones for whom there is <u>now</u> no condemnation:

*That the righteousness of the law might be fulfilled in us, who walk **not** after the flesh, but after the Spirit. For they that are after the flesh do mind the things of the flesh; but they that are after the Spirit the things of the Spirit. For to be <u>carnally minded</u>* [walking according to the flesh] *<u>is death</u>; but to be spiritually minded* [walking after the spirit] *is life and peace. Because the carnal mind is enmity against God: for it is not subject to the law of God, neither indeed can be. So then **they that are in the flesh cannot please God.*** Romans 8:4-8

> Salvation requires that we live according to the Spirit.

Even though reading the entire Chapter of Romans 8 gives the context to clarify the meaning of verse one, few take the time to do that. In fact, many reading this book will skip over many of the quoted Scriptures, especially if they are long passages. Additionally, what may be feeding some of these unscriptural teachings is that many Christians who read from the new versions of the Bible seem unaware that there is anything missing from their Bibles. Others, who do know there may be something wrong, seem to be anesthetized to these changes made by man to God's pure and holy Word.

## There's a difference in the lifestyles of saved and lost persons.

It has already been proven through Scripture that when a person is saved, he walks in the spirit rather than in the flesh. He will become convicted of sinful lifestyle practices and repent from them. That's the true-life application of Romans 8:1 and 2 Corinthians 5:17. Continuing to walk "after the flesh" is a sign that a person may not be saved—at least that is what many Scriptures teach. There are many other sins, but this book is focused on the sin of adultery. Thus, the application for these teachings is that **if** a person is saved, he must carefully examine his lifestyle. Living in the lifestyle of the sin of adultery is an example of walking in the flesh:

> God's Word shows us that living in an adulterous marriage is an example of walking in the flesh.

*This I say then, **Walk in the Spirit**, and ye shall not fulfil the lust of the flesh. For the flesh lusteth against the Spirit, and the Spirit against the flesh: and these are contrary the one to the other: so that ye cannot do the things that ye would. But **if** ye be led of the Spirit, ye are not under the law. Now the works of the flesh are manifest* [We can recognize them. They may not always be readily recognizable, but that doesn't mean they aren't manifest.], *which are these; **Adultery**, fornication, uncleanness, lasciviousness.* Galatians 5:16-19

*And they that are Christ's **have crucified** the flesh <u>with the affections and lusts</u>. **If** we live in the Spirit, let us also **walk** in the Spirit.* Galatians 5:24-25

*For as the body without the spirit is dead, so faith without works is dead also.* James 2:26

***If** a man abide <u>not</u> in me, he is cast forth as a branch and is withered; and men gather them, and cast them into the fire, and they are burned.* John 15:6

So, does God hold Christians "accountable" to a covenant-marriage made before salvation? Yes. Salvation does not change the state of marriage for anyone.

## Marriage was instituted from the beginning.
## God recognizes one-flesh marriages between both those who are saved and those who are not.

Some people confuse two covenants: the covenant of marriage and the covenant of salvation. Both covenants rely on many similar characteristics. Marriage doesn't save or "unsave" anyone; however, what man does to live out his marital commitment can affect his salvation.

> God's two covenants have similarities.

It doesn't matter if a person were married before or after he is saved, the covenant of marriage is binding. Marriage is God's institution which He created <u>from the beginning</u>. It is not exclusively a Christian institution, and it encompasses every person whether he be lost or saved. Mark 10:6-9 (shown below) teaches:

<u>*But from the beginning of the creation*</u> *God made them male and female. For this cause shall a man leave his father and mother, and cleave to his wife; And they twain shall be one flesh: so then they are no more twain, but one flesh. What therefore God hath joined together, let not man put asunder.*

There are many examples of unsaved husbands and wives throughout the Old and New Testaments whose marriages are recognized in the eyes of the LORD. Some are listed below:

- Cain, after he murdered his brother, went out from the presence of the LORD and *knew his wife* ... (Genesis 4:17).
- Potiphar and his wife (Genesis 39).
- Ahab and Jezebel (1 Kings 21).
- Felix and Drusilla (Acts 24).
- Gomer: She sold herself to others as a prostitute and even "remarried"; yet, God instructed her covenant husband, Hosea, to buy her back and extend unconditional love to her. (Hosea 2 and 3).
- Philip and Herodias (Luke 3).

## Why was John the Baptist maliciously murdered?

The circumstances surrounding the tragic and brutal ending of John the Baptist's life is given twice in the New Testament: Matthew 14:1-11 and Mark 6:14-28. He ... *was a man sent from God* ... (John 1:6) of whom Jesus said, *Verily I say unto you, Among them that are born of women there hath not risen a greater than John the Baptist* ... Matthew 11:11. John was a devoted servant who was **chosen by God** to prepare the "way" for the coming of Jesus—to tell people to repent from sin: He straightforwardly preached: ... *Repent ye: for the kingdom of heaven is at hand.* Matthew 3:2 John, however, was murdered for standing firm on God's "law of marriage." This was because he boldly preached the message of covenant-marriage to two people who were not only "remarried," but they were not saved:

*For Herod had laid hold on John, and bound him, and put him in prison for Herodias' sake, his brother Philip's wife. For John said unto him, It is not lawful for thee to have her.* Matthew 14:3-4

John the Baptist publicly rebuked Herod and Herodias. Can you imagine telling powerful political leaders to their face that they are in an adulterous "marriage," one that violates God's "law of marriage"—or even a close friend or a relative, the same thing; or what would be the consequences for a pastor to boldly preach before his congregation the words of John the Baptist as they apply to many who may be sitting in front of him? How many of these do not really understand what the Word of God teaches about adulterous "marriages"?

Herod and Herodias were very wicked, lost people; yet, John told Herod it was not lawful for him to have ("married") his brother's wife. Herod was not a Jew. Herod was not a Christian. Herod was a typical representative of the middle-eastern culture. John was talking about God's *universal* law—the law which from the beginning was one man and one woman until death parts them. John said to Herod, *"It is not lawful for you to have her."* Matthew 14:4 This is because Herod was taking someone else's wife to be his "wife." That meant God's "law of marriage" applied equally to Herod and Herodias (as it does to all people, whether they are saved or not saved). God's law doesn't change even if a person is a powerful political leader, or an unknown person with no political power, or if a person is a ministry leader with thousands of followers. It doesn't matter if people were saved or were lost before, during, or after a marriage or "re-marriage." God's "law of marriage" is no respecter of persons.

John was jailed by Herod for his "preaching" of the Word on marriage to these two lost people—Herod and Herodias. That, however, wasn't enough to satisfy wicked Herodias. She was so embittered that she asked for John's head to be cut off and brought to her on a platter. This insidious request was carried out after Herod ordered it.

The example of John the Baptist with his rebuke of Herod and Herodias and how it angered those to whom it was given should also caution those who are willing to uncompromisingly teach the Truth on covenant-marriage. This is one teaching that is often not favorably received. Yet, recall there are also strong warnings from God against those who do not warn people about sin in their lives, especially in Ezekiel 33. This is because people <u>need</u> to know Truth.

It should be clear that God recognizes <u>one-flesh marriages</u> between both saved and unsaved spouses. It's not the marriage of one's salvation; it's the marriage of one's covenant. It is unbiblical thinking to believe that the LORD doesn't recognize marriages of those who are not saved. Carrying through that line of skewed thinking, whenever unsaved married spouses are saved, they would need to get married because they supposedly were not married while they were not saved. This line of unscriptural reasoning would also wrongly assume they were living in a state of adultery or fornication. If God did not recognize those marriages between unsaved spouses, it would also mean that any children birthed of that relationship would have been born out of wedlock because the parents were not married in God's sight. That's nonsense.

Even though the church and society have lost sight of the high regard held by God for His "law of marriage," God has not. It's one man for one woman until death separates the two. Everyone—*whosoever*—is held accountable to "*What* therefore God hath joined together," until the physical death of one of the spouses separates them.

## "The Bible says to remain in the marriage I'm in when I got saved."

This statement is a continuation of principles discussed above and the confusion between one's salvation and God's one-flesh creation. This "loophole" statement, however, is slightly different. It's when those who are in an <u>adulterous "marriage"</u> are saved, they believe they should remain in that "marriage." However, neither Jesus nor any of those He inspired to record Scriptures told any person to remain in an adulterous lifestyle. That included the woman at the well, the woman caught in the act of adultery; and even through His beloved John the Baptist who spoke Truth to Herod.

Neither the woman caught in an act of adultery nor the woman at the well was told by Jesus that He approved of their sins. They, instead, were not to continue in these sins. The woman caught in an act of adultery was warned by Jesus to *go, and **sin no more*** John 8:11. Jesus also did not accept the sinful lifestyle of the woman at the well. Without her sharing any details, Jesus revealed to her that He knew all she had done—that she had had five husbands: *and he whom thou now hast is not thy husband.* John 4:18 She came under conviction admitting that Jesus knew she was living in a sinful lifestyle: *The woman saith unto him, Sir, I perceive that thou art a prophet.* John 4:19

This new convert immediately left what would have been her treasured waterpot, went into the city, and unashamedly witnessed to the men there: *Come, see a man, which told me all things that ever I did* ...Through her witness many of these men ... *went out of the city, and came unto him* [Jesus]. John 4:29-30 Everyone is to flee all sin.

The first criterion for evaluating Scripture should be to examine the context and then to be sure any interpretation does not violate other Scriptures on the same or related topics. When questions arise about marriage and divorce, Luke 16:18 is a good solid verse to use to evaluate most loopholes:

***Whosoever** putteth away his wife, and marrieth another, **committeth** adultery: and **whosoever** marrieth her that is put away from her husband **committeth** adultery.*

## 1 Corinthians 7:20 and 7:24 are misused to say that a person should remain in an adulterous marriage.

Two other Scriptures recorded by Paul that are often taken out of context to justify adulterous "marriages" include 1 Corinthians 7:20 and 1 Corinthians 7:24:

*Let every man abide in the same calling wherein he was called.* 1 Corinthians 7:20

*Brethren, let every man, wherein he is called, therein abide with God.* 1 Corinthians 7:24

In 1 Corinthians 7:20 and 24, Paul is not justifying adulterous marriages. He knows these are sinful relationships. He, instead, is teaching *principles* of faithfulness, through the examples of circumcision and servanthood as they relate to salvation.

Circumcision and servanthood were topics well understood by the audience Paul was addressing. In these examples, he isn't teaching directly on marriage but is using his comparative teaching to illustrate, through two entirely different topics (circumcision and servanthood), points of comparison to convey understanding about commitment.

## 1 Corinthians 7:20 is an illustration about circumcision.

We will look at these two Scriptures 1 Corinthians 7:20 and 7:24 individually. It's vital to read the Scriptures that come immediately prior to verses 20 and 24 to gather the context. Paul's pattern is the same for both of these metaphoric teachings on circumcision and servanthood. He first gives the example and then applies the principle. Study 1 Corinthians 7:20 in its context of verses 18-19. That is, read them together to see that they do not conflict. Each complements the other, which is the pattern of all inspired Scripture:

*18 Is any man called being **circumcised**? let him not become uncircumcised. Is any called in uncircumcision? let him not be circumcised. 19 Circumcision is nothing, and uncircumcision is nothing, but the keeping of the commandments of God. **20 Let every man abide in the same calling wherein he was called.***

It should be obvious that it's impossible to become uncircumcised. Paul knew that. The teaching point is that it is also ridiculous to think that works of man such as circumcision affect or are evidences of one's salvation. It is *the keeping of the commandments of God*, not the works of man that Paul is addressing. (Likewise one's state of salvation does not affect the validity of a marriage-covenant.) The context given in 1 Corinthians 7:18-19 shows what Paul is not teaching. He is not saying when God calls a person to serve Him **who is circumcised** that a condition of salvation is that he must be uncircumcised, nor should he believe that a requirement of salvation is that he must become circumcised if he has not been circumcised. Circumcision was an Old Testament work of the flesh required under the ceremonial law. It no longer applied when Paul wrote these verses of Scripture. Jesus fulfilled the works of the ceremonial law. Such works of man have nothing to do with salvation. However, even though circumcision was part of the "works" of the Old Testament law, it wasn't wrong to circumcise in New Testament times. Both Jesus and John the Baptist were circumcised. (See Luke 2:21 and 1:59.) Again, Paul was not teaching against circumcision. He was teaching that physical circumcision wasn't a "works" requirement for salvation.

**Physical circumcision is a work of man. Salvation is a work in the heart of man through the Holy Spirit.** The Scriptures confirm this; that is, it is our heart that must be circumcised. We must repent from sin—from the works of the flesh and DO the works of the spirit:

*And the LORD thy God will circumcise thine heart, and the heart of thy seed, to love the LORD thy God with all thine heart, and with all thy soul, that thou mayest live.* Deuteronomy 30:6

*Circumcise yourselves to the LORD, and take away the foreskins of your heart, ye men of Judah and inhabitants of Jerusalem: lest my fury come forth like fire, and burn that none can quench it, because of the evil of your doings.* Jeremiah 4:4

How might the principles taught about circumcision be related to 1 Corinthians 7:15? That is, how is it that a person can "abide in the same calling wherein he was called" if "the unbelieving depart"? A <u>faithful</u> brother or sister is to remain in an unmarried state or return to his spouse when and if that is possible. The state of marriage does not change because one of the spouses deserts the marriage. <u>However</u>, it assuredly does not mean that anyone is to remain in sin—in a marriage that is not a covenant-marriage. That is not the LORD's calling!

## 1 Corinthians 7:24 is an <u>illustration</u> about servanthood.

Paul uses another comparative example in verses 21-24 to illustrate that salvation does not negate *righteous* obligations made before a person is saved. Verses 21-23 give the context for verse 24:

*21 Art thou called being a servant? care not for it: but if thou mayest be made free, use it rather. 22 For he that is called in the Lord, being a servant, is the Lord's freeman: likewise also he that is called, being free, is Christ's servant. 23 Ye are bought with a price; be not ye the servants of men. 24 Brethren, let every man, wherein he is called, therein abide with God.*
1 Corinthians 7:21-24

First Corinthians 7:24, gets its context from verses 21-23. It is here that Paul is instructing those persons who were servants when they were saved (*were called*). If that be the situation, such a person, a servant when he got saved, was being instructed to not run away or try to wrongfully free himself. He should continue to be a faithful servant. He should pay his indenture (debt).

This is the "calling" in which that person should remain. It is the context for the teaching in 1 Corinthians 7:24 to ... *let every man, wherein he is called, therein abide <u>with God</u>*. This Scripture, however, is not a "call" to remain in sin. It is a "calling" to faithful servanthood and to not misuse one's faith to negate righteous secular obligations.

Most new versions translate *"servanthood"* as *slavery*. Societal standards have greatly changed since the time of Paul's writing. When 1 Corinthians was penned, servanthood was not always the oppressive environment many today envision it to be. Many people voluntarily sold themselves into "servanthood." It was also a way of being provided a home in which to live and food to eat. That's why it's translated *being a servant;* that's the overriding context for this teaching.

Does this have anything to do with marriage? Paul isn't advocating that people should be faithful to adultery. That would violate context. If a person divorces his spouse or deserts a covenant-marriage that work of the flesh does not affect God's marriage-covenant. However, neither of the two "let-every-man abide" statements in 1 Corinthians 7:20 and 7:24 is directing people to remain in an adulterous "marriage," or any other sin. It is the principle of commitment to righteous obligations to which every man should abide—and serve.

**"I think people should not get divorced. They promised under oath and should keep their promises."**

Here is an example where context reigns supreme. People should not get divorced IF they are in a covenant-marriage. People should never make ungodly vows and should not keep ungodly vows, even those taken under oath. We should not make or keep vows which violate God's Word. Sinful promises require repentance—not commitment. If a person makes a vow to marry someone who is already a covenant spouse, that is an ungodly vow in which God will not partake. Neither should we make, keep, or in any way partake in such ungodly vows.

| God holds man accountable for godly vows; that is, we are to keep them. We should not make or keep ungodly vows. There are eternal punishments for ungodly vow-making. ||
|---|---|
| *When thou vowest a vow <u>unto God</u>, defer not to pay it; for he hath no pleasure in fools: pay that which thou hast vowed. Better is it that thou shouldest not vow, than that thou shouldest vow and not pay. Suffer not thy mouth to cause thy flesh to sin; neither say thou before the angel, that it was an error: wherefore **should God** be angry at thy voice, and **destroy the work of thine hands**?* Ecclesiastes 5:4-6 | *Thou shalt not bear false witness ...* Exodus 20:16 |
| | *They have spoken words, **swearing** **falsely** <u>in making a covenant</u>: thus judgment springeth up as hemlock in the furrows of the field.* Hosea 10:4 |
| | When two people vow to enter into an adulterous marriage, that is a form of swearing falsely. They are swearing falsely, under oath, to partake in something God hates. |
| The **context** of the above vows (vows unto God) is those which are righteous. All one flesh marriages come under righteous vows which every person should "pay"; that is, should honor or keep. | *Whereupon he* [Herod] *promised with an oath to give her* [Herodias] *whatsoever she would ask.* Matthew 14:7 |
| | Herod should not have kept his ungodly vow to murder John. |

Again beware of applying Scriptures out of context. For example, there have been examples in this text to show that if man persists in sin, God will turn him over to a reprobate mind; that is, he will allow him to continue in that sin. The LORD allows man to sin, but He does not approve. That's God's punitive judgment. There are usually eternal destructive ramifications when this depth of depravity is reached:

## Chapter 21

*Thus saith the LORD of hosts, the God of Israel, saying; Ye and your wives have both spoken with your mouths, and fulfilled with your hand, saying, We will surely **perform our vows** that we have vowed, to burn incense to the queen of heaven, and to pour out drink offerings unto her: ye will surely accomplish your vows, and surely perform your vows.* Jeremiah 44:25

Jeremiah 44:25 is another example of making vows but vows of which God disapproves. God had taught His spiritual wife Israel that she was not to make vows with the heathen nor to their pagan gods and goddesses. The people, however, refused to obey Him. They made vows in direct rebellion to God. Likewise, God tells everyone today not to enter into adulterous marriages. Doing so is vowing but making false vows that God hates. It is much like what the Israelites did who had spoken with their mouths that they would surely be faithful to their ungodly vows to serve the queen of heaven. Here's what God's judgment was for their making and keeping these abhorrent vows:

*Behold, I will watch over them for evil, and not for good: and all the men of Judah that are in the land of Egypt shall be consumed by the sword and by the famine, until there be an end of them.* Jeremiah 44:27

It's important to repeat the fact that Paul is not saying that sin and wrongful living are sanctioned when he writes, in both 1 Corinthians 7:20 and 24, to *Let every man abide in the same calling wherein he was called.* That would be presenting conflicting teachings in his writings. He is not saying, "If you are a murderer, continue being a murderer." He is not saying, "If you are a liar, keep on lying." He isn't suggesting that if you are an adulterer to continue living in the sin of adultery. He's not saying if you are a covenant-breaker that you should continue being a covenant-breaker.

### Paul's Teachings Are Taken Out Of Context.

Sadly, many desert their call to salvation and righteous living when it comes to forsaking the sin of an adulterous "marriage" relationship. They, instead, cover their sin with the "violence" of a "re-marriage":

*For the LORD, the God of Israel, saith that he hateth putting away* [divorcing]*: for one **covereth violence** with his garment, saith the LORD of hosts: therefore take heed to your spirit, that ye deal not treacherously* [divorce]. Malachi 2:16

*And others save with fear, pulling them out of the fire; hating even the garment spotted by the flesh* [sin]. Jude 1:23

Commitment to godly vows doesn't change because of salvation or circumstances. All one-flesh covenant marriages are binding and are only dissolved by physical death. The validity of a marriage-covenant has nothing to do with sinful sexual intimacy, circumcision, or one's servitude—and certainly not one's salvation.

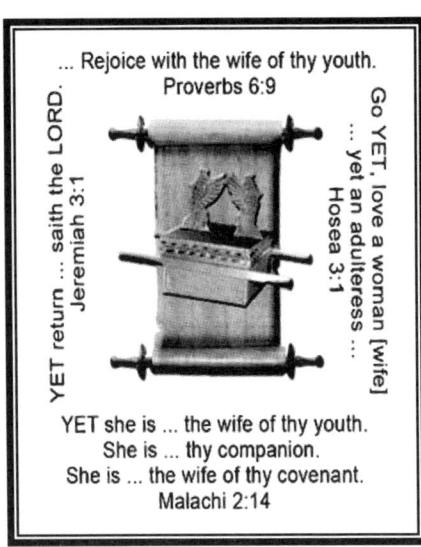

Marriage is a **covenant,** a one-flesh joining by God of a man and a woman, neither of whom has a living one-flesh spouse. Notice the repetition of the word *yet*. Even if there is a man-made dissolution, YET (still) she is the wife of thy covenant. Review pages 252 through 254.

# 22

# *Come Now, And Let Us Reason Together...*

This statement from Isaiah 1:18 is the launching pad for the final chapter. Three loopholes are discussed to add additional principles and to provide examples to apply to what has already been presented. There is an endless list of man's reasonings that could be included. However, I hope that by presenting the principles that will be covered in this chapter, along with those already discussed, that you will have ample information to ward off any unscriptural error about God's joining of one man and one woman until death they do part. That is, no matter what the question about covenant-marriage, there will be something within this book which will direct you to a Scriptural response. Feel free to write us at Restoration of the Family if you have any questions on the defense of marriage and why it is that Jesus says whosoever divorces a one-flesh spouse and marries another committ**eth** adultery.

## Is adultery a state or a single act?

The Bible clearly says that whenever what most people call a "re-marriage" occurs, God calls it adultery. He calls it this when a one-flesh spouse marries someone else while his covenant-spouse is still living. Some Scriptures which confirm this include: Matthew 5:32, 19:9; Mark 10:11-12; Luke 16:18, and Romans 7:2-3. Adultery is identified in every passage where the "re-marriage" of divorced persons is mentioned. Another important question is this: "Does adultery take place in the **act** of becoming 're-married,' or does it exist as an on-going **state** of adultery, or both?"

If adultery is just the act of "re-marriage," then a couple who is "re-married" can go to the Lord, confess that sin, and be forgiven, and go on living together and not be guilty of adultery until such a time ... when they split up, get "re-married," and go to the LORD again and confess that sin and be free again ... and become "re-married" ... until they split up and confess again ... If adultery is merely a single act, then that is how the process can work. The *act* can be forgiven like any other sinful *act*. However, that's not what the Scripture teaches. A major missing link is an understanding of the confessing and forgiving process. A person who asks for forgiveness is one who repents. This means he acknowledges that he isn't going to continue committing the sin for which he is asking forgiveness.

Chapter 22

## It all starts with an <u>act</u> of adultery.

An act of adultery occurs when a spouse looks with lust at another person to whom he is not married, or he has what society refers to as an affair but what God calls adultery. However, any time the flesh gets so out of control that a person would commit such an egregious sin against his spouse and against God, there should be great concern.

<u>Sexual sin is something from which millions never recover.</u> They become caught in the web of it—deceived—sadly thinking, as with other highly addictive practices, like alcoholism and drugs, that they can control themselves and stop whenever they tire of that habit. Perhaps they dabbled with fornication in their youth and overcame it so they think they can do it again and recover themselves ... *out of the snare of the devil* ... 2 Timothy 2:26 Anyone who is even entertaining such foolish thoughts is urged <u>daily</u> to read the two sections from Proverbs below and consider the warnings that God feels are necessary to record. **FLEE any pastor, counselor, or friend who suggests that recurring lustful thoughts, such as those that are recorded in the Scriptures below are normal and acceptable for someone who is walking in righteousness.** They are not acceptable:

> There is a major difference between an act and state of adultery.

*Lust not after her beauty in thine heart; neither let her take thee with her eyelids. For by means of a whorish woman a man is brought to a piece of bread: and the **adulteress will hunt for the precious life** ... So he that goeth in to his neighbour's wife; whosoever toucheth her shall not be innocent. But whoso committeth adultery with a woman lacketh understanding: he that doeth it **destroyeth his own soul** A wound and dishonour shall he get; and his reproach shall not be wiped away. Proverbs 6:25-26, 29, 32-33*

*With her much fair speech she caused him to yield, with the flattering of her lips she forced him. He goeth after her straightway, as an ox goeth to the slaughter, or as a fool to the correction of the stocks; Till a dart strike through his liver; as a bird hasteth to the snare, and knoweth not that **it is for his life** ... **Her house is the way to hell**, going down to the **chambers of death**.* Proverbs 7:21-23, 27

*But every man is tempted, when he is drawn away of **his <u>own</u> lust**, and enticed. Then when lust hath conceived, it bringeth forth sin: and sin, when it is finished, bringeth forth death. **Do not err**, <u>my beloved brethren</u>.* James 1:14-16

Court divorce records are littered with millions of examples of those who have entertained feelings of repeated lust. Perhaps they thought wrongly that sexual sin was normal or somehow justified. Even many respected and seemingly strong Christians with long-term marriages and children fall prey to the deception to ... *take fire in his bosom* ... Proverbs 6:27. Be not deceived. They destroy their own souls!

As you continue to study, recall the teaching from Chapter 12. Pronouns and nouns in most Scriptures are generic. They apply equally to both men and women, even when only one is mentioned.

## God's focus is on a <u>state</u> of adultery.

As a review, consider again the recurring phrase "committ**eth** adultery" in the gospel accounts (Matthew, Mark, Luke, John) and Romans. This phrase grammatically indicates a present on-going **state** because of the *eth* ending on *commit*. This is reflective of the underlying Greek grammar from which the Scriptures are translated. Additionally, in Romans 7:2-3 Paul uses the continuous action tense contextually when it says, "she **shall be called** an adulteress:"

Chapter 22

*For the woman which hath an husband is bound by the law* [This is God's "law of marriage."] *to her husband **so long as he liveth**; but if the husband be dead, she is loosed from the law of her husband. So then if, while her husband liveth, she be married to another man, **she shall be called an adulteress**: but if her husband be dead, she is free from that law; so that she is no adulteress, though she be married to another man.* Romans 7:2-3

*They have spoken words, swearing falsely in making a covenant: thus judgment springeth up as hemlock in the furrows of the field.* Hosea 10:4

**An Adulterous Ceremony:
This is what God cannot join
because the first marriage is still binding.**

In the graphic above, the two people in the foreground are depicted as getting married. That is how they picture this <u>act</u>, as do many of their friends and family. However, that is in their eyes. The Bible tells us that they have entered into a sinful state called *adultery*. Jesus says they are an adulteress and an adulterer. This is because, in this image, the man has a living covenant wife. She is shown in the background. Scriptures teach not only that the "re-marriage" of divorced persons is adultery, but why it is so. <u>It's adultery because the first marriage is still binding</u>. Luke 16:18 and other Scriptures reconfirm that *what* God

357

joins together is not dissolved when a person divorces or if that person marries someone else:

*Whosoever* [1] *putteth away his wife, and* [2] *marrieth another, committeth adultery: and whosoever marrieth her that is put away from her husband committeth adultery.* Luke 16:18

There's no big hidden theological meaning here. Nor are the words difficult to understand. How long is a person "bound" or joined to a one-flesh spouse? It's as long as he or she liv**eth**. Again, the *eth* ending indicates an on-going action, or what becomes a STATE of being—a state of marriage. This is part of the built-in Biblical grammar throughout the Bible which differentiates for the reader the difference between an *act* and a *state*—the addition of the *eth* ending.

What man does cannot dissolve *what* God has created in the spiritual realm. Man looks at everything in the physical for that's the environment in which he has been trained. He isn't normally trained to "see" the spiritual "disconnect" of what occurs in a "re-marriage." For example, think on what would normally come to mind when an invitation to a wedding is received, even if it's one for a "re-marriage." What do most envision? The bridegroom waits at the front, straining to get a glimpse of his veiled bride. The wedding march plays. Everyone stands and turns as the bride enters, walking slowly, but anxiously, down the aisle. She is beautifully adorned in her white, floor-length gown, arm in arm with her father. But STOP. God looks through all "veils" of human deception, and that's what Paul has clearly recorded in Romans 7:2-3:

## Chapter 22

*For the woman which hath an husband is bound by the law to her husband so long as he liveth; but if the husband be dead, she is loosed from the law of her husband.* Romans 7:2

Even though Romans 7:2 is very clear, Paul says the same thing again in Romans 7:3 by repeating and expanding it. He clearly says that those who rebel against God's "law of marriage" put themselves into an on-going **state** of adultery. How long is that state? It's as long as that person is married to another spouse. How do we know that? We know because of the carefully selected contextual words: *while, liveth, be married, shall be:*

> *So then, if, **while** her husband liv**eth**,*
> *she **be married** to another man,*
> *she **shall be** called an adulteress ...*
> Romans 7:3

The *exception* to allow those in a one-flesh marriage to marry another spouse is: ***but if** <u>her husband be dead</u>, she is free from that law; so that she is no adulteress, though she be married to another man.* Romans 7:3
However ...
*... **if** a woman shall put away her husband, **and** <u>be married</u> to another, she committ**eth** adultery.* Mark 10:12

Did you notice the word *and* which is used to not only join two actions but, as the study in Chapter 4 showed, the word *and* is not only used as a connective but it also indicates there is some indeterminate period of time between the two acts? That time here is between when the wife "put away her husband," and she "married" another person. To "be married" should be clear. It is again that wording which indicates an on-going continuous action. Scripture will never conflict with Scripture. Romans 7:2-3 is in total agreement with what Jesus taught in the *Sermon on the Mount* and in other Scriptures.

## Are they loopholes?

Below are additional ways Scriptures are taken out of context with man-made loopholes which are used in efforts to justify adulterous marriages. As noted above, even though there are others, the three examples presented below and the Bible verses already covered should provide ample information which can be applied to any other situation. These teachings have as their foundation covenant, one-flesh marriages: one man for one woman until physical death parts them. There will be some review, repetition, and even redundancy of information as there has been throughout this text, but something new will be added. It is important to regularly reinforce what the Word says and how the guidelines studied are applicable. (See Isaiah 28:10.)

## *1* Loophole: "He committed adultery so our marriage is dissolved."

Many divorced spouses say, "Our first marriage is dissolved. The covenant has been broken. He committed adultery." Such comments are usually made because one or both spouses have been involved in adultery, or there has been a state-issued divorce decree, or a church annulment. However, a marriage-covenant is not dissolved in God's eyes because someone violates its terms or if a judge strikes his gavel granting a divorce indicating, in his eyes, that a one-flesh marriage is dissolved. As long as both the one-flesh spouses are alive, God says the marriage cannot be dissolved.

A person driving a car can break or violate the law. However, doing so doesn't change or dissolve the law. Likewise, if a husband or wife violates or breaks the terms of God's marriage-covenant, this does not change the permanency of God's joining. Sin does not change or dissolve God's "law of marriage:"

> *The wife is bound by the law* [of marriage] *as long as her husband liveth; but if her husband be dead, she is at liberty to be married to whom she will; only in the Lord.* 1 Corinthians 7:39

However, according to Hebrews 13:4, those who sin against the marriage bed will be judged IF they do not repent:

> *Marriage is honourable in all, and the bed undefiled: but whoremongers and adulterers God will judge.* Hebrews 13:4

## Two acts create an adulterous marriage.

When one of the spouses separates from the other and "re-marries" someone else, those acts do not free him from the *state* of his one-flesh marriage. Instead, such *acts* place him into an on-going *state* of adultery. There are two aspects of an adulterous "marriage" relationship. First, it is the divorcing of a one-flesh spouse and then the act of marrying another that then puts the "spouses" so involved into on-going states of adultery. A married person who has lustful thoughts or affections toward someone not his one-flesh spouse commits an act of adultery; but the *act* of "re-marrying" puts both persons so involved into an on-going *state* of adultery. Just as the act of becoming married leads one into an on-going state of matrimony, the act of becoming "re-married" results in an ongoing state of adultery. This is a serious sin against God not recognized as such by millions of Christians:

> *Whosoever (1) putteth away his wife, **and** (2) marrieth another, committeth adultery: and whosoever marrieth her that is put away from her husband committeth adultery.* Luke 16:18

*For the woman which hath an husband is bound by the law to her husband so long as he liveth; but if the husband be dead, she is loosed from the law of her husband. So then if, while her husband liveth, **she be married to another man**, she **shall be called an adulteress**: but if her husband be dead, she is free from that law; so that she is no adulteress, though she be married to another man.* Romans 7:2-3

The truth about divorce and "re-marriage" is clear and consistent with God's unchanging perspective on marriage. The adulterous relationship resulting from a second "marriage" (if there is a living one-flesh spouse) is not a one-time <u>act</u> of adultery. It is, instead, a continuing <u>state</u> of adultery. According to what the Word of God says, "Whosoever do**eth** it committ**eth** adultery." Adultery is a serious sin.

Both Joseph and Job, who were godly Old Testament men, clearly understood the dangers of defiling themselves with sexual sin. Joseph, for example, fled sexual sin when his master's wife tried to seduce him to have sex with her. He jeopardized what seemed like his entire political and financial career to honor God rather than his flesh. Joseph, however, as all men must do, controlled his flesh. He didn't let lustful thoughts overtake him and sin against God.

Potiphar and his wife were not saved; yet, their marriage was valid in God's eyes, and Joseph knew not to touch such a "holy thing"—the marriage-covenant: ... *because thou art his wife: how then can I do this great wickedness, and **sin against God?*** Genesis 39:9 Joseph's rejection of Potiphar's wife's advances angered her. She lied telling her husband that Joseph tried to seduce her. As a result, Potiphar retaliated and had Joseph put in prison:

*And it came to pass, when his* [Joseph] *master heard the words of his wife, which she spake unto him, saying, After this manner did thy servant to me; that his wrath was kindled. And Joseph's master took him, and put him into the prison, a place where the king's prisoners were bound: and he was there in the prison.* Genesis 39:19-20

Even though all sin against God is serious, adultery is specifically recorded twice as *a sin against God.* The first example was given on the previous page with Joseph's statement. Additionally, the high priest Eli had two rebellious sons who: *... lay with the women that assembled at the door of the tabernacle of the congregation.*

Eli asked his sons why they did such evil and said: *If one man sin against another, the judge shall judge him: but if a man **sin against the LORD**, who shall intreat for him? Notwithstanding they hearkened not unto the voice of their father ...* 1 Samuel 2:22, 25 Eli, however, **did nothing to punish his sons** for these vile sins. That was honoring them above God: *Wherefore kick ye at my sacrifice and at mine offering, which I have commanded in ... and honourest thy sons above me...* 1 Samuel 2:29 Many honor their sinful lifestyles and those of their children above God's Word. God warned Eli this would end his priesthood and his future generations would be cut off. Shortly thereafter both Eli and his sons died on the same day.

Everyone, like Joseph, should be willing to be jailed rather than to sin sexually and especially to flee having an affair with a married man or a married woman—an egregious sin against God. Job, too, understood the cost of sexual sin. He described adultery as *... a fire that consumeth to destruction, and would root out all mine increase.* Job 31:12

Those who think they can flirt with others of the opposite sex with "friendly" hugs and kisses, should follow Job's example: *I made a covenant with mine eyes; why then should I think upon a maid?* Job 31:1

## 2. Loophole: "I have <u>repented</u> of my first marriage."

"I have repented of my first marriage. God has forgiven me of that marriage." These are common statements of those who are in an adulterous "marriage"; that is, they have in the eyes of society, "remarried." Thus, they feel God's "law of marriage" doesn't apply.

Even some strong Christians seem confused on the definition of repentance. Repentance is more than saying you are sorry for sinning. Many say they are sorry when they are caught doing something they should <u>not</u> have done. Children are very good at saying, "I'm sorry," to appease a parent or to possibly plea-bargain a punishment. Adults act somewhat the same. For example, a husband, after being caught in an act of adultery, said to his wife: "I'm sorry, but I love her. I love you, but not as a wife." That man was not expressing godly sorrow. His words were steeped in sin, rebellion, and deception. God defines repentance as not just confessing the sin by saying you are sorry but by totally turning from and forsaking the sin in godly **sorrow**. This applies whether it is an act or a state of adultery. Whenever there is a question about spiritual matters, the answer must be based on Scripture. Review how God defines repentance:

> *He that covereth his sins shall not prosper: but whoso confesseth **and forsaketh them** shall have mercy.* Proverbs 28:13 *For godly sorrow worketh repentance to salvation not to be repented of: but the sorrow of the world worketh death.* 2 Corinthians 7:10

To repent, it must first be determined that the act is sin. Then, Scripture tells us there are two requirements before any sin can be forgiven. The two requirements are (1) confessing and (2) forsaking sin. It's impossible to repent without turning **from** sin and turning **to** the LORD. True repentance requires godly sorrow and having nothing further to do with the sin that had been committed:

*Now I rejoice, <u>not that ye were made sorry</u>, **but** that ye sorrowed to repentance ...* 2 Corinthians 7:9

***If** my people, which are called by my name, shall humble themselves, and pray, and seek my face, and **turn from their wicked ways**; <u>then</u> will I hear from heaven, and will <u>forgive</u> their sin, and will heal their land.* 2 Chronicles 7:14

*I tell you, Nay: but, except ye repent, ye shall all likewise perish.* Luke 13:3
*But **if** the wicked will **turn** from all his sins that he hath committed, and **keep all my statutes**, and do that which is lawful and right, he shall surely live, he shall not die. All his transgressions that he hath committed, they shall not be mentioned unto him: in his righteousness that he hath done he shall live ... But when the righteous turneth away from his righteousness, and committ**eth** iniquity, and do**eth** according to all the abominations that the wicked man doeth, shall he live? All his righteousness that he hath done shall not be mentioned: in his trespass that he hath trespassed, and in his sin that he hath sinned, in them shall he die.* Ezekiel 18:21-24

## A covenant-marriage is created by God. It is not sin.

A person cannot "repent" of a one-flesh marriage because it isn't sin, and neither can God forgive a person because He has joined two people into one flesh via His supernatural, invisible permanent joining. *There may be acts leading up to a covenant joining from which a person should repent*; however, the joining of a man and a woman by God, neither of whom has a living one-flesh spouse, is not a sin.

Unlike a covenant-marriage, God deems **an adulterous "marriage" sin.** Adultery is the sin from which a person who wants to be forgiven must repent. That's the fallacy of this loophole: "I have <u>repented</u> of my first (covenant) marriage."

When a person repents, he repents <u>from</u> something that is sin. So the question must be asked how a person can repent from a covenant-marriage. The answer should be obvious. That's impossible because a covenant-marriage is not sin. The latter is created by God. God has nothing to do with sin; that is, He does not create sin. All His acts are righteous. Thus, the loophole that says someone can repent of a previous marriage is false—assuming it is one created by God as God only creates a one-flesh union between a man and woman when neither of them has a living one-flesh spouse.

## 3 Loophole: "We no longer have sex so we are not committing adultery. We are married for tax reasons and companionship."

This has no biblical basis. There are several major errors with this loophole. ¹Sex is not what marries or "unmarries" two people. ²We don't marry for tax reasons. Adultery is not the kind of companionship God has designed. It's a covenant spouse for whom God has designed this kind of companionship. ³We are not to give the appearance of evil. ⁴Marriage is to glorify God. Study below and on the next page:

¹*Whosoever (1) putteth away his wife,* **and** *(2) marrieth another, committ***eth** *adultery: and whosoever marrieth her that is put away from her husband committ***eth** *adultery.* Luke 16:18 (See next page for superscripts [2, 3, 4].)

Luke 16:18 says nothing about sexual intimacy. It states that whosoever divorces AND marries a different spouse "committ**eth** adultery." It's the putting away **and** marrying another that creates an adulterous "marriage." This is the aspect of adultery that is misunderstood by many who are involved in a "re-marriage." That doesn't mean it isn't also sin—adultery or fornication—when two unmarried people live together and participate in sexual intimacy or have inordinate affections toward one another:

*²Yet ye say, Wherefore? Because the LORD hath been witness between thee and the wife of thy youth, against whom thou hast dealt treacherously: yet **is she thy companion**, and the **wife of thy covenant**.* Malachi 2:14

A covenant-marriage is what is designed for companionship as well as to replenish the earth, and to glorify God. It's not for tax reasons!

*³Abstain from all appearance of evil.* 1 Thessalonians 5:22
*⁴And God blessed them, saying, Be fruitful, and multiply ...* Genesis 1:22
*For we are members of his body, of his flesh, and of his bones. For this cause shall a man leave his father and mother, and shall be joined unto his wife, and they two shall be one flesh. This is a great mystery: but I speak concerning Christ and the church.* Ephesians 5:30-32

## It's clear what God loves and what God hates.

God put in place "in the beginning" an invisible spiritual supernatural mechanism—a covenant—through which a man and a woman are joined until physical death dissolves it. This joining, like the spinning of the earth on its invisible axis, cannot be changed by man. The LORD recorded, through the hands of holy men in two testaments, the importance, permanence, and immutability of this joining. He chronicled this through the nation Israel, His spiritual wife, and through the lives of men and women made one flesh by this covenant, permanently, which was esablished in the garden of Eden. God begs, pleads, and commands man to not "touch" this covenant and lovingly shows through Scriptures that man cannot break His established covenants. He hates any act which has as its purpose the putting apart of what His covenant has joined. Study Jeremiah 33:20-26.

It seems inconceivable that anyone would purposely do something that God hates and then think that the LORD will somehow approve. It's impossible for God to do something that violates His Word. He cannot join someone with a living spouse to someone else. But, man, in his childlike attitude, will ask how he has offended God. Yet, God clearly tells us what He loves and what He hates:

| If we love God, we do not do what He hates. ||
|---|---|
| John 14:15<br>*If ye <u>love</u> me, keep my commandments.*<br><br>John 14:23-24<br>*Jesus answered and said unto him, **If a man <u>love</u> me**, **he will** keep my words: and my Father will love him, and we will come unto him, and make our abode with him. He that **<u>loveth me not</u>** <u>keepeth not my sayings</u> ...* | Malachi 2:16<br>*For the LORD, the God of Israel, saith that **he <u>hateth</u> putting away:** ... therefore take heed to your spirit, that ye <u>deal not treacherously</u>* [Do not divorce.].<br><br>Matthew 19:6<br>*Wherefore they are no more twain, but one flesh. What therefore God hath joined together, <u>let not</u> man put asunder.* |
| Malachi 2:17<br>*Ye have wearied the LORD with your words. Yet ye say, Wherein have we wearied him? When ye say, Every one that doeth evil is good in the sight of the LORD, and he delighteth in them; or, Where is the God of judgment?* ||

In his futile efforts to defend his sin, man, instead of pointing to the *sayings* (Word) of God as the standard for marriage, points to the many in leadership who in the eyes of man have prosperous ministries but are living in adulterous "marriages." He also considers the many others who are in long-term adulterous "marriages" who seem to be successful and happy as examples God has joined. Confused man misinterprets free will. He feels that because God *allows* so many to continue in the sin of adultery—adulterous "marriages"—that either

## Chapter 22

He isn't judging or won't judge them. Those are misconceptions: *... the LORD seeth not as man seeth; for man looketh on the outward appearance, but the LORD looketh on the heart.* 1 Samuel 16:7 They are covenant-breakers. God, through the apostle Paul, describes covenant-breakers in Romans 1:28-32 as those who have been turned over to a reprobate mind, and as shown above, He specifically names *putting away* (divorce) as something He hates in Malachi 2:16-17.

**Breaking a marriage-covenant is a very serious sin.** Those who commit adultery have violated a sacred vow. The warnings against this sin are found throughout the Bible. Three references are listed below, but many others are given throughout this book:

*When thou vowest a vow unto God, defer not to pay it; for he hath no pleasure in fools: pay that which thou hast vowed. Better is it that thou shouldest not vow, than that thou shouldest vow and not pay. Suffer not thy mouth to cause thy flesh to sin; neither say thou before the angel, that it was an error: wherefore should God be angry at thy voice, and destroy the work of thine hands?* Ecclesiastes 5:4-6

*... Therefore take heed to your spirit, and let none deal treacherously against the wife of his youth.* Malachi 2:15

*And I gave her space to repent of her fornication; and she repented not. Behold, I will cast her into a bed, and them that commit adultery with her into great tribulation, except they repent of their deeds.* Revelation 2:21-22

## You may be surprised who it is that God has turned over to a reprobate mind.

There have been many examples throughout this book of Scriptures that have been doctrinally changed. These affect the message readers are learning about God's perspective on marriage and divorce as well as the demise of those who continue in the sin of adultery. Another example is given below, Romans 1:28-32. Are the **underlined and bolded** words in your Bible?

*28 And even as they did not like to retain God in their knowledge, <u>God gave them over to a **reprobate** mind</u>, to do those things which are not convenient; 29 Being filled with all unrighteousness, fornication, wickedness, covetousness, maliciousness; full of envy, murder, debate, deceit, malignity; whisperers, 30 Backbiters, haters of God, despiteful, proud, boasters, inventors of evil things, disobedient to parents, 31 Without understanding, **<u>covenantbreakers</u>**, **<u>without natural affection</u>**, implacable, unmerciful: 32 Who knowing the judgment of God, that they which commit such things are worthy of death, not only do the same, but have pleasure in them that do them.* Romans 1:28-32

Romans 1:28-32 contains some very strong language. God describes all those who commit these sins as those whom HE has turned over to a reprobate mind. I leave it to the reader to open a dictionary and read what is described as a reprobate. It's surely nothing with which anyone would purposely wish to be identified. Scripture tells us:

*Examine yourselves, whether ye be in the faith; prove your own selves. Know ye not your own selves, how that <u>Jesus Christ is in you</u>,\* **except** [unless] ye be reprobates?* 2 Corinthians 13:5 *\*You are "in Christ."*

The underlying Greek text for both the King James Bible and that for the new versions include the Greek words which should be translated *covenantbreakers* and *without natural affection*. See below:

| ἀσυνέτους,<br>Without understanding,<br>801<br>asunétous | ἀσυνθέτους,<br>covenantbreakers,<br>802<br>asunthétous | ἀστόργους,<br>without natural affection,<br>794<br>astórgous |
|---|---|---|

**Both the TR and NA have<br>Greek words AND translations as shown above.**

However, these two sins *covenant-breakers* and those *without natural affection* have been removed—haven't been translated as such in most new versions of the Bible. Study the table below to see the common pattern followed in several new versions of the Bible. The King James translation is given first in which the translators have correctly translated the full text of Romans 1:31.

| | ***Covenantbreakers* are omitted from most Bibles.** |
|---|---|
| | *Without understanding, covenantbreakers, without natural affection, implacable, unmerciful.* King James Bible |
| Bible* | Romans 1:31 |
| NIV | *they are senseless, faithless, heartless, ruthless.* |
| NKJV | *undiscerning, untrustworthy, unloving, unforgiving, unmerciful.* |
| NASV | *without understanding, untrustworthy, unloving, unmerciful;* |
| ESV | *foolish, faithless, heartless, ruthless.* |
| HCSB | *undiscerning, untrustworthy, unloving, and unmerciful.* |
| Lamsa | *They have no respect for a covenant. They know neither love nor peace, nor is there mercy in them.* |
| ICB | *They are foolish, they do not keep their promises, and they show no kindness or mercy to other people.* |
| *NIV: New International Version; NKJV: New King James Version; NASV: New American Standard Version; ESV: English Standard Version; HCSB: Holman Christian Standard Bible; Lamsa: The Holy Bible; ICB: International Children's Bible | |

## Here's the <u>false</u> "story," <u>in part</u>, that most new version Bibles tell.

Most new version Bibles, and many pastors, give a flawed picture about marriage, adultery, and adulterous "marriages." Their teachings conflict with the pure Word of God; that is, with doctrine that reflects the underlying, consistent, and contextually agreeing Scripture. This is because of their paraphrasing. Thus, they say:

- God made a helper for man rather than an help meet.
- God made a woman suitable or comparable for man.

- The sin of adultery, marital unfaithfulness, immorality, or desertion can be reason to divorce a one-flesh wife.
- There's no such thing as a covenant-breaker (in their texts).
- It is not good for man to marry.
- A second, third, or fourth marriage is valid when there is a living covenant spouse.
- A person can divorce for any reason and "re-marry."
- Fornicators are <u>not</u> included in those listed who will not enter the Kingdom of God.
- There's no condemnation by God for living in a sinful lifestyle.
- Marriage is a "work" of man.

These attacks on the Word of God are no different, in principle, than the attack which started in the garden of Eden when the Serpent changed the Words of God <u>from</u>: ... *thou shalt surely die.* Genesis 2:17 <u>to</u>: *Ye shall not surely die.* Genesis 3:4

Sadly, the Serpent's message is the same one that is being given to those who study from the new Bible versions: *Ye shall not surely die ...* if you refuse to turn from your adultery, from your adulterous "marriage," and re-turn to the LORD:

*Seeing thou hatest instruction, and castest my words behind thee. When thou sawest a thief, then thou consentedst with him, and hast been partaker with adulterers. Thou givest thy mouth to evil, and thy tongue frameth deceit.* Psalm 50:17-19

The topics presented in this book can be a matter of spiritual life or death. You may benefit from reading two other books: *It's A Matter of Life or Death; Wrong Thinking About Marriage Leads to Destruction* and *The Miracle of Marriage*. These are also available from Restoration of the Family: www.RestorationOfTheFamily.org.

Chapter 22

# The famine in the land
# is quickly sweeping around the world.

No man has the power to create or to destroy God's covenants. Yet, man tries to do both. He joins what God says cannot be joined, and he thinks he dissolves what cannot be dissolved. Not satisfied with those acts against God, man removes evidence from the Bible that upholds the LORD's perspective on marriage. These doctrinal changes are directly related to the famine warned of Amos almost 3,000 years ago. This famine, mentioned several times throughout this text, is a famine unlike that for food and water—a physical hunger and thirst. The famine God prophesied through Amos is manifest in ways that, tragically, are not recognized by most Christians. This famine is one crafted through anemic Bibles—those in which God's "living water" has been infused with man's words.

*Behold, the days come, saith the Lord GOD, that I will send a famine in the land, not a famine of bread, nor a thirst for water, but of **hearing the words of the LORD**. Amos 8:11*

This famine is a strong message that the LORD gave to me as I was *wrestling* with the Holy Spirit 20 years ago about interlinking teachings on marriage and divorce with errors I was discovering in the new versions. I tried to "explain" to the LORD that I was already grieved and over-burdened with the heaviness of teaching on the much-rejected Biblical perspective of one man for one woman. However, the thoughts that came to me were that I had faithfully carried the torch for many years, focusing my efforts on teaching about one-flesh marriage. I had lived it, taught it, and fervently defended it. However, my teaching was too narrow. It is the entire

Word that is at peril. I must expand my ministry to encompass both teachings within the ministry that the LORD assigned to me: Bible versions and marriage. Thus, this book includes the interlinking of these two difficult messages as best I can with my limited understanding. I'm well aware that these are messages which offend relatives, friends, pastors, laypersons, and many people I may never meet. But I must be faithful to God. He is the One Who has held me up and provided in supernatural ways to bring to you, the reader, what is written upon the pages of this book.

Thus, I again share with you that warning about the famine taught through the prophet Amos. Is it not being played out with the proliferation of hundreds of versions of God's Word? Man refuses to ... *earnestly contend for the faith which was once delivered unto the saints.* (Jude 1:3), or ... *to receive the love of the truth* ... so God has sent *a strong delusion that they should believe a lie.* 2 Thessalonians 2:10-11 **The pure Word of God is disappearing from the Bibles, from the pulpits, and from the heart of man.**

Perhaps the famine of hearing the words of the LORD is being sent by God because that is the desire of millions who are supporting the practice of "re-writing" the Word of God. Man has rejected the preserved Biblical language written in English on the sixth-grade level as he searches for something he feels is easy to read. His flesh searches for loopholes—untruths about marriage "supping on" words which say that it is man who hates and divorces his wife instead of the LORD being the one that ... *saith that he hateth putting away.* Malachi

2:16. Thus, those who study from the NIV would not know that it is God who says He hates divorce. Is this another area where the LORD has given man over to a reprobate mind? (See Romans 1:28-32.)

God has warned throughout the Bible not to change His Word—not to add to it or subtract from it in any way—and that every "jot" and "tittle" is there for a reason. There is one God, and there is one Word. That pure Word is not littered with doctrinal error.

Review the six "Extra Points of Interest." There is a common thread among these six teachings, but especially William Tyndale's murder, the "unlawful" copyrighting of God's Word, and the thousands of God's words that have been replaced by authors of the new versions. Does God's Word belong to any one man? Should man control God's Word? The answer should be, "No," to each of these questions. If it is God's Word, then it belongs to God. It is meant to be read freely by man: *the word of God is not bound.* 2 Timothy 2:9 What happens when man controls the Word of God? William Tyndale saw firsthand the abuses that come when men control God's Word. The priests of his day changed the text to fit their ungodly lifestyles, told the people what they wanted them to hear, and passed a law that made it a crime punishable by death to translate the Bible into English. That control became so oppressive that a woman and six men were burned at the stake for teaching their children the Ten Commandments from the Bible translated into English by William Tyndale. And where did this all begin? Satan started with changing only one word—*not*.

Paraphrasing or dynamic equivalency—whichever term it might be given—is exchanging God's words for man's. This book focused on only a few changes that have been made to God's Word—those related mostly to marriage. Another even longer book could be written on how the new versions make changes to the name, character, and deity of Jesus Christ—even the number of times the LORD's name is removed; but, I leave that to the reader to research further and to carefully assess the table and image below.

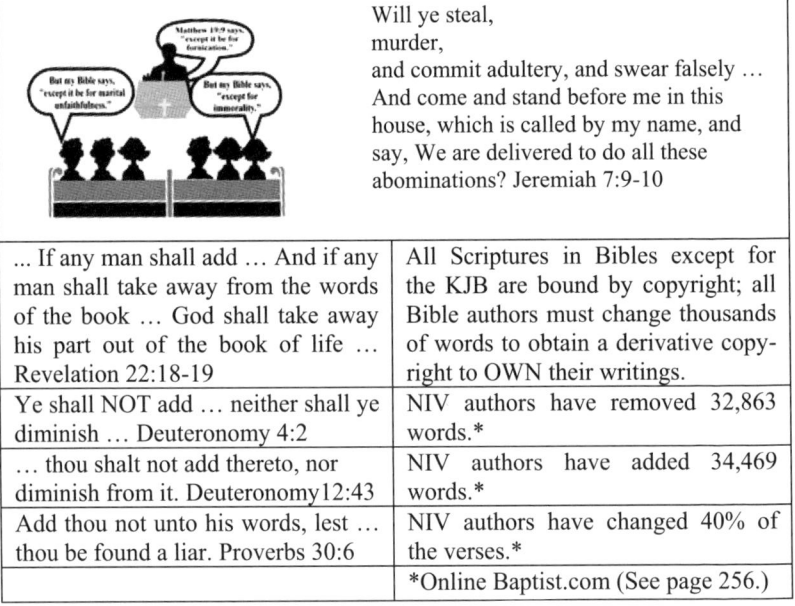

| | |
|---|---|
| ... If any man shall add ... And if any man shall take away from the words of the book ... God shall take away his part out of the book of life ... Revelation 22:18-19 | All Scriptures in Bibles except for the KJB are bound by copyright; all Bible authors must change thousands of words to obtain a derivative copyright to OWN their writings. |
| Ye shall NOT add ... neither shall ye diminish ... Deuteronomy 4:2 | NIV authors have removed 32,863 words.* |
| ... thou shalt not add thereto, nor diminish from it. Deuteronomy 12:43 | NIV authors have added 34,469 words.* |
| Add thou not unto his words, lest ... thou be found a liar. Proverbs 30:6 | NIV authors have changed 40% of the verses.* |
| | *Online Baptist.com (See page 256.) |

Please consider the last words Jesus left for every Christian—a serious warning against any type of partaking in changing His Word; yet, most do not feel it applies to them. That is a grave deception. Read again God's closing words laden with warnings from Jesus:

*For I* [Jesus] *testify unto **every man** that heareth the words of the prophecy of this book, If **any man** shall add unto these things, God shall add unto him the plagues that are written in this book: And if **any man** shall take away from the words of the book of this prophecy, God shall take away his part out of the book of life, and out of the holy city, and from the things which are written in this book. He which testifieth these things saith, Surely I come quickly. Amen. Even so, come, Lord Jesus.* Revelation 22:18-20

The famine in the land is part of what is called in this book God's *punitive judgment*. Fortunately, it's not too late to delay God's punitive judgment of famine. It's up to Christians around the world to pray and fast and DO the works—to teach Biblical Truths and to read and teach from Bibles that do not contain doctrinal error:

*The words of the LORD are pure words: as silver tried in a furnace of earth, purified seven times. Thou shalt keep them, O LORD, thou shalt preserve them from this generation for ever.* Psalm 12:6-7

*Thou therefore which teachest another, teachest thou not thyself? thou that preachest a man should not steal, dost thou steal? Thou that sayest a man should not commit adultery, dost thou commit adultery? thou that abhorrest idols, dost thou commit sacrilege? Thou that makest thy boast of the law, through breaking the law dishonourest thou God?* Romans 2:21-23

*But the Word of the LORD endureth for ever ...* 1 Peter 1:25

## *Summary and Conclusions*

### Does the Bible teach there are loopholes or exceptions to God's "law of marriage"?

It's now time to see if you have learned any new concepts from the teachings in this book. Review the table given in Chapter 1, pages four and five, of this book. If you made a copy of it, complete it again and compare your answers. Can you defend your answers from Scripture?

None of the loopholes listed in that table is a Biblical loophole; and thus, we come to the meaning behind the title for this book: ***Finding Loopholes in the Bible on Divorce and "Re-marriage" is Like Riding a Bike to Jamaica.*** Both are impossibilities. The Bible contains no loopholes. There is no Biblical loophole to divorce a covenant spouse. There is no loophole to allow for a "re-marriage"— adultery. These loopholes are man-made. **God doesn't make loopholes.** He says a marriage is only dissolved when one of the spouses physically dies. And ... there is no way to ride a bicycle on the waters between the United States and the island of Jamaica!

May you go forth to teach and defend God's perspective on marriage and have the desire to ... *Be not afraid of them: remember the LORD, which is great and terrible, and fight for your brethren, your sons, and your daughters, your wives, and your houses.* Nehemiah 4:14

## As it was in the beginning, so now it is!

*And the LORD God caused a deep sleep to fall upon Adam and he slept: and he took one of his ribs, and closed up the flesh instead thereof; And the rib, which the LORD God had taken from man, made he a woman, and brought her unto the man. And Adam said, This is now bone of my bones, and flesh of my flesh: she shall be called Woman, because she was taken out of Man. Therefore shall a man leave his father and his mother, and shall cleave unto his wife: and they shall be one flesh.* Genesis 2:21-24 But ***from the beginning*** *of the creation God made them male and female. For this cause shall a man leave his father and mother, and cleave to his wife; And they twain shall be one flesh: so then they are no more twain, but one flesh.* **What** *therefore* <u>*God hath joined together,*</u> **let not man put asunder.** Mark 10:6-9

May you feel equipped, or know how to equip yourself, through the Word of God, to love and cherish your one-flesh spouse. It's each person's decision to love or not to love; to remain faithful or not to remain faithful. Whatever your "station" in life, it's important, whether you are married or single, to continue to equip yourself to teach others some of these Truths which the Word of God admonishes every believer to do. You can do this by sitting down with others and going over the Scriptures. Share a copy of this book with others so they can study for themselves many of the teachings that require additional study and prayer:

### Where do you stand with the LORD?

Have you given your life over to serving and following the LORD? If not, please bow your head wherever you are and pray to God the Father in the name of Jesus Christ: *I come to you in the name of Jesus Christ, to ask for your help and forgiveness. I want to receive you as Saviour and Lord of my life. I don't fully understand all I have read, but I know I want to spend eternity in a place with Jesus—away from torment, and experience joy and peace in this life and forever. Please help me to begin to read your Word with understanding and to build a relationship with Jesus. I know that I have sinned much and now ask you to forgive me of my sins. Help me to turn from anything in my life which is sin. In the name of Jesus Christ, I pray. Amen*

**Read our tract online or write to us if you have further questions:**

http://restorationofthefamily.org/Articles/receive_jesus_christ_now.htm

# Scripture Bibliography

Genesis 2:18-25 is embedded in the word *Truth* above.

**OLD TESTAMENT**

**GENESIS**
1:1-7: 31
1:2: 34
1:9: 94
1:22: 367
1:27: 52
1:27-28: 218, 325
2:8-9: 34
2:17: 64, 136, 372
2:18: 51, 106, 144
2:18, 20: 54, 55, 57-60, 105
2:18-25: 381
2:20-22: 34
2:21-22: 35
2:21-24: 29, 315, 378
2:22: 30, 33
2:22-24: 27
2:23: 288
2:24: 17, 26, 144, 211, 221, 222
3:1: 90
3:4: 64, 90, 372
3:15: 140
3:24: 35
4:17: 213, 341
12:19: 292
20:17: 213
29:18: 109
39:7-9: 212
39:9: 47, 362
39:19-20: 363

**EXODUS**
18:4: 57
20:7: 155
20:14: 44, 101
20:14, 17: 44
20:16: 350
20:17: 165
22:7: 189, 190

**LEVITICUS**
18:6: 159

**NUMBERS**
4:15: 205
23:19: 53, 122

**DEUTERONOMY**
4:2: 64, 77, 326, 376
12:43: 376
20:7: 92, 144, 293
22:22-23: 97
22:22-24: 293
22:23: 92, 189, 190, 294
24:1: 100, 101
24:1-4: 245
24:2: 236, 238
24:4: 239, 245, 246
30:6: 347
33:7: 57

**JOSHUA**
17:15: 189, 190
24:15: 39, 239

**1 SAMUEL**
2:22-25: 213
2:22, 25: 363
2:29: 363
15:23: 206
16:7: 369

**2 SAMUEL**
6:7: 205
12:1: 11
12:9-12: 12

**1 KINGS**
16:31: 213

**1 CHRONICLES**
22:12: 177

**2 CHRONICLES**
7:14: 365

**NEHEMIAH**
4:14: 378

**JOB**
1:1: 154
31:1: 154
31:1, 12: 363
31:4-12: 154
38:4: 61

**PSALMS**
11:3: 189, 190
12:6-7: 54, 171, 178, 290, 330

## Scripture Bibliography

**PSALMS continued**
12:6-7: 377
22:18: 87, 88
33:20: 57
50:17-19: 372
50:18: 233, 234
50:18-19: 217
51:3: 11
51:4: 47
70:5: 57
101:2-3: 154, 155
105:8: 171
115:9: 56
115:10, 11: 57
119:89: 18, 228
121:2: 57
124:8: 57
138:2: 21, 171

**PROVERBS**
6:9: 352
6:25-26, 29, 32-33: 355
6:27: 356
6:29: 165
6:32: 101, 246
7:21-23, 27: 356
7:25-27: 323
12:6-7: 54
20:27: 208
28:13: 274, 364
30:5-6: 319, 330
30:6: 376
31:10: 290
31:10, 12: 52

**ECCLESIASTES**
1:9: 242
5:4-6: 350, 369

**ISAIAH**
1:18: 353
5:20-21: 74, 309
7:14: 141
28:9-10: xvi, 134, 177, 225
50:1: 286, 287
54:1: 294
56:4-5: 311
59:19: 236, 307
61:10: 88

**JEREMIAH**
3:1: 144, 239, 244, 245, 246, 248, 250, 251, 253, 259, 260, 285, 286, 352
3:6-9: 283
3:8-9: 285
3:12-14: 283, 285
4:1: 252, 253
4:4: 347
5:8: 165
7:9-10: 136, 376
17:9-10: 23
44:25: 351
44:27: 351

**LAMENTATIONS**
4:2: 59

**EZEKIEL**
16:8: 249, 282
18:4: 207
18:21-24: 365
18:30-32: 284
20:24-26: 240
33:7-9: x
42:1: 59

**DANIEL**
11:45: 56

**HOSEA**
1:1-3: 282
3:1: 162, 250, 284, 352
4:6: 241
4:12-14: 240
10:4: 350, 357
13:9: 57

**AMOS**
3:3: viii
8:11: 373
8:11-12: 71, 89, 136

**MALACHI**
2:13-17: 285
2:14: 52, 93, 249, 288, 352, 367
2:15: 218, 369
2:16: 19, 23, 62, 205, 234, 256, 352, 369
2:16-17: 217, 368
3:5: 101
3:7: 252, 288

# NEW TESTAMENT

**MATTHEW**
1:18: 103
1:18-19: 92, 98, 186
1:18, 19, 24: 291
1:18-20: 110, 294
1:19: 138
1:20, 24: 96, 138
1:20, 24, 25: 95
1:23: 24
1:24: 110, 282
1:25: 142
3:2: 341
4:3: 67, 68, 70, 189, 190
5:18: 76, 78, 80, 83, 84, 191
5:27: 259, 264, 269
5:27, 28: 44, 46
5:28: 153, 156, 169, 259
5:29-32: 46
5:31: 231, 259, 264
5:31-32: 45, 260, 268
5:32: 40, 117, 123-125, 130, 144, 147, 149, 158, 181, 231, 232, 238, 261-265, 268, 272-276, 295
7:28-29: 48
8:34: 106
11:11: 341
12:46-47: 142
13:19: 261, 262
13:55-56: 142
14:3-4: 341
14:4: 342
14:7: 350
15:19: 149
16:11-12: 72
18:3: 223
18:4-6: 129
18:6-7: 235
18:21-22: 51, 323
19:3: 42, 50, 65, 67, 69, 70, 72, 183, 187, 196, 197
19:3, 7: 16
19:4: 16, 28
19:4-6: 17, 29, 196
19:5: 17, 211, 221, 222
19:6: xii, 112, 168, 258, 368
19:7: 16, 196, 198, 246
19:7, 8: 18, 44, 197
19:7-9: 102
19:8: xvi, 28, 231
19:8-9: 196
19:8-12: 302
19:9: 38, 40, 42,

## MATTHEW Continued

49, 99, 110, 117, 119-125, 130, 131, 137-139, 144, 147-149, 157, 169, 181-184, 189, 193, 197-198, 229, 231, 273, 274, 276, 291, 295
19:9-12: 305
19:10: 304
19:10-11: x
19:10-12: 306
19:12: 300, 307
22:15: 71
22:25: 144, 296
23:13, 14, 16, 17: 72
23:27: 72
23:33: 72
25:11-12: 115
27:5: 9, 161
27:19: 213
27:35: 87

## MARK

3:25: 189, 190
6:17: 213
7:7: 43, 48
8:21: 24
9:43: 63
10:2: 65
10:2: 9-12: 302
10:6: 28
10:6-9: 29, 340, 378
10:8: 35, 211, 221, 222, 288
10:8-9: xii, 94
10:9: 26, 93, 112
10:10: 303
10:11: 152
10:11-12: 40, 104, 122, 304, 306
10:12: 158, 359
14:13: 106
15:34: 24

## LUKE

1:34-35: 141
1:35: 140
6:31: 9, 161
8:21: 261, 262
11:34-35: 156
13:3: 365
14:20: 95, 296
16:18: 34, 152, 157, 165, 345, 358, 361, 366
22:1: 24
23:34: 87
24:19: 266
24:45: 176

## JOHN

1:1, 14: 21, 262
1:6: 341
1:19: 24
1:41: 24
3:16: 152
4:18, 19: 344
4:29-30: 345
5:2: 24
6:60-61: x
6:63: 71, 176, 319
8:3-4: 158
8:9: 144
8:11: 157, 344
8:37: 70
8:41: 140, 141, 143
8:41-42: 142
10:10: 68
10:35: 53, 86
11:35: xvi
12:9: 24
14:15: 284, 368
14:23: 316
14:23-24: 368
15:6: 340
15:12: 316

17:22: 260
18:36: 189
19:13: 24
19:17: 24
19:23-24: 87
19:36: 88

## ACTS

8:29: 111, 112
13:49: 261, 262
15:7: 261, 262
15:20: 164
17:11: 228
17:30: 13
18:7: 112

## ROMANS

1:22-32: 241
1:28-32: 370
1:29: 163
1:31: 144, 163, 371
2:21-23: 377
4:18: 223
6:1-2, 12: 168
6:16: 19, 287
7:1-3: 332
7:2: 122
7:2-3: 151, 165, 356, 357, 359, 362
7:3: 157, 183, 256, 8:1: 334-337
8:4-8: 338
8:31: 189
15:18: 266

## 1 CORINTHIANS

2:13: 52, 116, 134, 228
2:13-14: 177
5:1: 158, 159
5:1-2: 265
6:9: 50, 131, 147, 220
6:9-10: 23, 130, 268
6:13: 212
6:15-17: 208, 209
6:16: 210, 211, 221
7:1: 325, 326
7:1-2: 327, 330
7:2: 144, 159
7:5: 218
7:10-11: 218, 247, 285
7:11: 252, 310, 315, 319
7:12-13: 315
7:13: 152
7:15: 144, 150, 314, 315, 317, 320
7:16: 213, 319
7:18-20: 346
7:20, 24: 345, 351
7:21-24: 348
7:27: 296, 320, 321, 322
7:28: 326
7:32: vii
7:32-35: 310-311
7:39: 21, 315, 318, 319, 321, 322, 361
8:9: 223
10:21: 234
12:13: 187
13:4-8: 316
13:8: 219

## 2 CORINTHIANS

2:14: 261
5:17: 334-335, 337
5:18: 1
6:14: 14, 210
7:9: 365
7:9-10: 310
7:10: 364
9:11: 261
10:4-5: 13
11:2: 107, 113-115, 116, 297
11:2, 3: 110-111

## Scripture Bibliography

**2 CORINTHIANS**
continued
11:3-4: xv, 26, 278
13:5: 370

**GALATIANS**
1:6-7: xv
1:6-9: 278
3:28: 276
5:16-19: 339
5:19: 50, 144, 149
5:19-21: 23, 130
5:24-25: 339

**EPHESIANS**
4:12: 175
4:16: 112
4:22-24: 336
5:3: 163
5:21: 62
5:23-31: 116
5:25-33: 219
5:30-32: 298, 367
5:31: 112, 211, 221

**PHILIPPIANS**
3:5: 113
4:8: 134

**COLOSSIANS**
3:5: 164
3:17: 266

**1 THESSALONIANS**
5:22: 367

**2 THESSALONIANS**
2:10-11: 374
2:10-12: 241

**1 TIMOTHY**
2:3-4: 305
5:22: 234

**2 TIMOTHY**
2:9: 178, 375
2:15: viii, 86, 176, 199, 261, 329
2:24-26: 324
2:26: 355
3:16: 124
3:16-17: 6
4:2-4: xi

**TITUS**
1:2: 122, 237
1:2-3: 53
2:3-4: vii

**PHILEMON**
1:6: 223

**HEBREWS**
11:1: 93
12:15-17: 160
13:4: 20, 47, 166, 236, 283, 361
13:8: 21, 124

**JAMES**
1:6: 134
1:6-7: 8
1:13: 68
1:14-16: 44, 157, 356
1:21: 208
2:19-20: 195
2:20: 265
2:26: 340

**1 PETER**
1:25: 377

**2 PETER**
1:20-21: 192, 288
1:21: 88, 122
2:14: 156

**1 JOHN**
3:1: 151
3:18: 266
5:7-8: 21

**2 JOHN**
1:10-11: 234

**3 JOHN**
1:4: v

**JUDE**
1:3: 374
1:7: 159
1:22-23: 39
1:23: 324, 352

**REVELATION**
2:7: 260
2:21-22: 149, 369
3:10: 261, 262
6:9: 255
9:21: 163
12:17: 255
13:12, 16: 261
18:5: 235
19:2: 159, 169
19:7: 144, 297
19:7-9: 115
19:10: 255
21:8: 330
22:18-19: 151, 376
22:18-20: 255, 377
22:19: 77